# The New Democratic Frontier:
## A Country by Country Report
## on Elections in Central

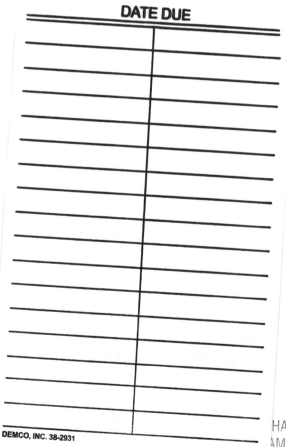

**DATE DUE**

Library of Congress Cataloging-in-Publication Data

The New democratic frontier: a country by country report on
  elections in Central and Eastern Europe / edited by Larry Garber
  and Eric Bjornlund
      p.        cm.
   ISBN  1-880134-09-8 : $12.95.
   1. Elections--Europe, Eastern.  2. Elections--Central Europe.
3. Europe, Eastern--Politics and government--1989-  4. Central
Europe--Politics and government.  I. Garber, Larry.  II. Bjornlund,
Eric, 1958-  .
JN96.A956N48   1992
324.94'0558--dc20                                                92-2960
                                                                 CIP

# Table of Contents

# Foreword

## J. Brian Atwood

It is rare that any institution has an opportunity to work with people who are changing the course of history. We at NDI were well aware that our colleagues from Eastern and Central Europe, many of whom had been prisoners of conscience or underground dissidents, were making history in 1989-90. This book tells their story, not a story of the victory of West over East, or of capitalism over communism, but the triumph of the human spirit. To have participated even in a small way in that epoch was an extraordinary privilege. To share our experience, we believe, is nothing less than NDI's obligation to future generations of democrats.

The editors of this book and the authors of its chapters have worked very hard to interpret the cataclysmic events of this region. They have viewed the elections and the environments within which they took place in the context of contemporary political situations, the history of the region's nations and, importantly, through the prism of their own experiences, both in their own countries and on the ground in Eastern and Central Europe as part of NDI's international network. Their insights and analyses do justice to the courageous and committed citizens of this region.

The editors of this book are two talented lawyers who have chosen to apply their considerable legal skills to the democratic development work of NDI. Larry Garber is NDI's Special Counsel for Electoral Processes and Eric Bjornlund, Senior Program Officer. While this was a labor of love for them, it was at the same time arduous work. They conceived the format, guided the authors, edited texts and constantly prodded those drafting chapters, including me, to meet deadlines. Both continued to carry a full NDI workload, managing projects on even newer democratic frontiers in Africa and South Asia. They deserve great credit for seeing this project through and for enabling our Institute to contribute to a better understanding of the history of this time.

Finally, it is gratifying to be associated with an effort that analyzes and explains important aspects of the democratization mission. Western political leaders trumpet democracy-building as a major tenet of foreign policy. Yet, the operational work is only vaguely understood, its definition often distorted. A frequently heard criticism is that elections are highly superficial indicators of democratization. This is, of course, correct, but many who repeat this increasingly trite insight fail to acknowledge that elections are an essential starting point. And they routinely underestimate the difficulty of holding meaningful elections in fragile new democracies. If this book contributes to a more sophisticated discussion of these issues, it will have served an important secondary purpose.

# Acknowledgements

This book is the product of hard work by a large number of people. The National Democratic Institute for International Affairs (NDI) thanks in particular the authors of the different chapters for their contributions. (Author biographies are listed at the back of the book.) The Institute also thanks all the participants in its training and observer missions in the region. Their insights and dedication contributed enormously to the quality of this work.

NDI President J. Brian Atwood conceived and initiated the idea of a country by country study of the 1990 elections in Eastern and Central Europe and ensured that the project remained an NDI priority. NDI Executive Vice President Kenneth Wollack carefully reviewed the entire manuscript.

In addition to editing each of the chapters, NDI Public Information Director Sue Grabowski was responsible for the volume's format and design. She also endured the seemingly never-ending process of rewriting, editing and production.

The editors also acknowledge the significant contribution of NDI Program Assistant Joseph Hennessey. In addition to his thorough editing, Mr. Hennessey was responsible for developing outlines for several thematic chapters and for regularly communicating with authors located on four continents.

Amy Tate checked facts for several of the chapters and prepared the tables of election results included as an appendix to this volume. Britta Bjornlund also assisted with the fact-checking. Jacqueline Dorsey capably handled the time-consuming job of typing and retyping the many drafts, often with barely legible edits. Karen Clark, Patricia Keefer, Lisa McLean, Thomas Melia and Gerald Mitchell also edited one or more chapters.

This book was produced with funds provided through a grant from the National Endowment for Democracy. The observer delegations to Hungary, Romania, Czechoslovakia and Bulgaria were organized with funds provided by the United States Agency for International Development.

*Larry Garber*                                    *Eric C. Bjornlund*

*Chapter 1*

# Introduction

## Larry Garber and Eric C. Bjornlund

The dramatic events in Eastern and Central Europe from autumn 1989 to spring 1990 mark a watershed in European and world history. As the Cold War waned, the authority of totalitarian governments crumbled virtually overnight. Re-energized populations found their voices and regained control of their governments. Elections opened a new phase of politics throughout the region.

Between March 18, 1990, when East Germans freely elected a Christian Democratic government with a mandate for German unification, and June 10, 1990, when Bulgarians narrowly returned the renamed Communist Party to office, the people of Eastern and Central Europe went to the polls to choose their leaders in more or less free elections. During this short, four-month span, six of the former Warsaw Pact countries, counting Yugoslavia, held their first genuinely competitive elections since the end of World War II. A seventh, Poland, which launched the trend a year earlier with partially free national elections, became the first country in the region to hold competitive local elections during this timeframe. The combination of these extraordinary elections in one concentrated period and in one part of the world made this one of the most unique and dramatic times of the 20th century.

The Eastern and Central European elections of 1990 were largely successful in allowing sufficient political space for opposition forces to contend for political power. With the significant exception of Romania, the 1990 elections also succeeded in creating governments that derived their legitimacy from the free choices of the people. The elections occurred with little violence. They allowed populations subjected to decades of political repression their first meaningful opportunity to express political views. They encouraged and enabled significant political participation for the first time in years. The elections provided, in effect, an opportunity for these publics to participate in a country by country series of referendums on the communist system.

# I

As the sequence of events in Eastern and Central Europe from late 1989 through mid-1990 illustrates, elections seldom distinguish the beginning of a democratic transition or a revolutionary transformation. Rather, a schism in the government or the military, a severe economic crisis, a catastrophic war or even the unification of opposition forces generally initiates a transition process. The combination of such circumstances leads to calls for meaningful elections, which, when they occur, signal a second phase of a democratic transition.

Throughout 1989, the communist governments in the region, sometimes of their own accord and sometimes in response to mass protests, relinquished their monopolies on political power and allowed opposition groups to form and mobilize, thus marking the first stage of the transition process. These events were relatively peaceful, although insurrection against Romanian President Nicolae Ceausescu at the end of 1989 brought this chapter to a bloody denouement.

A second phase commenced when the communist regimes, or their remnants, and opposition forces established rules for competitive elections and then permitted their occurrence. This was no small achievement because none of the countries in the region had held truly multiparty elections in more than 40 years.

# II

This book is intended to be a resource for scholars, activists and policy-makers alike. It reports on the elections of 1990, and it analyzes the ongoing political transitions in which these elections played such a key role. Focusing in particular on elections, the book describes how opposition political leaders and democratic activists affected dramatic political change in seven countries of Eastern and Central Europe in an extremely short period of time.

This book was conceived in the spring of 1990 as part of the response of the National Democratic Institute for International Affairs (NDI) to the second phase of the dramatic democratic developments in the region. NDI, a nonprofit, U.S.-based institute, conducts nonpartisan political development programs overseas. By working with political parties and other institutions, NDI seeks to promote, maintain and strengthen democratic institutions and pluralistic values in new and emerging democracies. In its democratic development projects around the world, NDI draws upon the expertise of prominent political leaders, government officials, journalists, academics and civic leaders from across the democratic spectrum and from established and emerging democracies around the world.

Through its activities, NDI has developed a reputation as a leading nongovernmental organization in the field of election observing and election processes. Since 1986, NDI has sponsored large, high-profile international delegations that have observed and monitored more than 20 of the most important and controversial elections that have occurred around the world; smaller NDI teams have been present for elections in many other countries. NDI has also provided technical assistance to political parties and nonpartisan civic organizations that have conducted voter and civic education campaigns and have organized election monitoring programs, such as poll-watching and independent counting systems.

NDI observer missions and other programs have enhanced confidence and encouraged participation in the electoral process, promoted understanding of international standards for free and fair elections, deterred fraud and manipulation, and reported to the international community about the conduct of the elections and the extent of election-related abuses. International observers have focused attention on the process before, during and after election day. By recruiting high-profile leaders and expert delegates, developing specific techniques for identifying fraudulent practices and issuing comprehensive election reports, NDI has significantly influenced the development and application of international standards for free and fair elections and for election observing.

NDI began its activities in Eastern and Central Europe in 1989 with programs in Poland, where NDI co-sponsored a conference on the organizational and decision-making process of the parliament, and Hungary, where NDI organized a party training program in the fall. In January 1990, at the request of President Vaclav Havel, the Institute sent to Czechoslovakia a multinational team of technical experts to advise the new government on the relative merits of different election systems. Subsequently, in anticipation of the spring 1990 elections, NDI sponsored training programs for emerging democratic political parties in Hungary and Czechoslovakia and helped establish nonpartisan civic organizations in Bulgaria and Romania.

Between March and June 1990, NDI organized major observer delegations for elections in Hungary, Romania, Czechoslovakia and Bulgaria. These delegations were co-sponsored by NDI's Republican counterpart, the International Republican Institute, formerly the National Republican Institute for International Affairs (NRIIA). The delegations included parliamentarians, political party leaders, election officials, journalists and democratic activists from more than 35 countries. A number of prominent world political leaders led these delegations, including: NDI Chairman and former U.S. Vice President Walter Mondale; U.S. Senators Joseph Lieberman (D-CT), Christopher Dodd (D-CT) and John McCain (R-AZ); former U.S. Senators Charles Mathias (R-MD) and Harrison Schmitt (R-NM); Representative Robert Lagomarsino (R-CA); Governor Madeleine Kunin of Vermont; Prime Ministers James Mitchell of St. Vincent and the Grenadines, Garrett FitzGerald of Ireland and Steingrimur Hermannsson of Iceland; political party leaders Jan Carnogursky of Czechoslovakia, Roy Hattersley of Great Britain, and Senator Robert Hill of Australia; and Honduran first lady, Norma Gaborit de

Callejas. Each delegation issued a post-election statement that assessed the entire electoral process, from the pre-campaign period until after the after the announcement of the official results. NDI and NRIIA jointly published comprehensive, book-length post-election reports that analyzed the elections in Romania and Bulgaria in detail.

Drawing on the observations of these delegations, as well as those of smaller NDI delegations sent to the March 1990 national elections in East Germany, the April 1990 elections in Slovenia, Yugoslavia, and the May 1990 local elections in Poland, this book reviews and assesses the political context and the electoral process in the seven countries. In the following chapters, international experts and democratic activists who have participated in NDI's programs in the region analyze aspects of the elections and their social, political and historical context. The appendix at the end of the book provides results for each of the elections covered in this volume.

This book provides insights into the ongoing transitions to more democratic governments in Europe. The chapters describe how the transition processes were effectuated: the workings of the roundtable negotiations, the choice of election systems and mechanisms for administering elections, the formation and functioning of political parties and electoral coalitions, the role of civic organizations, and the contributions of the international community. Here are lessons for democrats in other countries still struggling for freedom against repressive regimes.

The transitions have not solved many problems confronting the countries in the region. The consolidation of democratic government and the transformation to free market economies remain daunting tasks.

The chapters of this book were written between late 1990 and early 1991. While political developments in the region have continued to move forward rapidly, other regions are only now entering the critical electoral stage of democratic transitions. By focusing on the election phase the book will inform the debate and discussion of historians, political scientists and policy-makers around the world.

# III

In hindsight, there exists an easy wisdom that the dissolution of the communist regimes in Eastern and Central Europe was inevitable. This was not, however, the expectation of most scholars and experts writing even five years ago. Still, as Professor Madeleine Albright writes in the first chapter of the book, a series of developments, beginning with the signing of the Helsinki Accords in 1975 and including Gorbachev's ascension to power, made peaceful transitions in most of the region possible. In her contribution, Albright, who formerly served as NDI's vice-chair, provides the framework for understanding the circumstances surrounding the momentous 1990 elections.

Chapters 3 through 9 describe the historical contexts and electoral processes of the seven Eastern and Central European countries that held elections in the spring of 1990. While these countries share the experience of communist domination, differing political, social and cultural conditions shaped their transitions.

In the German Democratic Republic, the question of German unification dominated the political debate during the electoral campaign. This factor significantly distinguished the East German elections from the others in the region. In their chapter, Daniel Gordon and Fred Reinke describe the unique political situation in Germany and the dominance of West German political parties and resources over the East German electoral process. They report on what were the only truly competitive elections in East German history. In the end, the March 1990 elections in East Germany became a referendum on unification and marked only one step, albeit an extremely important one, in the process of incorporation into the Federal Republic.

Hungary benefitted from a phased transition process, emerging as the only country in the region with ideologically oriented, indigenous political parties. In Chapter 4, Thomas Melia analyzes Hungary's recent political history, leading up to and following the historic March 1990 parliamentary elections. He notes that, until the sudden transitions elsewhere in the region in late 1989, events in Hungary preceded parallel events elsewhere. The chapter considers some reasons for the relative success and strength of Hungary's democratic transition.

Edward McMahon's account of the April 1990 elections in Slovenia highlights the complex mix of democratic and nationalist politics that characterized all of the Yugoslav republics on the eve of Yugoslavia's disintegration and the outbreak of civil war. He describes the complicated governmental institutions, both within the republic and in Yugoslavia as a whole, that were designed to hold together and govern this multi-ethnic, multinational state. Within Slovenia itself, the chapter reports that the elections resulted in a careful balance between new democrats and reformed communists and between democratic and nationalist ideologies.

After the bloody overthrow of Ceausescu, Romania held elections in May 1990, but Thomas Carothers, relying on the findings of the NDI/NRIIA international observer delegation, concludes that the electoral process was severely flawed. Carothers assesses the significance of the December 1989 revolution and considers whether the National Salvation Front, which assumed power during the revolution, was ever truly committed to democratic reform. He describes a myriad of problems that made the electoral process systematically unfair, even while balloting on election day proceeded in a relatively smooth and peaceful manner. The chapter suggests that the flawed electoral process portends serious impediments to a genuine democratic transition in Romania.

The partially free 1989 national elections in Poland were a precursor of further, and more dramatic, liberalization in the other countries. Indeed, the drama of Poland's democratic opening seems almost anachronistic from the perspective of subsequent developments in the region. Nonetheless, as Maya Latynski recounts in Chapter 7, the 1990 local elections, the first completely open elections in Poland, were a critical step in the country's consolidation of democracy and provided the stimulus for efforts at decentralization and democratization at the local level, a pattern followed by other countries in the region. Latynski expresses concern about voter apathy and about certain demagogic tendencies in Polish politics, but she describes an important phase of what looks to be a genuine democratic transition.

The June 1990 elections in Czechoslovakia marked a continuation of the almost surreal quality of the "Velvet Revolution." In Chapter 8, Robin Carnahan and Judith Corley recall the events that suddenly swept intellectual Vaclav Havel from leading dissident to government leader. Unlike the other countries in the region during the election period, in Czechoslovakia the communists or their successors did not control the media or the election machinery. As the chapter reports, the elections themselves were not controversial and served only to confirm Civic Forum, and its Slovak counterpart Public Against Violence, in government.

The June elections in Bulgaria, which concluded the 1990 election season, demonstrated that a reformed and renamed Communist Party could compete successfully in multiparty elections. This pattern of victory by a reformed communist party was later repeated in Serbia and Albania.[1] Nonetheless, as Larry Garber relates in Chapter 9, subsequent developments revealed the ruling party's inability to govern effectively, even with a legislative majority. The chapter also describes the complicated electoral system and the important role of a nonpartisan, election monitoring organization, the Bulgarian Association for Fair Elections.

# IV

Certain common themes emerge from the country chapters, including the key role played by dissidents and other mediating institutions in shaping the transition, the complicated process of negotiating the modalities of a new election system, the emergence of political parties in anticipation of elections and the important role played by the international community. These themes form the basis for the analysis in Chapters 10 through 15.

In Chapter 10, Professor Shlomo Avineri, a renowned scholar of Marxism, describes the critical role that broadly based, social mediating institutions played in developing a democratic culture and making possible a meaningful electoral process and democratic transition. Professor Avineri asserts that the presence of social and

---

[1]  See, National Democratic Institute for International Affairs, *The March 31, 1991 Elections in Albania* (1991). See also, National Republican Institute for International Affairs, *The 1990 Elections in the Republics of Yugoslavia* (1991).

cultural institutions, such as Solidarity in Poland and Charter 77 in Czechoslovakia, facilitated meaningful elections in those countries and made successful the first stages of their transitions. In contrast, the absence of such institutions and of a democratic culture in Romania and to a lesser extent in Bulgaria has made the transitions in those countries more questionable, or at least more troubled.

Judge Antonio Vitorino, who serves on the Constitutional Court of Portugal, describes and assesses in Chapter 11 the critical contribution of the roundtables. In most of the countries, ruling and opposition political forces and other representatives of many sectors of society sat down together to discuss political reform. The roundtables took on a legitimacy completely unavailable to the existing governmental institutions. They urged sweeping constitutional and legislative changes. And they proposed the holding of free and fair elections to resolve political conflicts and confer legitimacy on the resulting governments.

Vitorino also compares the process of transition in Eastern and Central Europe in 1989-90 to the transition process in Southern Europe in the 1970s. Similarly, Genaro Arriagada, a Chilean political scientist and democratic activist who coordinated the opposition forces in the 1988 plebiscite campaign in Chile, suggests parallels between the political situation in Eastern and Central Europe in 1989-90 and in Latin America in the 1980s. Arriagada addresses the complex challenges and opportunities that a flawed, imperfect electoral process presents for democratic forces in an authoritarian political environment. He considers the danger that leading democratic activists may lose touch with the larger public and the need for democratic activists to marry moral principles with practical politics.

One of the most important decisions for the roundtable participants involved selecting an election system and formulating the mechanics of administrating elections in countries where distrust in authority, naturally, was widespread. In Chapter 13, Antonio Nadais, a Portuguese lawyer, reflects on the significance of various choices about election systems made by each country. He further describes the administrative safeguards that were introduced to inspire confidence in the process.

A healthy democracy requires not only a fair election system, but also competitive political parties. In Chapter 14, Andrew Ellis, a leader of Britain's Liberal Party, analyzes the development and importance of political parties in the region. Ellis assesses the critical need for opposition political forces to unite in order to depose the entrenched communists and establish the foundation for a successful transition, even as he describes the inevitable and powerful forces pulling political coalitions apart.

In his chapter on the role of international observers, NDI Senior Counsel Larry Garber credits the international community with strengthening the electoral processes in these emerging democracies. The chapter notes that the 1990 elections in the region marked the climax of a relatively recent innovation in international relations: mutually supportive interactions among democratic activists across national boundaries. Acting in the immediate aftermath of these elections, the 35 countries then party to the Conference on Security and Cooperation in Europe (CSCE) institutionalized the practice of election observing. Garber reviews the significance of this development, which obligates CSCE members, under the terms of the Copenhagen Declaration, to facilitate visits by international observers for all national elections in their countries. More important, perhaps, the declaration sets standards by which the quality of an election process can be evaluated.

Finally, in the book's concluding chapter, NDI President Brian Atwood assesses the successes and limitations of the transitions to date. He addresses in particular the importance of a democratic civic culture, genuine pluralism and credible intermediary institutions, a representative and workable election system, strong and ideologically oriented political parties, and democratic and effective governing institutions. Speaking for all of the book's contributors and editors, Atwood finds the progress toward democracy encouraging, but he also concludes that significant challenges remain.

*January 1992*

## Chapter 2

# The Glorious Revolutions of 1989

## Madeleine Albright

We used to call them satellites. We used to talk about them as Warsaw Pact members or the Soviet bloc. Today, even the appellation Eastern Europe sounds wrong. Moreover, in describing Poland, Hungary, Bulgaria, Romania, it may be appropriate to use the familiar names of these countries. In the case of the German Democratic Republic and Czechoslovakia, officially renamed the Czech and Slovak Federal Republic, it is not.

History, which seemed to stand still for almost half a century, is now accelerating at double time for those who lived under communism and who are now trying to catch up with post-war political and economic growth. Those forced into uniformity are demanding that attention be paid to their individual differences.

Communism, based on the class concept, derided nationalism; however, for pragmatic reasons orthodox communists unable to curb national aspirations have at times either permitted them to emerge or have actually harnessed them for their own purposes. The new Europe, however, is demonstrating, quite dramatically, that nationalism is a movement that over time cannot be suppressed or manipulated. In the 20th century it has manifested its potency over all other movements.

# I

After the second world war, while other colonial empires were disintegrating and nationalism was on the rise, Stalin built an empire out of the ethnically diverse but war-numbed peoples of Central and Eastern Europe. Communism never enjoyed legitimacy in Eastern Europe, as it was imposed from the outside by the Red Army and political commissars.

The Soviets established their post-war empire for three reasons. Their first priority was security. They never again wanted to be invaded from the west and the empire was seen as a buffer zone.

The empire also served economic needs. Following World War II, whole factories in some instances were transplanted from Eastern European countries to the Soviet Union. Later, the Soviet Union assured itself a steady supply of products in exchange for cheap oil. In contrast to classic empires, in the Soviet case the mother country provided the raw materials while the colonies took care of manufacturing.

Finally, Stalin wanted an empire to showcase the appeal of communism for countries in other regions. Having eschewed Trotsky's permanent revolution concept, which envisioned communism spreading throughout the world, Stalin spent the 1930s developing the Soviet Union itself, choosing a policy of "socialism in one country." After World War II, however, he believed the time had come to demonstrate that communist ideology could spread first to Eastern Europe and later, he hoped, to Western Europe.

For more than 40 years, communist leaders purchased their legitimacy, to a greater or lesser degree, by promising the people a better standard of living and by providing them with a minimum of consumer goods. Their position was obviously the most tenuous in those countries where they did not have enough of an economic cushion to deliver on their end of this very bizarre social contract.

# II

In reflecting on the more than 40-year period, it now seems clear that the communist rulers never succeeded in suppressing each nation's individuality despite efforts to homogenize the region with orthodox economic and political policies carried out by successive purges. Although they appeared as generally isolated events, problems within the bloc surfaced regularly each decade. For short periods of time, seemingly every 10 years, the illegitimacy of respective regimes was exposed. Interestingly enough, those challenges that caused the most problems were somehow associated with changes in Soviet leadership or attempts by the Soviets to alter policies.

The first defection from the communist empire occurred in 1948, as a result of actions taken by the only legitimate leader in the region. Yugoslavia's Tito had actually mobilized his fellow citizens to fight against the Germans and therefore commanded a power base from which to question *diktats* from the Kremlin. In the other countries of the bloc, national leaders were purged and Soviet advisers helped local communists fashion totalitarian systems that replicated the one in Moscow.

The next change occurred shortly after Stalin's death in 1953, when workers rioted first in Pilzen, Czechoslovakia, then in the German Democratic Republic, and finally in Poland. When Stalin's successor Georgi Malenkov enunciated his "New Course," a policy designed to reorient the Soviet economy from heavy industry to consumer goods and establish a more collegial governing style, formerly forbidden dissent surfaced in Eastern Europe, particularly in Poland and Hungary. In November 1956, Soviet tanks rolled into Budapest to crush the Hungarian revolt against the communist system.

Malenkov was succeeded by Nikita Khrushchev, who not only exposed Stalin's crimes, but also came to espouse a theory, in the sixties, that permitted different paths to socialism. Khrushchev and others realized that growing economic difficulties were caused, in large measure, by the uniform imposition of a rigid foreign system on countries with very different political cultures and levels of economic development.

The attempt by communists to reform their own systems culminated with Czechoslovakia's "socialism with a human face" in 1968. An uncensored press that unearthed past crimes, grassroots movements that stood up to the Soviets, and various calls for some type of multiparty political system persuaded Soviet and Czechoslovak hardliners that the reform movement had gone too far. Once again, Soviet tanks were dispatched to put down locally inspired change.

# III

Poland precipitated the most dramatic events of the 1970s. They were associated with three events: Brezhnev's policy of detente, the signing of the Helsinki Final Act in 1975 and the election of a Polish Pope in October 1978.

The Poles had shown their restiveness repeatedly since the end of World War II. Polish farmers never submitted to collectivization. The Catholic Church, closely linked with the fate of the Polish nation, never lost its appeal. The workers and the intelligentsia never forgot that the changes they had fashioned in 1956 were forcibly taken away from them. The workers riots of 1976 marked the beginning a new phase that culminated with the birth of Solidarity in 1980.

Brezhnev's policy of detente opened the door to Western political and economic influence in Eastern Europe. Nowhere was the impact more evident than in Poland, the recipient of Western credits and the beneficiary of increased contacts; the former ultimately created economic chaos, the latter whetted reformers' appetites for more freedom.

Detente brought East and the West together at the Conference on Security and Cooperation in Europe, which produced the Helsinki Final Act. When it was signed, the Final Act was criticized by many in the United States for having acquiesced to Soviet wishes to recognize the permanent division of Europe. The truth is that the Final Act proved to be a double-edged sword. While it did indeed codify the status quo, it also placed human rights on the international agenda, and thus gave hope to dissidents in Eastern Europe that their voices would be amplified more broadly. In Czechoslovakia, specifically, the Final Act led to the birth of Charter 77, whose original purpose was to press the Czechoslovak government to respect its own constitution and the obligations of the international document it had signed. In Poland, it helped to catalyze the forces for change, which climaxed with the 1980 strikes in Gdansk and the emergence of Solidarity.

The election of Karol Cardinal Wojtyła, the archbishop of Krakow, as Pope John Paul II in October 1978, inspired and strengthened those being denied their rights in Poland. When the Pope returned to his homeland the following summer, his trip totally orchestrated by parishes, generated previously unimaginable crowds. It revealed to the Polish people how many faithful nationalists there were, and it taught them that they could accomplish great things if they took matters into their own hands. While not as Catholic as the Poles, other Eastern Europeans were also fortified by a Slavic Pope who, with numerous signs, made clear that his mission was to liberate them from communism and make them, once again, an integral part of Europe.

# IV

Gorbachev's ascension to power in 1985 initiated a new, and it turns out overwhelming, wave of change in the bloc. *Glasnost* and *perestroika* revealed the flaws of a centralized economy and legitimized the search for new approaches to resolving problems in the Soviet Union and in Eastern Europe. Although Gorbachev's name will be forever identified with the dismantling of the Soviet empire and the demise of the Soviet Union, the Soviet leader did not intend these results. In fact throughout his tenure, he continued to believe in communism and in Stalin's three tenets: that Eastern Europe was necessary to the Soviet Union for security, economic and ideological purposes. The problem was that security cost too much, the economies were more a liability than an asset, and the leadership of the six old men running the Eastern European countries was more sclerotic than ideologically imaginative.

During his first year in office when traveling around the bloc, Gorbachev indicated that his ruling style would combine firmness with a liberal amount of understanding for local conditions. He encouraged reform of inefficient economic systems, sustained discipline and economic cooperation. At the same time, he wanted Warsaw Pact members to recognize that the Soviet Union would continue to shape relationships with the West. Bloc countries could strive for lessening tensions toward the West, but only on the basis of bloc unity directed from Moscow. Thus, Gorbachev strengthened COMECON and renewed the Warsaw Pact for at least another 20 years.

Later in 1986 and 1987, Gorbachev grew impatient. As he again travelled around Eastern Europe, signs were evident that he wanted reforms to accelerate. On the other hand, Gorbachev did not directly interfere. Thus, confusion arose about the amount of space created by Moscow's *laissez faire* leadership. Soon each country adopted its own pace of reform: Poland and Hungary moving forward quickly, the GDR and Czechoslovakia dragging their feet, Bulgaria misunderstanding what Gorbachev wanted, and Romania rejecting everything emerging from Moscow.


# V


Outside events also energized change in each of the countries. The communications revolution and the Chernobyl disaster, for example, played important roles in hastening change.

Voice of America, Radio Free Europe, and BBC had long broadcast into the Soviet bloc. These voices from the West served as an alternative communications network for those living in societies where official news was controlled. They provided information and hope to those who were struggling against repressive regimes. Western assistance also helped nurture and develop underground news networks. Dissidents plugged into the communications revolution by using audio cassettes and contraband computers.

While the international information network revealed to people in these countries that they were not alone, another phenomenon exposed how inextricably all were linked. The Chernobyl disaster posed immediate danger to those living in neighboring countries and long-term jeopardy to all who encountered contaminated food. Environmental disasters had happened before. They were always known to the local population, but were never publicly divulged. The immensity of Chernobyl ultimately leaked out. Chernobyl thus added strength to environmental movements, which further undermined the governments in the region.

# VI

Ironically, in the mid-1980s a Soviet leader was viewed as the symbol of openness rather than of repression; Gorbachev's desire for change bolstered the aspirations of those in each country who also sought reform. The threat of Soviet intervention was removed because Gorbachev by his actions was repudiating the Brezhnev Doctrine, which had legitimized Soviet meddling and intrusion in the affairs of the satellite countries. As the leaders of Eastern European countries sorted out Moscow's signals on the limits of allowable change, dissident groups of various sizes in each of the countries began to push the bounds of permissible opposition. The absence of fear and the presence of a thirst for freedom coalesced in 1989, the year of glorious revolutions.

The year begins in Prague when Vaclav Havel and more than 800 others are arrested following human rights protests in January. In February, as Havel is being sentenced to nine months in jail, roundtable talks begin in Poland between opposition and government leaders after months of strikes and police repression. In March, 75,000 people gather in Budapest on the anniversary of the 1848 revolution, calling for a withdrawal of Soviet troops and free elections.

In April, Solidarity and the Polish government reach agreement in their roundtable talks; it is decided that in the next elections 35 percent of the seats in a new Sejm and all 100 seats in the Senate are to be contested. In May, Janos Kadar is removed as head of state, and Hungary begins to dismantle the Iron Curtain along its border with Austria. Havel is released from jail.

In June, Solidarity wins a tremendous election victory in the first free elections in the communist bloc. In August, for the first time since 1948, negotiations between Solidarity and the communists result in a non-communist heading a government in Eastern Europe. The same month, almost 400 are arrested in Prague after a demonstration marking the anniversary of the Soviet invasion. In September, the German exodus begins when Hungary opens its borders with Austria for more than 13,000 East Germans, while another 17,000 flee via West German embassies in Warsaw and Prague. The Hungarian government and the opposition parties agree on the creation of a multiparty system.

In October, demonstrations in East Germany lead to the resignation of Erich Honeker. The following month, the GDR ends travel restrictions. Millions of East Germans pour across the border into West Germany. The Berlin Wall falls. Bulgaria's Todor Zhivkov steps down; 50,000 people demonstrate in Sofia to call for further reforms. Czechs and Slovaks take to the streets, and the government collapses.

In December, President Husak swears in Czechoslovakia's first non-communist government since the February 1948 coup, with Vaclav Havel as president. Proposals for free elections emerge in Bulgaria, and mass demonstrations occur in Timisoara and in Bucharest. The tumultuous year ends with the execution of Nicolae and Elena Ceausescu.

Timothy Garton Ash deserves credit for producing the best sound bite about the revolutions of 1989. While observing the Velvet Revolution in Czechoslovakia, he commented that the transition process took 10 years in Poland, 10 months in Hungary, 10 weeks in the German Democratic Republic, and 10 days in Czechoslovakia. One can add, that events in Romania took 10 minutes, and Bulgaria's experience is not neatly categorized. Ash's quip is more than a crisp summary, it also provides the context for explaining the extent to which the process varied among countries. The differences in each country's emergence from communism were reflected in its reaction to its immediate post-revolutionary period. And it is accurate to say that the characteristics of each country's re-birth continue to affect its current behavior.

With the revolutions of 1989, the countries of Eastern Europe ended a very painful period in their histories. Since these events, we have seen that their struggle for freedom and democracy has only begun.

When Vaclav Havel addressed the U.S. Congress before a joint session in February 1990, he said a great deal very eloquently. He emphasized that:

> [W]e still don't know how to put morality ahead of politics, science, and economics. We are still incapable of understanding that the only genuine backbone of our actions — if they are to be moral — is responsibility. Responsibility to something higher than my family, my country, my company, my success. Responsibility to the order of Being, where all our actions are indelibly recorded, and where and only where, they will be properly judged.

Having left these countries to their own devices for almost half a century, the West, too, has a responsibility toward the newly emerging democracies.

## Chapter 3

# East Germany
# March 18, 1990

## Daniel I. Gordon and Fred W. Reinke

*This chapter draws on the observations of a four-member NDI-sponsored team that visited East Germany at the time of the March 18, 1990 elections. The team included Daniel Gordon and Fred Reinke, Washington, D.C.-based attorneys, and Peter Galbraith and Frank Sieverts, staff members to the U.S. Senate Foreign Relations Committee. The team met with political party leaders, election officials and representatives of nongovernmental organizations and monitored the balloting process in Berlin and Dresden.*

At the end of World War II, the victorious allies, the United States, the Soviet Union, the United Kingdom and France, divided Germany into four zones of occupation; the capital, Berlin, was similarly divided. The division was initially intended to be temporary, but increased tensions between the Western powers and the Soviet Union led the former to unify their three zones into a separate political entity that, in 1949, became the Federal Republic of Germany (FRG or West Germany). In October of the same year, the Soviet Union and its local collaborators declared the Soviet zone of occupation to be the German Democratic Republic (GDR or East Germany). The Soviet zone of Berlin (East Berlin) was declared the capital of the GDR.

The GDR was, from its inception, the Soviet Union's most loyal ally in Eastern Europe. In large part, this affinity was due to the ideological basis of the state's existence: while the communist regimes in other East European countries could attempt to blend socialist ideology with local nationalism, the GDR's existence as a separate state was predicated on rejection of German unity. In the place of German nationalism, the East German regime stressed socialist ideological purity and opposition to perceived revanchist and neo-Nazi tendencies in West Germany.

In other ways, the oppressive political and economic system established in the GDR mirrored regimes created with Soviet help throughout Eastern Europe. During the 1950s, the state usurped control of the economy, particularly the agricultural and heavy industrial sectors. The government completed its domination of the economy through a series of expropriations, which continued into the early 1970s. An all-powerful secret police, the *Staatssicherheits-dienst*, or "*Stasi*," built an omnipresent internal spying system that used psychological, economic and physical means to eliminate opposition.

Led by the Socialist Unity Party (SED), a coalition of self-proclaimed anti-fascist parties officially held the real power in the GDR. The SED was formed in 1946 by the involuntary union of the Communist and Social Democratic parties (KPD and SPD, respectively) and was clearly dominated by the Communist Party members in the SED. The SED's coalition partners were the so-called "bloc parties," rumps of Weimar-era (pre-1933) parties that were allowed to exist on the pretext that they provided representation for different social groups. The bloc parties were the Christian Democratic Union (CDU), the Liberal Democratic Party of Germany (LDPD), the National Democratic Party of Germany (NDPD) and the Democratic Farmers' Party of Germany (DBD). Despite their bureaucracies and representatives in parliament (*Volkskammer*), the bloc parties maintained no independence and served as little more than facades for SED rule.

Although the GDR regularly held elections, those elections were not free. The ballot consisted of a list of candidates drawn according to a predetermined percentage selected from each bloc party. Voters had no choice among the candidates; they could only accept or reject the list presented to them. A negative vote was difficult because voting was expected to be public. Although the privacy of a voting booth was available and the election laws provided for a secret ballot, using a booth was considered suspect, and voters rarely did so.

# I

During its 40-year history, the GDR faced three major crises. The first was in June 1953, when a revolt against the regime broke out in Berlin. The revolt was brutally repressed.

The second major crisis occurred in 1961, when unfavorable economic and political developments led a growing number of East Germans to use the open border between the occupation sectors in Berlin to flee to the West. With the support of the Soviet Union, the East German regime built a wall around the three western zones of occupation in West Berlin that became the foremost symbol of the Iron Curtain. Anyone who tried to escape was shot.

The construction of the Berlin Wall effectively, if brutally, stemmed the exodus from the GDR and in that sense resolved the country's second major crisis. As a result of the stabilization that followed, the East German economy grew in the 1960s. By the beginning of the 1970s, East Germany was considered one of the most prosperous Soviet-bloc economies. Both its collectivized agriculture and its state-owned industry were viewed as more successful than those of any other communist state, including the Soviet Union. As a further sign of the regime's success at solidifying its situation, most Western countries, including the United States, established diplomatic relations with the GDR during the 1970s.

By the 1980s, it appeared that East and West Germany had become permanent features of European political geography. Yet, just as the GDR's 40th anniversary was approaching in 1989, the third major crisis erupted, a consequence of political liberalization that swept Eastern Europe in the late 1980s. That crisis led to the end of the GDR.

# II

Mikhail Gorbachev's softening of Soviet control over Eastern Europe made the GDR's hard-line, essentially Stalinist, regime seem out of step with history. By May 1989, embryonic East German opposition groups, based primarily in the churches, felt strong enough to encourage citizens to vote "No" in local elections held at that time. More important, church-related peace groups organized citizens to witness the counting of the ballots − a process that was theoretically permitted, but one that was viewed as potentially dangerous for observers. Notwithstanding the obstacles imposed by government officials, particularly members of the *Stasi,* the observers reported "No" votes on the order of 20 percent nationwide.

While the local polling station results appear to have been accurately reported to the regional level, apparently the numbers were distorted at some higher point. At the national level the official count showed fewer than 1 percent "No" votes. The widespread recognition that fraud had occurred increased public alienation from the regime.

During the summer of 1989, limitations imposed on the freedom of East Germans to travel became the focus of opposition to the regime. In an effort to reduce feelings of isolation (and indeed imprisonment) resulting from the Berlin Wall, the government had gradually relaxed travel restrictions to certain Eastern Bloc countries. Travel was allowed only to countries considered "reliable" in the sense that their regimes would prevent East Germans visitors from continuing to the West. That system began to unravel when, in the summer of 1989, the Hungarian government allowed East German tourists to escape across the Austrian border.

By early autumn 1989, church-based groups in Leipzig had established a tradition of Monday evening protest marches. The marches, originally attended by only a few people, grew in response to the heightened frustration over travel restrictions and a sense that the regime was more and more isolated from the reforms associated with Mikhail Gorbachev.

By late September, with the GDR's 40th anniversary celebrations just days away, the world press was filled with pictures of the West German embassy in Prague overflowing with East Germans seeking to escape their country. Hoping to resolve the issue on a one-time-only basis, the GDR reached an agreement with the governments of Czechoslovakia and West Germany to allow the refugees to ride trains through East Germany and then on to West Germany. When the trains passed through East Germany, riots ensued in train stations along the way as people attempted to board the trains to the West.

As the Monday evening demonstrations continued in Leipzig, apprehension arose concerning the possibility of violent repression by the police. The environment surrounding the state's 40th anniversary in early October was marked by suspense and uncertainty. At the festivities in East Berlin, tension was evident between SED chief Erich Honeker and the visiting Soviet leader Mikhail Gorbachev, who warned his hosts of the risks inherent in failing to join the tide of liberalization.

In late October 1989, Honeker was replaced by Egon Krenz, widely viewed as Honeker's protégé and also a hardliner. Krenz was unable to stave off the deterioration of the situation. In early November, with demonstrations growing in Leipzig and other cities, the government spokesperson made an ambiguously phrased announcement at the end of a press conference that many interpreted as lifting the restrictions on travel. Shortly thereafter, the Berlin Wall was breached.

Although Krenz may have hoped to stem the demands for reform by granting free travel, the SED's position continued to erode, particularly in light of new revelations of corruption and abuse of power by the SED elite. The tide of emigrants to the West continued to grow. By December, a roundtable forum was created to help maintain stability. The roundtable included church groups as well as various new civic organizations, particularly the New Forum citizens movement. In the closing days of 1989, language relating to the leading role of the SED (itself reconstituted as the Party of Democratic Socialism, PDS) was stricken from the country's constitution.

Free elections to the *Volkskammer* were promised for May 6, 1990. Thousands of East Germans continued to move each week to the West during December and January, however, and a sense of continuing uncertainty eroded the roundtable's efforts at stabilization. Consequently, in late January, the date for the parliamentary elections was moved forward to March 18, 1990 (although May 6 remained the date for local elections). The shift in the election date did not appear to have been made for the purpose of favoring any one party or group of parties.

# III

As a result of the date change for the parliamentary elections, the original plan to circulate a draft election law for full public debate had to be scrapped. Instead, the *Volkskammer* enacted an extremely simple election law. It is worth noting that the law differed considerably from the West German electoral system, where the voter is required to vote twice, once for a party list and once for an individual candidate, and generally requires a 5 percent minimum for a party to gain representation in the federal parliament. The new East German election law, used only for the March 18 elections, created a proportional representation system. The 15 administrative units of the country (*Bezirke*) served as election districts (*Wahlkreise*), with voters in each district choosing among the lists of the parties competing in that district.

Voters selected from among party lists rather than individual candidates, in keeping with German, GDR and indeed general continental European tradition. It should also be noted that, unlike the democratic movements in Poland and Czechoslovakia, the GDR counterpart lacked well-known leaders, a circumstance that may have played a part in the formulation of the voting system.

To obtain a seat, no minimum percentage of votes was required. This condition was created to ensure that the fledgling citizens organizations, which were fragmented and lacked organizational experience, would not be excluded from the new parliament. The decision thus mirrored the consensus approach heralded by the establishment of the roundtable forum in December 1989.

East German citizens over 18 years old were automatically eligible to vote without registering; voter rolls were based on the government's list of residents. Voters received notification of their eligibility through the mail, although those who did not receive the notice were given time to add their names to the rolls. Because completely current lists of residents were unavailable, some former GDR citizens who had emigrated to West Germany were eligible to return and vote; an Electoral Commission spokesman stated that this was not a significant problem.

People could vote only at their local polling station. If voters knew in advance that they were going to be away on election day, they had to obtain special voting certificates (*Wahlscheine*) from the local election committee before election day. With that document, which functioned as a modified absentee ballot, people were allowed to vote at any polling station in the country. Approximately 200,000 such certificates were issued. Citizens were allowed to obtain voting certificates until Friday, March 16, two days before the elections.

A voter using an absentee certificate was required to surrender the certificate upon voting, a measure that prevented repeat voting. Special arrangements were made for invalids, soldiers and other qualified voters unable to visit their local polling stations. Citizens who were outside the country on election day were permitted to vote in GDR embassies abroad. Approximately 24,000 absentee ballots were mailed to such East German citizens working in foreign countries. These votes were tallied in the Berlin voting district.

In contrast to previous elections in East Germany, secret voting was mandatory. Voters were required to enter a polling booth to mark their ballots. Only paper ballots were used; there were no electronic voting machines.

# IV

Twenty-four party lists appeared on the March 18 ballot, ranging from the Party of Democratic Socialism (PDS), the SED's successor, to the Beer Drinkers Union, which appeared on the ballot only in the northern Bezirk of Rostock. The larger parties fielded lists in every district; the smaller ones did not.

The truncated campaign period hindered both the new parties and the established ones seeking to separate themselves from the previous regime.  More important, the shadow of the past forced several old parties to underscore their differences with their pre-November 1989 predecessors.  Although this factor was obviously most important for the PDS, it played a role for the former bloc parties — the Christian Democratic Union, the Liberal Democratic Party, the National Democratic Party, and the Democratic Farmers' Party — as well. The Party of Democratic Socialism worked to distance itself from the SED primarily by playing on the reformist reputation and perceived integrity of its two leaders, Hans Modrow, the prime minister who succeeded Egon Krenz in December 1989, and Gregor Gysi, who succeeded Krenz as head of the party.

The East German CDU did not shake off its association with the prior regime until West German Chancellor Helmut Kohl campaigned in the country in late winter, when the partnership with the West German CDU apparently replaced in people's minds the East German CDU's longtime alliance with the SED.  Kohl's impact on the East German CDU highlighted perhaps the most significant factor impeding the development of indigenous political parties: the influential role of the West German parties.  The roundtable made a largely ineffectual appeal for the West German parties to refrain from any activity, including funding, during the East German campaign.  The relationship between East German parties and groups in the West became a key issue in the campaign.

In the case of the Social Democratic Party, the East Germans initially formed a clearly separate party, even using a slightly different name (SDP instead of SPD) in order to make their independence clear.  By January 1990, however, the East German party apparently decided that it would be advantageous to associate with the West German SPD, and so the name was made identical. The West German SPD ultimately came to play a more prominent role in the East German campaign.  For example, at the SPD's election-eve rally in Rostock on March 17, Willy Brandt assumed a higher profile than Ibrahim Böhme, the chairman of the East German SPD.

The West German SPD had an easier time establishing its partnership with its East German counterpart than did the two other large West German parties, the West German CDU and the West German Free Democratic Party (FDP).  From December 1989 to January 1990, the West German CDU and FDP confronted the difficult task of selecting their East German partners. Each was faced with a bloc party eager to be the chosen partner: the East German CDU with the West German CDU, and the LDPD, which was supposed to be the liberal party in the East, with the FDP. Newly formed parties, however, most of which arose during the course of the October-November 1989 political turmoil, were also seeking partnership roles with the two West German parties. Those new parties and groups were able to claim a clean slate, free from the taint of association with the SED regime.

For the CDU, as noted above, Chancellor Kohl played a key — even decisive — role. He pressed for the establishment of the Alliance for Germany, composed of the East German CDU, the Democratic Awakening (a group created during the autumn 1989 events) and the DSU, a new party closely aligned with the Bavarian-based Christian Social Union (CSU). Similarly, the FDP eventually supported an alliance of three liberal groups. The liberal groups, in fact, succeeded in uniting so closely that the alliance presented one joint list on the ballot, whereas the Alliance for Germany's three parties each fielded separate lists.

Most of the other lists facing the voters on March 18 comprised new groups organized during the heady days of October and November 1989. These included Bundnis 90 (Alliance 90), a coalition of three of the most active protest groups (including the New Forum), and an alliance of the Greens and the Independent Women's Union.

One party, the right-wing Republican Party, was barred by the *Volkskammer* from participating in the elections because of its allegedly anti-democratic character. The West German Republican Party, which had been widely criticized as neo-Nazi, was successful in organizing noisy, if not numerous, supporters in East Germany during the winter months. Following its prohibition, the Republican Party essentially disappeared from the scene and made no effort either to influence or to disrupt the elections. Little if any criticism of the ban on the Republicans was voiced.

# V

As noted above, the campaign period was shorter than originally anticipated. Nonetheless, it appeared that the parties had adequate opportunity to air their views, and the voters had substantial exposure to party platforms. Issues were discussed and debated without any appearance of intimidation or harassment.

Issues shifted during the course of the winter, but they were substantive throughout the campaign. In December 1989, the campaign focused on ridding the country of the SED regime, including in particular the omnipresent *Stasi*. This issue never completely disappeared. Indeed, on the eve of the elections in March 1990, Wolfgang Schnur, the leader of Democratic Awakening, one of the CDU's partners in the Alliance for Germany, was forced to step down because of allegations that linked him with the *Stasi* under the old regime. (Similar charges against Ibrahim Böhme forced him to resign from the SPD leadership shortly after the elections.)

By early January 1990, the primary issue had become whether the GDR should continue as a separate political entity or whether the two German states should be unified. As the elections approached, that question was overtaken by events: all major parties, including the PDS, agreed that unification was inevitable. As a result, the issue before the voters in the final weeks of the campaign concerned the terms of unification.

The parties in the Alliance for Germany, particularly the CDU, stressed their desire for unification as quickly as possible. They supported unification through use of Article 23 of the West German Basic Law, which would allow the East German parliament (or the regional legislatures to be established in the course of 1990) to vote on whether to join the Federal Republic; unification would then occur instantaneously. The CDU sensed that the mood of the country favored unification as quickly and painlessly as possible.

The PDS was more cautious toward a rapid unification process. It stressed the economic disruption — including higher rents, devalued pensions, higher unemployment and loss of free health care — that East Germans would allegedly suffer at the hands of the West Germans. The party emphasized its commitment to maintain the sense of "social security" that the GDR had developed over the years. The PDS also emphasized the integrity of its two leaders, Hans Modrow and Gregor Gysi, and projected their superior images as leaders needed in a time of chaos. Indeed, Modrow avoided politicizing his reputation by refusing to campaign before the elections.

By the end of the campaign, the SPD was unable to distinguish itself from its rivals. It was not perceived as the best party for quick reunification because it advocated, in contrast to the Alliance for Germany, slower unification via the more cumbersome Article 146 of the Basic Law (requiring negotiations over a new constitution for the unified nation, rather than simple incorporation of East Germany into the Federal Republic through Article 23). Nor was the SPD recognized as the best party to bolster the economy, since the CDU's partner controlled the purse strings in Bonn.

In addition, the SPD suffered (for reasons that are not altogether clear) from disorganization and lack of direction. Thus, a few days before the elections, when the Berlin headquarters of the Alliance for Germany and the PDS were teeming with activity, the SPD's leaders, Markus Meckel and Ibrahim Böhme, were found virtually alone in the party's Berlin campaign office. The party, which in December 1989 and January 1990 had been picked as the certain winner of the elections, seemed aware that it was on the way to defeat.

In the final days of the campaign, opponents charged the West German CDU with "buying" the elections, not only through the resources it was providing the Alliance for Germany, but more fundamentally through its pledge to make an even exchange of East German marks for West German marks when economic union became a reality later in the year. The West German polling organization, Forschungsgruppe Wahlen, based in Mannheim, put it more concisely in a paper written after the election by its director, Wolfgang Gibowski: "The data show that the reasons for this outcome of the election are due to the great attractiveness of the political and economic system of West Germany." In the end, the results showed that most voters had more faith in the willingness and competence of the West German CDU, and especially Chancellor Helmut Kohl, to move rapidly toward reunification.

# VI

The role of the West Germans was aired thoroughly during the campaign, but it appears never to have become a decisive issue. To some East Germans, the West Germans were still seen through the lens of SED propaganda, primarily as predatory capitalists with no concern for the unemployed, the sick and the less fortunate. Voters holding this view tended to support either the PDS or the small independent left-wing parties. Still, despite significant resentment in many segments of East German society against the perceived insensitivity of West Germans, and notwithstanding some political missteps by Kohl during the campaign (particularly regarding the German-Polish border question), it is clear that GDR voting decisions were not determined by their feelings toward the West Germans.

The PDS, in particular, placed great emphasis on protecting GDR "national pride"; the GDR flag was proudly displayed at its rallies, even while the wrongs of the previous regime were denounced. Indeed, the flags people hung from their apartment balconies varied across the country: in the south, few GDR flags were observed, while West German flags and the green and white flag of Saxony were much in evidence; in Berlin and its suburbs, the GDR flag predominated. On election day, consistent with these observations, the PDS made its best showing in Berlin.

The West Germans played a critical role in financing East German partner parties – the Alliance, the SPD and the Free Democrats. This support provided these parties an advantage over indigenous protest groups bereft of such sponsorship. This factor appeared to grow more significant as the campaign continued. Thus, in December 1989 and January 1990, the East German CDU had a very low profile, while groups such as the New Forum (part of whose support eventually went to the Alliance 90 list) and Democratic Awakening appeared stronger.

By February 1990, the effect of the West German funding was evident: the East German CDU, the SPD, and the liberals had flashy posters and abundant campaign literature and buttons, all of which appeared to be printed in West Germany, although they were tailored to the East German situation. West German foundations (*Stiftungen*) affiliated closely with the major West German political parties also sent volunteers and party professionals to the GDR to assist East German parties in organizing rallies, handling the press and soliciting voter support.

One press report asserted that the West German Ministry for Intra-German Relations contributed three times as much in election support grants to the Alliance for Germany than to the East German SPD or FDP. That report alleged that three Alliance-affiliated West German foundations each received DM 1.5 million whereas only one SPD and one FDP foundation each received a DM 1.5 million contribution. The PDS, meanwhile, was estimated to have spent approximately DM 5.5 million, all drawn from East German government coffers, for its election campaign.

To a certain extent, some West German resources may have been too much for the East German system to absorb. One such example involved the delivery, a few days before the elections, of personal computers to SPD headquarters in East Berlin, where virtually no one was present to receive, much less to take advantage of, the equipment. In any event, even though the SPD may have received less West German assistance than the CDU, the much stronger showing of the CDU on March 18 appeared to be primarily issue-related. Certainly the eventual electoral support for the CDU was disproportionate to any financial advantage it may have enjoyed over the SPD and the liberals. It should similarly be noted that the PDS, which did not appear to receive outside assistance, did much better than expected in the elections. While it is true that the PDS enjoyed access to substantial domestic resources, its success seemed to be the result of its positions on the issues.

# VII

Election administration was handled by a National Electoral Commission composed of 48 members — two representatives each from the 24 political parties that appeared on the ballot. The Commission formed district electoral commissions in all of the 15 districts, each of which in turn included approximately 1,000 to 1,500 polling stations. Altogether, 22,000 polling stations were established throughout East Germany.  Each polling station was assigned between 800 and 1,200 eligible voters (with 1,500 the legal maximum).  A polling station was administered by a local election commission consisting of seven to 10 members.

Although the Electoral Commission was not an unfamiliar institution in the GDR — such commissions had administered elections since 1963 — its commitment to free elections was quite new.  The Commission quickly established a reputation as a fully independent, completely nonpartisan body.  It maintained a high profile during the campaign, and its members enjoyed ready access to both the print and electronic media.  The Commission used that access to explain the electoral process to the voters.  For example, during one television program viewers called in questions, while members of the Electoral Commission explained how people could vote outside their residential district, and why only one "X" could be marked on the ballot.

The Electoral Commission issued non-mandatory guidelines that election campaigning cease at 9 p.m. on Friday, March 16, and that no campaigning occur in Leipzig during its biannual trade fair, March 12-16.  West German Chancellor Helmut Kohl ignored the latter guideline by speaking in Leipzig to a crowd of 120,000 on Wednesday, March 14; Willy Brandt and Ibrahim Böhme similarly disregarded the Commission guidelines by holding final rallies in Rostock and Stralsund on Saturday, March 17.

The Electoral Commission supervised the reporting of both the preliminary results (announced Sunday night and Monday, March 18 and 19) and the final results (announced Friday, March 23).  The Commission appeared to display initiative and to demonstrate complete independence from all partisan influence; no criticism of its work was voiced.

The roundtable, the extra-parliamentary forum established in December 1989 to provide a channel of communication between the regime and the various political and church groups in the country, played only a limited role in the administration of the election process.  At various times during the spring, the roundtable took positions concerning appropriate conduct during the campaign.  Those positions, however, particularly the roundtable's opposition to activity and funding by West German parties, remained largely ineffective.  The West German television stations, however, did obey a roundtable prohibition on election advertising on West German television.

# VIII

Although many parties were extremely active in the days preceding March 18, election day itself was surprisingly quiet. Very few party workers were visible on the streets, even in the vicinity of polling stations. In contrast to the situation in other emerging democratic countries, there was a general expectation that the polling and reporting of the results would be free and fair. That confidence was borne out by events.

The NDI team visited polling sites at random and without advance notice in Berlin, as well as in other locations. At each polling station visited, the observer group was welcomed into the voting station. The election officials at the sites were friendly and more than willing to answer questions and provide information about the polling procedures. The officials also seemed to take their task very seriously and followed closely the voting procedures developed by the National Electoral Commission.

As indicated above, a seven- to 10-member local election commission managed each polling station. Commission members were volunteers and generally included both party and non-party members. Members were apparently required to be residents in the neighborhood served by the polling station. Some local commission members had performed similar functions during prior elections, including the May 1989 nationwide elections held under dubious circumstances. Several of those interviewed expressed pleasure at having the opportunity to assist in fair and free elections. Although not all parties were represented at every polling station (indeed, in some cases, only one party was represented), the commission members seemed to have performed their roles properly; no complaints were heard, either on election day or afterward, about their work.

The local election commissions appeared well-prepared for the elections, due in part to a determination to conduct the elections fairly "this time." At briefings for local Berlin election officials during the week prior to the elections, for example, the Berlin district electoral commission answered questions about the eligibility of voters, the validity of ballots, procedures for assuring secret ballots and correctly

counting votes and similar issues.  Each local election commission
also met a few days before the election to discuss voting procedures.

# IX

On election day when the polls opened in the morning, local
commission members waited until at least two voters arrived and then
showed the empty ballot boxes to the voters who acted as witnesses.
The ballot boxes were then sealed shut (except for the slot for ballots)
and the voting commenced.

Upon presentation of a personal identity card or absentee voting
certificate, the voter was given a ballot and directed to a voting
booth.  Upon entering the booth, the voter marked the ballot and then
took it out of the booth and deposited in the ballot box.  The voting
process, using a secret ballot in a voting booth, a strict requirement
in these elections, contrasted with prior elections when *Stasi* or other
officials apparently took note when a voter insisted on using the
voting booth to vote secretly.  With very few exceptions, the voters
appeared to understand how to vote and, indeed, were determined to
take the opportunity to participate in free elections: at several polling
stations more than 50 percent of the eligible voters had cast ballots by
noon.

At 6 p.m., the polls closed, and the counting process began,
which the public was permitted to observe.  Throughout the day, one
election official continuously tallied the number of individuals who
had voted.  The final number thereby derived was then compared
with the total number of ballots counted in order to ensure that no
extra ballots had been added.  (Each voting site was provided a
precise number of ballots that permitted some extras to be available
in case a large number of voters from outside the district voted, and
the local commission was required to account for all unused ballots.)

After the vote counting was completed, the chair and vice-chair
of the local electoral commission and at least three other commission
members were required to sign a form that contained the total number
of used and valid ballots, the total number of used ballots declared
invalid and the number of votes for each party list.

A complex reporting procedure was used to safeguard correct transmittal of the local results to the regional and national levels. The complexity of that procedure was clearly the result of the bitter experience in May 1989, when the results of the local elections were fraudulently altered in transmission between the local polling stations and the national level. After the tally form was signed, the local commission chair opened an envelope (received earlier from the district electoral commission) containing a telephone number and a code. The chair called the telephone number, used the code to identify him/herself and reported the voting results of the polling site to the district electoral commission.

Each of the 15 districts in East Germany maintained a central statistics office to receive calls from the local polling stations. Each of those offices compiled the results at the district level and then transmitted these results by computer to the national Electoral Commission in Berlin. The ballots themselves were delivered to the National Electoral Commission in sealed envelopes over the two days following the elections and were recounted to determine the final results announced on Friday, March 23.

There were no signs of vote fraud during the balloting process, nor any indications that the brief campaign negatively affected election administration. The dramatic results of the elections tend to support the proposition that vote fraud, if any, was minimal, particularly since the PDS, the incumbent party most interested in retaining power and in the best position to perpetrate fraud, lost heavily. The spokesman for the National Electoral Commission, while admitting the occurrence of certain minor irregularities throughout the country, took the view that such irregularities would potentially affect no more than votes "up to three figures," *i.e.*, fewer than one thousand votes.

The final results showed an overwhelming victory for the Alliance for Germany, which obtained 48 percent of the vote and 192 seats. The SDP trailed with just under 22 percent and 88 seats, while the PDS obtained 16 percent of the vote and 66 seats. The 54 remaining seats were divided among eight smaller parties. Eleven parties obtained no representation.

With the elections completed, the pace of German unification moved even more quickly. On April 24, 1990, West German Chancellor Kohl and newly elected East German Prime Minister

Lothar de Maiziere announced that July 2 would be the date for monetary, economic and social union. On July 1, 1990, Chancellor Kohl announced a one-to-one exchange of East German marks for West German marks, which effectively unified the economies of East and West Germany. Negotiations with the four World War II powers followed and, to the surprise of many, an agreement was speedily reached. On October 3, 1990, the treaty became effective and East Germany ceased to exist.

Because of its links with West Germany, East Germany enjoys many benefits not shared by the other emerging democracies in Eastern Europe. While the economic benefits of the West German connection may be most obvious, East Germany's transition to democracy has also been eased. Indeed, since October 3, 1990, the question of East Germany and its democratic development is no longer germane: East Germany has become part of the FRG's well-established democracy. For this reason, little concern was raised about the freedom and fairness with which the December 1990 pan-German elections were conducted. Similarly, the development of indigenous political parties, a key issue throughout Eastern Europe, has been preempted by the role of the Federal Republic's parties throughout all of united Germany.

At the same time, the challenge of democratic development in East Germany has been submerged rather than eliminated. During the campaign, expressions of concern were heard regarding the democratization process in the GDR. The *nomenklatura* remains entrenched. The governmental bureaucracies, particularly at the local level, are staffed with civil servants left over from the SED regime; their adherence to democratic values has yet to be tested. Similarly the educational system is staffed by teachers and administrators who had served the SED and who continue in place, both because no replacements exist and because firing them would aggravate the already difficult unemployment problem.

It may well be that East Germany's incorporation into the Federal Republic will allow the democratization process to take place minus the risk or the tension present in other East European countries today. But while the mechanics of democratic self-governance may be ensured by the Federal German framework, the substance of democratic development remains a challenge. Although East Germans experienced democracy vicariously for years by watching

West German television, they now need to learn how democracy actually works, just as they are learning how the West German economy works.

In economic matters, there is a risk that economic stagnation may lead to frustration among East Germans. The current high unemployment figures are causing considerable anxiety among East Germans accustomed to total job security, and political developments, such as the absence of East Germans from the united country's governing elite, may lead to doubts about the benefits of the democratic system. In the East, there is widespread talk of West Germany having "annexed" East Germany and treating it as a colony of the West. Unless democracy and the Western economic system prove beneficial for the East Germans, the former GDR may become the economic and political backwater of a united Germany, rather like Sicily and the south of Italy, marginalized from the country's prosperity and alienated from its political life. The challenges to democratic development may be less daunting in the ex-GDR than they are in the other countries of Eastern Europe, but they are formidable nonetheless.

*Chapter 4*

# Hungary
# March 25, 1990

## Thomas O. Melia

*This chapter is based on the election monitoring activities undertaken by NDI in Hungary from November 1989 through April 1990. During this period, NDI together with the National Republican Institute for International Affairs, sponsored a five-member delegation to observe the November 1989 constitutional referendum, a 60-member international delegation to the March 25, 1990 legislative elections and a two-member team to the April 8, 1990 run-off elections. NDI Chairman Walter F. Mondale served as the principal leader of the international delegation. Before the elections, NDI also conducted training workshops for leaders of six of the political parties contesting the elections. After the elections, NDI continued its work in Hungary, organizing seminars for the newly elected legislators on parliamentary procedure.*

*The author of this chapter, NDI Program Director Thomas Melia, participated in each of the election observation missions and coordinated the NDI training programs. He is also the author of a forthcoming study of the Hungarian transition, to be published in 1992 by NDI.*

Thirty-five years after the unsuccessful revolution of 1956, and a year after the historic 1990 elections, Hungary possessed the best articulated democratic political system in the post-communist world and the most stable national government. Strains within the governing parliamentary coalition were evident, to be sure, and political formations were by no means permanently settled. But national and local elections had dispersed power and enabled several parties and diverse localities to assume responsibility for governing.

Economic restructuring remains a difficult and controversial challenge for Hungary. Hungarians generally have avoided the bolder shock therapy approach of some neighbors, although the entrepreneurial energies of the nation have been unleashed and a consumer society has emerged. Rising inflation and unemployment concern a great many, but the stability of the *forint* and the relatively sophisticated commercial and industrial infrastructure have made Hungary an attractive locus for Western investment.

Major debates rage about control of the state broadcast media; these are fully reported not only in privately owned and increasingly professional daily newspapers, but on television as well. While ethnically animated strife in adjacent Romania and Yugoslavia have raised security concerns, as did the arrival of thousands of refugees from the south and east, Soviet troops are departing, and Hungary has been admitted to the Council of Europe.

Overall, Hungary seems to be making the transformation from a one-party system with a state-directed economy to a pluralist, market-oriented democracy with equanimity and deliberation. An intricate election law provided voters with a wide range of choice and winnowed the field to a comprehensible few parties capable of assembling majorities in parliament and in city councils. An early consensus has been achieved regarding elemental state structures, and a system is in place that clarifies decision-making authority. Major sectors of society, including the formerly ruling Communist Party, have acknowledged the pre-eminence of parliament even as the actions of the president or the Constitutional Court have at times qualified that primacy. Consequently, political debate focuses on the particulars of specific policies rather than on the legitimacy of those enacting the policies.

Certainly, Hungary's progress compares favorably with its erstwhile Warsaw Pact allies, which are characterized variously by the continuing control on the part of denizens of the *anciens régimes* or by political turmoil that makes unclear whether anyone is in control at all. For those whose principal point of reference is the aftermath of the thwarted 1956 revolution, or who failed to discern since then the profound differences among Moscow's European satellites, Hungary's current situation may seem an unlikely reality.

Mikhail Gorbachev's ascension to power in Moscow in 1985 indisputably accelerated the transition from totalitarianism in Hungary, and ultimately his policies ensured that Hungary would regain its sovereignty. Yet by 1985, the transition was already underway, as Hungarians sought discreetly to disengage from the Soviet embrace. It proceeded steadily during the era of *perestroika* in the late 1980s, even while international attention more intensely focused on Poland, historically the boldest and most confrontational of all the countries dominated by the Soviets.

By the time the 1989 European revolution unfolded in October and November — when Gorbachev pulled the plug on entrenched Soviet henchman such as Hoenicker and Zhivkov — the Hungarians had on their own retired Janos Kadar, Communist Party boss for more than three decades. The regime was divided about just how much freedom it could tolerate and still remain in power. The democratic opposition had fully emerged and had begun to campaign for free elections and other democratic staples in increasingly uninhibited fashion. Indeed, by 1989 the Hungarian opposition was so confident of the imminent demise of communist rule that its leaders did not believe it necessary to coalesce under one banner — such as was the case with Solidarity in Poland, Civic Forum in the Czech Republic, Public Against Violence in Slovakia and the Union of Democratic Forces in Bulgaria. On certain occasions, Hungarian democrats coordinated their activities, but the non-communist political parties were fairly well defined when they entered negotiations on the political transition.

This early differentiation among democrats was unique in the region and is a further reflection that the Hungarian transition was not as dramatic or sudden as the others. Over several years, various groups undertook different initiatives to challenge the regime and arrived at numerous compromises or accommodations. In the absence of an apocalyptic confrontation, no charismatic hero-figure emerged comparable to Lech Walesa or Vaclav Havel.

The critical events of the transition occurred between May 1988, when the Communist Party replaced Janos Kadar with a new generation of pragmatic leaders, and May 1990, when the freely elected government of Prime Minister Jozsef Antall was sworn into office. Democratic pluralism and competitive elections displaced one-party rule. Only in the context of the 1989 European revolution could such sweeping changes in so brief a period be characterized as deliberate rather than dramatic. This is the story of the negotiated revolution.

# I

The four most important anniversary dates in Hungarian political history are March 15, June 4, June 16 and October 23. Ironically, all of them recall profound setbacks for the Hungarian nation. Still, each of these dates provided an opportunity for Hungarian democrats to seize the limelight during the exuberant year preceding the landmark elections of 1990.

On March 15, 1848, during the whirlwind of revolution that spread from Paris across Europe, Hungarians led by Lajos Kossuth launched their revolt against the Austrians. After a year of embattled independence, the combined armies of the Hapsburgs and the Russian czar defeated the Hungarians and returned Hungary to the control of Vienna.

Following World War I, the victors who gathered at Versailles disassembled the Hapsburgs' Austro-Hungarian empire. Under the terms of the Treaty of Trianon, agreed to on June 4, 1920, two-thirds of the territory that had been Hungary was ceded to Austria, Romania and the newly established states of Czechoslovakia and Yugoslavia. The polyglot population of Hungary thus fell in a day from 21 million to 7 million. About 3 million ethnic Hungarians suddenly found themselves minorities in other states — creating, in the plight of their kin, a grievance that is vivid in the minds of Hungarians to this day.

On October 23, 1956, security forces opened fire on students demonstrating in front of the state radio station. This assault ignited a revolution that led initially to the defeat of the Soviet military in Budapest by Hungarian irregulars and to the radicalization of the Hungarian leadership, which sought in vain U.N. and Western protection. In mid-November, however, the Soviet and other Warsaw Pact armies invaded Hungary *en masse* and crushed the revolution. As many as 30,000 Hungarians were killed in the fighting or executed afterward, and 200,000 more fled the country. Eighteen months later, on June 16, 1958, revolutionary Prime Minister Imre Nagy was executed in Budapest.

In the meantime, the Soviets installed Janos Kadar as paramount communist leader in 1956, where he remained in charge until 1988. His 32-year rule ranged from severe political repression, which was known euphemistically in the early years as "the period of national reconciliation," to tolerance of economic experiments. Particularly after the 1968 Soviet invasion of neighboring Czechoslovakia ended Dubcek's "socialism with a human face," Kadar's more modest "goulash socialism" seemed to represent the practical limit to liberalism within the communist world. The principal political effect of the economic reforms was to bring more and more Hungarians into contact with Westerners.

# II

In legislative elections held between 1949 and 1967, voters could cast ballots only for or against an entire national list of candidates. In 1967, however, individual election districts were created that allowed more than one candidate to be nominated for the same seat. Yet few multi-candidate races were run in the four national elections held under this system. Political power remained in the hands of the Communist Party, in any event, and the Hungarian National Assembly was quite obviously a rubber-stamp body, meeting just a few days each year in *pro forma* session.

In an effort to promote increased voter participation, the 1983 electoral law mandated multiple-candidate races for all election districts. In addition, to ensure that key individuals would not find themselves inadvertently removed from the legislature, a modified version of the national nominating list was re-introduced, whereby voters voted yes or no for a list of prominent personalities to fill 10 percent of the seats.

The 1985 elections produced several important results. First, 78 independent candidates were nominated, even though the law stipulated that all nominees be formally presented by the People's Patriotic Front (PPF), the communist-controlled umbrella organization that recruited a slate of candidates nominally reflecting all sectors of society. Public meetings were convened by the PPF in each constituency, and those candidates who received a positive vote from the crowd in attendance were placed on the general election ballot. Only occasionally, however, did the independents manage to get their supporters into these gatherings.

Eventually, 34 independents — that is, candidates not hand-picked by the communist authorities — were elected to the National Assembly. None of them, however, could fairly be described as a dissident because all enjoyed some standing in official society. But several of the new legislators, such as television personality Zoltan Kiraly, were authentic independents, willing and able to use their new public positions to criticize government policies. Still, even after the 1985 elections, the parliament remained a rubber-stamp body, meeting twice a year to enact, without amendment, legislation prepared by the Central Committee of the Hungarian Socialist Workers Party.

# III

The Soviet Union's shifting posture toward its satellites critically affected Hungarian domestic politics in the late 1980s. The new *glasnost* and *perestroika* policies of Mikhail Gorbachev, his preoccupation with economic and social crises within the Soviet Union, and his manifest disinterest in using military force to ensure the survival of East European communism, combined to quicken the pace of reform in Hungary.

Instrumental in this process was a small group of reformers within the communist establishment, led most frequently by Imre

Pozsgay, and opponents of the regime who divided generally into two overlapping groups — the urbanists and the populists. During most of the period from 1985 to 1990, mutual suspicions about motives prevented these three groups from collaborating effectively. Instead, they interacted at various forums, raising demands and mobilizing public opinion to support their initiatives.

In June 1985, however, individuals from all three groups gathered for an historic meeting in Monor, a village on the outskirts of Budapest. Although they did not reach a common approach to the process of securing a democratic transition, the varied personalities began the process of demand, dialogue and compromise that characterized the next five years.

On September 27, 1987, the first independent, non-communist, legal political organization in Hungary, the Hungarian Democratic Forum (MDF), was launched at a backyard meeting in Lakitelek in south central Hungary. Imre Pozsgay, then head of the communist Patriotic People's Front, attended the meeting, along with a curious combination of reform-minded Communist Party dissidents and non-party intellectuals, populists and nationalists. The urbanists who had been present in Monor were not invited to Lakitelek, because Pozsgay and the others from the regime thought them too insistent on radical, immediate reform.

The Hungarian Democratic Forum soon emerged as a broad coalition of democratic proponents and formerly communist reformers. Shortly after forming, the MDF pressured the government to assert and defend the rights of the large Hungarian minority in Romania. To everyone's surprise, the government began to complain about the domestic policies of a socialist ally. Indeed, the MDF eventually became a distinctly anti-communist organization and marginalized the communist reformers who had sponsored its creation.

On March 17, 1988, a number of the urbanist leaders signed a declaration that formed the basis for the creation of the Network of Free Initiatives. The declaration recognized that the internal economic crisis and the loosening Soviet grip created a clear opportunity for a broader dialogue with the government about the direction the country should take.

Originally formed to connect a number of freely formed clubs and organizations based on what its leaders called "social liberal" principles, the Network soon became a radical alternative to the legal and more moderate MDF.  The Network sponsored debates and demonstrations and issued press statements as part of a concerted effort to force the government to the negotiating table.  In particular, the Network organized a demonstration on October 23, 1988 to commemorate the 1956 revolution.  At the last minute, the government refused to allow the demonstration, leading the cautious MDF to retract its support for the gathering.  In the end, only a few hundred demonstrators took to the streets, and they were brutally dispersed.  On November 13, 1988, the Network transformed itself into a political organization called the Alliance of Free Democrats (SZDSZ).

In 1988, the Hungarian Socialist Workers Party (MSZMP) began its own political transformation.  On May 22, after more than 30 years in power, Janos Kadar was replaced as party leader by Prime Minister Karoly Grosz, who was viewed for a time by the West as a reform-minded technocrat.  The new Politburo included Imre Pozsgay, the increasingly well-known advocate of political pluralism and reform, and Reszo Nyers, the former Social Democrat who had been a leading proponent of economic liberalization in the 1960s.  By year's end, the government relaxed censorship and a legal free trade union federation was formed.

The pace of political liberalization accelerated throughout 1989.  The MSZMP attempted to ride this wave of democratization by embracing some of the opposition's demands as its own and initiating other reforms from above.  In January 1989, the rights to strike and to demonstrate freely were legalized.  The new Law on Referendum permitted a binding national vote to be called on almost any policy question presented in a petition signed by 100,000 Hungarians.  The Law on Associations allowed the establishment of non-communist and independent groups of various kinds.  Although such groups still could not register as political parties, many nevertheless announced their formation and soon discovered that they could operate without official hindrance.  In this remarkable month, too, the historic events of 1956 were officially redefined, at Pozsgay's initiative, as a "popular uprising" rather than a "counter-revolution," as the communist catechism had maintained for 33 years.

Changes continued throughout the year.  The MSZMP began to structure a transition to a multiparty state, sending delegations to examine Western constitutions, legal codes and economic laws. As with state officials in the Soviet Union, those in Hungary began to distinguish themselves from the party and to act with some autonomy from it — although, as the opposition continually pointed out, these newly independent officials had made long careers in the service of the party. Probably prompted by the example of the Polish Communist Party, the MSZMP invited opposition leaders to a national roundtable discussion to examine major issues. The principal opposition groups, however, declined to participate until certain conditions (explained below) were met. On March 15, Hungarians legally celebrated the anniversary of the 1848 war of independence against the Hapsburg empire for the first time since the communists assumed power.

In the most dramatic demonstration of national reconciliation, the bodies of Imre Nagy and others executed with him in 1958 were removed from their unmarked graves and ceremoniously reburied on June 16, 1989. This nationally televised event did not feature government officials, but instead spotlighted leading opposition political figures assembled by the Committee for Historical Justice. Hungarians seemed to have resolved a generation of acrimony. In this light, and in the aftermath of the partly free June 1989 elections in Poland, serious negotiations on the nation's future commenced.

# IV

The Association of Young Lawyers, a group of liberal attorneys in Budapest, prompted the creation of the Roundtable of the Opposition in March 1989. It grew out of the buoyant and unusual events of March 15, the traditional day of commemorating the Hungarian nation and its opposition to foreign oppression.

In early 1989, the government designated March 15 an official national holiday and organized a parade. The obvious goal was to transform the governing party's image from that of an agent of Soviet occupation to one associated with Hungarian national traditions. The emerging democratic groups — some of whose members had been harassed and beaten as recently as 1988 for celebrating March 15 — organized a rival demonstration. The official celebration in Budapest drew a crowd of 15,000 to 20,000, assembled in the time-honored communist manner of busing people from factories, while the opposition rally attracted a more spirited gathering of 50,000. The success of this event demonstrated to emerging democratic groups, parties and unions the utility of unified efforts to mobilize the public and pressure the regime for change.

Afterward, with the lawyers group acting as the principal staff and liaison for the coordinated effort, regular meetings began among representatives of eight organizations: Hungarian Democratic Forum (MDF), Alliance of Free Democrats (SZDSZ), Federation of Young Democrats (FIDESZ), Hungarian Social Democratic Party (MSZDP), Independent Smallholders Party (FKgP), People's Party (NP), Democratic League of Independent Trade Unions and the Bajcsy Zsilinszky Friendship Society. In June, following its revival, the Christian Democratic People's Party (KDNP) joined the Roundtable of the Opposition.

The Hungarian roundtable talks were designed to address the pace and direction of political and economic reform. Members of both the communist-controlled organizations and the opposition attended. Several preliminary issues, however, had to be resolved before the opposition consented to participate in discussions with the government. First, the parties agreed to use a square table for the negotiations, with the united opposition and the MSZMP facing each other. On a third side would sit three communist-controlled organizations: the Patriotic People's Front (PPF), the umbrella organization through which the MSZMP had long-administered many aspects of society; the official trade union organization (SZOT); and the communist youth group (KISZ). On the fourth side, as observers, would sit other groups, including Church officials.

Second, the MSZMP agreed to guarantee the passage of legislation necessary to enact any agreements that emerged from the talks. Until June, MSZMP officials promised only to recommend proposals to the legislature, which the opposition thought ludicrous since the MSZMP thoroughly controlled the parliament and could, if it wanted, arrange passage of all agreed changes. The government also withdrew pending legislation to reform election laws, party registration regulations and the constitution — proposals that had been prepared by the communist government without consultation with its emerging political rivals.

At the behest of the governing party, the roundtable organized itself into 12 sub-committees, six devoted to political issues and six to economic issues. The opposition groups, however, were reluctant to negotiate on any issues apart from those necessary for the election of a democratic parliament, contending that the new parliament should address all other topics including economic policy and constitutional reform. The MSZMP, on the other hand, wanted to secure opposition concurrence in various short-term policy decisions, especially those relating to economic restructuring because international financial institutions now wanted assurances that the next government would not repudiate measures the current government might enact.

During three months of negotiations, several divisions emerged among the opposition. First, the People's Party was not considered by the other members of the opposition to be truly independent of the MSZMP. Although some opposition forces regretted having included the People's Party in the group, they took no steps to exclude it. In addition, a clear rift began to grow between the revived "nostalgia" parties (Social Democratic Party, Smallholders Party and Christian Democratic People's Party), which had existed before the communist era, and the new groups (MDF, SZDSZ and FIDESZ), which were generally more militant, younger and better organized. Moreover, even among the new parties, one could clearly distinguish the MDF, with its extensive field organization and its inclination to promote Hungarian national traditions and social conservatism, from the SZDSZ and FIDESZ, which were more Budapest-based, culturally liberal and internationalist (*i.e.*, supporting Hungary's quick integration into the European community). This last distinction between populists and urbanists echoed the traditional division between Hungary's principal intellectual and political currents.

While the roundtable negotiations continued during the summer and fall of 1989, by-elections were held for six parliamentary seats vacated by the recall or resignation of MSZMP incumbents. In these cases, local groups of opposition activists took advantage of an old, never-used provision of the election law that enabled the voters of a constituency to compel a recall election by collecting and filing 1,000 signatures. The process began in the town of Gödöllö in the spring, when townspeople were angered by the refusal of their representative in parliament to attend a town meeting that they had organized. She said she represented the Communist Party in parliament, not the people who had elected her in 1985. Rather than face a recall election, however, the several MPs chose to resign, leading eventually to the by-elections. These contests, organized in an essentially *ad hoc* manner — because it was clear to all that the old law was a dead letter and a new one had not yet been enacted — became the first competitive elections for public office in Hungary since 1947. Non-communist opposition candidates emerged victorious in four of the six races; in the two other districts, the seats remained vacant due to insufficient voter turnout.

On September 18, 1989, an agreement was signed between the MSZMP and some of the opposition groups. SZDSZ, FIDESZ and the Democratic League of Independent Trade Unions refused to sign the accord, believing that it conceded too much to the MSZMP, principally by agreeing to hold a direct election of a president before parliamentary elections. The Social Democrats signed the agreement, but noted reservations.

The timing and manner of the presidential election was a primary point of contention. The opposition claimed that other issues were equally important to them — the disposition of Hungarian Socialist Workers Party assets, the presence of MSZMP cells in work places and the dismantling of the Workers' Militia, a part-time paramilitary force created in 1956 to be the armed wing of the governing party. However, they were soon resolved to the opposition's satisfaction. The issue of whether and when to hold a presidential election was to be the first major contest decided according to democratic procedures.

# V

On November 26, 1989, Hungarians voted in the first free, nationwide electoral exercise since 1947 — a referendum to settle the principal political disputes that had remained unresolved when the roundtable agreement was signed on September 18. The referendum was called pursuant to one of the reform laws enacted in January 1989, which established procedures for referenda on local and national issues. A petition with 50,000 signatures obliged the National Assembly to consider whether to put a question to a binding popular referendum. One hundred thousand signatures mandated the government to organize a referendum.

SZDSZ initiated a campaign to compel a referendum and, toward that end, obtained more than 200,000 signatures in four weeks. The Federation of Young Democrats, the Independent Smallholders Party and the Social Democratic Party of Hungary joined SZDSZ in calling for the referendum. Although the Electoral Commission invalidated about half the signatures, 114,000 survived challenges. The referendum was scheduled for November 26, 1989.

While the November ballot featured four questions, the campaign concentrated primarily one issue: whether to hold the presidential election before or after the parliamentary elections. A decision to elect the parliament first effectively meant that the presidential election would be indirect, because the next parliament would ensure that a direct election would not occur. It is unclear, however, whether most people understood that they were voting on this distinct issue concerning the nature of the presidency because the vote was formally only on the timing of the election.

SZDSZ leaders believed the ruling Hungarian Socialist Party (MSZP)[1] would enjoy an unfair advantage if the presidential election were to be held early. They asserted that the governing party still controlled the mass media and the election apparatus, and the opposition would have little time to field a candidate strong enough to challenge the well-known and increasingly obvious MSZP candidate, Imre Pozsgay. SZDSZ did not want to imitate the recent Polish experience where a communist was installed as a strong president and then, once in office, resisted the accelerating process of democratization. SZDSZ preferred to leave the choice of president to the new, freely elected parliament — so that the office of the president would be weaker, and less likely to be occupied by a communist.

---

[1] The ruling Hungarian Socialist Workers Party (MSZMP) changed its name to the Hungarian Socialist Party (MSZP) at its Congress in October 1989. Shortly afterward, a rump group of hardliners declared that the MSZMP would continue, and they did present candidates in the 1990 elections under the old party name. But the principal personalities and considerable material assets of the old party reverted to the new Socialist Party.

The MDF, on the other hand, maintained that the president's powers were so limited that such an election would be relatively insignificant compared to parliamentary elections. MDF leaders also contended that the scheduling of a presidential election before parliamentary elections had been one of the conditions necessary to obtain the consent of the communists to hold free parliamentary elections. MDF asserted that it was necessary to honor the entire roundtable agreement in order to be able to hold the governing party to its commitments. Unwilling to advocate a position identical to that of the governing party (they were already being accused by some of entering into pacts with the communists), the MDF urged their supporters to boycott the voting. If the turnout was less than 50 percent of eligible voters, the referendum would be ruled invalid regardless of the voting results.

The referendum produced a very close result that represented a narrow defeat for the ruling party and a setback for the Hungarian Democratic Forum. With a 55 percent turnout, slightly more than 50 percent of the voters chose to postpone the presidential election until after elections for a new parliament. The Socialist Party-controlled government, led by a conspicuously gracious Imre Pozsgay, immediately acquiesced to the expressed will of the people and canceled presidential voting that had been slated for January 16.

On March 1, 1990, in one of its last acts, the MSZP-controlled parliament amended the constitution to provide for a direct presidential election. On this occasion, it was SZDSZ that called for upholding the roundtable agreement, which limited the outgoing parliament's actions to passing only legislation "essential for the democratic transition and economic stability." SZDSZ was still concerned that Imre Pozsgay would win a direct national election. While SZDSZ had grown by this time to become one of the strongest political organizations in the country, it did not yet have a candidate for president.

# VI

The election law provided for the election of 386 representatives to a unicameral legislature according to three methods. One hundred seventy-six deputies would be directly elected from single-member constituencies on a two-round majority basis (the first round would require a majority for victory; in the second round a plurality would suffice.) One hundred fifty-two deputies would be elected from 20 county party lists based on a proportional system (with a 4 percent national threshold). Fifty-eight seats would be filled from national party lists, also proportionally allocated from "unused" votes not needed to win a seat in a constituency or from a county list. Each voter would cast two ballots: one for the local constituency representative and one for the county list. If neither was needed to elect a legislator, it was added to the pool from which the 58 national party list seats were to be filled.

This election system thus represented a combination of direct election of individuals and proportional representation by party. The election law of the Federal Republic of Germany, as well as the Scandinavian Lague system, influenced the formulation of the somewhat more complex Hungarian variant. The communist-dominated parliament modified the law before enacting it to increase the number of single-member constituencies, a move that some incumbents believed would enhance their own re-election chances.

The law also reflected a balancing of the parties' respective understandings of their electoral strengths. The MDF preferred the single-member system because, according to public opinion polls at the time the system was adopted in October, the Forum enjoyed by far the most popular support. SZDSZ envisioned itself as a party that could obtain no more than 10 percent of the national vote and therefore supported proportional representation. The nostalgia parties, vaguely confident of broad nationwide support, also favored proportional representation because they were unsure whether their supporters were concentrated enough to enable them to win in single-member districts. Leaders of the MSZP thought they would do well in individual constituencies and knew that their national apparatus would allow them to profit from a proportional system. As a result, the MSZP was satisfied with a mixed system.

In accordance with the law, the government provided 700 million *forints* (U.S. $11.2 million) to political parties during 1990. In January and February, parties received grants based on their unverified claims of membership. The amounts received by the parties varied, with MDF, MSZP and the Independent Smallholders receiving 15 million *forints* (U.S. $240,000) each, based on membership claims in excess of 20,000. SZDSZ and the Social Democrats received 10 million *forints* (U.S. $160,000), FIDESZ 7 million *forints* (U.S. $112,000), and the Christian Democrats 4 million *forints* (U.S. $64,000). Not surprisingly, the smaller parties objected to the allocation of money based merely on unverified claims of membership, but the system endured.

In addition to the above grants, 100 million *forints* (U.S. $1.65 million) was set aside to subsidize the election campaign; each candidate who qualified to run in a single-member district received approximately 25,000 *forints* (U.S. $400). Private fundraising from sources inside and outside the country was permitted, though contributions from foreign governments were prohibited.

The total amount spent by the parties in the election campaign and the sources of that money remain largely unknown. Despite a legal requirement obliging all parties to account publicly for their financing and spending, few had done so by the end of 1990. Thus, the extent of foreign contributions also remains unclear, with most parties claiming to have received very little while charging their competitors with receiving large foreign subsidies. The Socialist Party and the Socialist Workers Party, the two rival successors to the once-monolithic state party, clearly enjoyed many infrastructural advantages, although the principal opposition parties were given substantial office space in Budapest and other towns between January and March 1990.

The law also allowed parties to buy television and radio time at commercial rates (Hungary being the only Warsaw Pact country to have established such a policy before the 1990 elections) and provided free television and radio time to 39 political parties that nominated candidates for parliament. A series of debates among representatives of the 12 major parties that qualified to present national lists was also broadcast before the elections.

The issue of media coverage and access was a source of constant acrimony throughout the campaign period and was animated largely by the fact that the broadcast media remained state-controlled. Parties and candidates complained regularly about uneven coverage. Irme Pozsgay, Socialist Party leader and parliamentary candidate, was removed from overseeing a theoretically independent media supervisory board in January 1990. SZDSZ and FIDESZ charged that Hungarian television favored the MDF and that the print media consistently failed to announce SZDSZ and FIDESZ events and under-reported attendance at their rallies. MDF countered that the media spent excessive time covering SZDSZ press conferences and otherwise showed favoritism toward its candidates.

While some parties enjoyed more success communicating through the media than others, by most standards it appeared that access to the media remained relatively nonpartisan. At the same time, the growing freedom of the press did not translate immediately into competent professional news reporting by Hungarian journalists, who were mostly veterans of the restricted press of the previous era. These journalists had as little experience covering political campaigns as the aspiring politicians had in organizing them. Especially in the early days of the campaign, newspapers and broadcast media were clumsy and uneven in making judgments about what constituted newsworthy material.

In early 1990, the Association of Young Lawyers collaborated with representatives from 12 political parties, the Hungarian News Agency and Hungarian Television in preparing the Hungarian Electoral Code of Ethics. The drafting organizations adopted the Code on January 23, 1990, and pledged to refrain from negative campaigning, which was defined to include attacks on opponents and defacement of rival campaign posters. By the formal start of the campaign, 33 political parties, including all the major ones, and most key news organizations had subscribed to the Code. Given the Code's broad, general language and the parties' apparent inability or disinclination to enforce specific provisions, it is difficult to estimate its effect on the activities of the parties and the media during the campaign.

# VII

Between the November referendum and the commencement of the official election campaign period on February 26, several specific issues or incidents captured the attention of the parties, the media and the public. The principal political debates focused on determining who was responsible for sustaining the unpopular communist regime and deciding who would be most effective at building the new social order. Non-communist parties and candidates sought to portray one another as historically or secretly aligned with the communist establishment and to minimize or discount the reformist record of leading Socialists. Within this general environment, several specific issues attracted attention.

"Duna-gate" (combining the Hungarian word for the Danube river, Duna, with the international suffix connoting political scandal) virtually monopolized media attention and political debate in January 1990. During the last week in December, an officer in the Hungarian secret police, fearing that the Hungarian security forces might follow the lead of their Romanian counterparts (who during the revolution that month had backed the dictator, Ceausescu, against popular demands for reform), divulged to an MDF legislator that the secret police continued to spy on members of the opposition and kept records on various meetings and events. With the help of the informant, a video crew entered the police headquarters in Budapest and filmed files recording the recent political activities of opposition parties.

In early January, SZDSZ, FIDESZ and other opposition groups publicized the footage and called for the immediate dismantling of the entire secret police. In response to the negative publicity, the government agreed to stop monitoring opposition political activities. The chief of the secret police and a deputy minister of the interior were dismissed, and control of the clandestine agencies was removed from the jurisdiction of the Interior Ministry and placed under control of the prime minister.

As election day approached, MDF, SZDSZ and the Independent Smallholders emerged as the leading contenders. Because the leading parties agreed on the need for a transition to a market economy, the only real economic debate surrounded the pace at which this transition should take place. In general, SZDSZ and FIDESZ favored a quick transition and immediate integration into the European community. Later in the campaign, the Christian Democrats and Social Democrats also featured European integration — and their links to kindred parties in the West — in posters and television ads. The MDF and the Smallholders, on the other hand, took a somewhat more cautious approach to economic reform and formal European integration.

The Smallholders emphasized radical land reform, calling for the simple and immediate return of property (not compensation) to pre-nationalization owners.  All other parties ridiculed this idea as unworkable, but the Smallholders support in the countryside increased in January and February as the party's position was publicized.

All of the parties, including the governing MSZP, sought to portray themselves as the most outspoken, long-standing or effective opponents of the totalitarian "party-state."  SZDSZ and FIDESZ asserted that MDF was too close to the governing party, and their candidates frequently alleged that "deals" had been struck between MDF and the Socialists.  One controversial SZDSZ campaign poster ominously proclaimed "Those who are not with us are with *them*." MDF rebutted these charges by claiming that SZDSZ and FIDESZ leaders, some of whom were in fact children of prominent communists, were themselves closely linked to the communist regime. The Socialists said they were the most effective at government and claimed credit for reforms already implemented.

Communist-bashing tactics remained popular throughout the campaign.  One MDF campaign poster portrayed the back of the head of a Soviet soldier, with the words "Good Riddance!"  Another depicted a trash can full of Stalinist and communist propaganda and offered "Spring Cleaning with the MDF."  The MSZP, meanwhile, attempted to bolster its own anti-communist credentials through frequent and visible meetings with Western political and government officials.

The issue of Hungarian national identity dramatically affected all of the parties and may have boosted the fortunes of the MDF during the week preceding the elections.  When the Romanian revolution broke out in December 1989 with a brave ethnic Hungarian cleric as its first hero, the leading Hungarian parties organized highly publicized relief caravans to deliver medicine and food to ethnic Hungarians in Transylvania. Even those parties that had sought to downplay old-fashioned nationalist sentiment, such as SZDSZ and FIDESZ, were compelled by their supporters to become involved. On March 20, just five days before the elections, and following a renewed outbreak of anti-Hungarian violence in Transylvania, tens of thousands of people from all parties joined together at a somber televised rally in Hero's Square in Budapest without a campaign banner in sight.  Since the MDF was well-established as the party that had most consistently enunciated Hungarian cultural nationalism, in particular denouncing the Romanian regime for its long-standing mistreatment of the Hungarian minority there, the upsurge of emotion in those days before the voting may have enhanced support for the MDF.

# VIII

Election day finally arrived on Sunday, March 25, 1990. The law provided four levels of election committees: national, county, constituency and polling place. These committees were designated to oversee the implementation of the law and regulations issued by the Interior Ministry. Each committee contained three non-party members appointed by the appropriate state governing body (national legislature or municipal council), as well as representatives from each party that had a candidate standing in that jurisdiction. The process worked smoothly, as all parties appeared to trust the integrity of the election officials, and there were no substantial reports of electoral manipulation. November's referendum had provided an important trial run for the election apparatus, and persuaded many skeptics that the votes would be counted accurately.

Sixty-six percent of eligible voters turned out for the elections; only five constituencies failed to meet the 50 percent threshold required to validate the elections. Five of the 176 majority seats were decided in the first round; the remainder were decided in run-off elections on April 8. MDF, capturing 24.7 percent of the vote in the county lists, scored a narrow victory over SZDSZ, which polled 21.4 percent. Four other parties met the 4 percent threshold necessary for representation in the legislature.

Despite the close contest between MDF and SZDSZ, both parties interpreted the first-round results as a decisive victory for MDF. In part, this observation stemmed from MDF's narrow plurality over SZDSZ in Budapest (28.38 percent to 27.13 percent), a city that had generally been expected to favor SZDSZ.

The two-week period between the first and second rounds of elections shaped up as a direct confrontation between MDF and SZDSZ candidates in virtually every electoral district. Although more than two candidates could appear on the second-round ballot (anyone with more than 15 percent of the vote in round one), FIDESZ candidates generally stepped aside in favor of SZDSZ, while KDNP and FKgP usually did the same for MDF. Unlike in the first round, when SZDSZ dominated the political debate and skillfully used the media to launch its attacks, in the second round MDF controlled the debate. MDF aggressively attacked SZDSZ as "leftists," "sons of Bolsheviks" and "communists." Uncharacteristically, SZDSZ leaders failed to respond vigorously or to launch any counter-attack during this critical two-week period. After the second round of elections, the MDF controlled 164 of the 386 legislative seats, SZDSZ garnered 92 seats, and 130 seats were divided among four other parties and a few independents.

A provision of the election law that called for the new National Assembly to elect eight additional members to represent specific ethnic minorities (Serbs, Croatians, Germans, Gypsies) was never implemented. There has been very little public discussion of this omission, and none of the parliamentary parties has sought the addition of these extra deputies.

The role of international observers turned out to be less significant than in other places where the legitimacy of the system or the fairness of the election environment is a subject of controversy. All Hungarian parties requested international observers, and the election administrators were very accommodating of them. The most important accomplishment in this regard was in the model that Hungary provided to observers from countries where the political process was less developed.

# IX

Despite some early speculation, a grand coalition between MDF and SZDSZ never developed. Instead, a more ideologically cohesive ruling coalition, which included the Smallholders and Christian Democrats, coalesced behind MDF leader Jozsef Antall who was elected prime minister on May 10. The coalition controlled approximately 60 percent of the seats in the National Assembly, leaving in opposition a very strong and vocal, and equally non-communist, bloc comprising primarily SZDSZ and FIDESZ parliamentarians. The presence of a strong governing coalition and a strong democratic opposition force in the National Assembly has succeeded in further marginalizing the role of former communists in Hungary's new National Assembly.

At Antall's initiative, MDF and SZDSZ reached an agreement to promote the stability of the new government. SZDSZ agreed to support a constitutional amendment to restrict the number of laws requiring a two-thirds majority. In addition, SZDSZ supported an amendment requiring the opposition to put forward a new name for prime minister if it introduced a motion of no confidence. This provision, the "constructive vote of no confidence," made it more difficult to bring down a government even if a prime minister lost a majority in the legislature, because the no confidence vote would simultaneously be a vote for an alternative prime minister.

In return for these concessions, the coalition parties agreed to support SDZSZ parliamentarian Arpad Goncz as the National Assembly's choice for president. This pact elicited a great deal of criticism from the press and from parliamentary parties who were not consulted. Indeed, there was considerable grumbling within the two major parties, as well. But it provided the new prime minister some working room, and it sent a message that even campaign rivals could find ways to work together in the interests of the stability of the new democratic regime.

The Socialist's first major political initiative after assuming their place in the parliamentary opposition (with 11 percent of the vote and 33 seats) was to revive the question of how to elect the country's president. They gathered the requisite signatures to compel a referendum which, if successful, would have provided for the direct, popular election of the president. But the voting was scheduled for July 29, a weekend at the height of the vacation season, and turnout was only 13 percent. The referendum was therefore ruled invalid and the proposal failed.

# X

In early August, the National Assembly enacted a local government election law, which paved the way for local elections on

September 30 and October 14. For the fifth and sixth times in a year, voters went to the polls — this time to elect municipal assemblies and, in settlements with fewer than 10,000 voters, to elect mayors directly. Half the municipal councillors were elected from party slates, and half were elected from candidate lists on a majority basis. In towns with populations larger than 10,000, the municipal assembly elected the mayor. In the special case of Budapest, voters cast their ballots to elect one of 22 district assemblies, as well as to elect 66 members of a city-wide municipal assembly. These districts then each elected one of their number to be district mayor (immensely complicating the difficult job of the mayor of Budapest elected by the municipal assembly). The district assemblies also each elected one member to join the municipal assembly, bringing its total membership to 88.

By and large, elections for local government authorities were a disappointment for the voters and the parties. Voter turnout averaged 40 percent in the first round and 29 percent in the second round. Several factors contributed to the low turnout. First, the Hungarian people were apparently weary of going to the polls. Second, without a law that fully defined the roles and responsibilities of the local governments, candidates found it difficult to conduct an effective campaign. The August law principally addressed elections; it did not provide for local government financing. In addition, many of the political parties had exhausted the funds needed to conduct an effective campaign. (No additional state financing was provided for these elections.) Finally, many of the parties were unable to recruit sufficient candidates. Still, with the implementation of local elections, the Hungarian people successfully completed a process of replacing a centralized totalitarian government with elected representatives at all levels of government.

# XI

Hungarian politics in the years following May 1988, when long-time strongman Janos Kadar was retired by his communist colleagues, constitute the third Hungarian revolution. Following the failures of 1848 and 1956, it is the first revolution to have succeeded in establishing a sovereign and democratic Hungarian state. Only in the extraordinary context of Eastern Europe after the fall of the Berlin Wall does it seem to have been a lengthy and placid process; during any other time in history, it would have been seen as tumultuous and dramatic.

Events in Poland clearly influenced Hungarians. Agreements reached in Warsaw made it easier for the Hungarian communist authorities to consider similar concessions, while also providing standards of accomplishment for democrats in Budapest to surpass. In 1956, a nationalist-minded Polish regime had compelled Khrushchev to retreat from Poland, and that made the Soviets a little too quick to crush the rebellion in Hungary a few weeks later. In the late 1980s, as in the mid-1950s, Hungarians wanted to be rid of Soviets and communists as much as did the Poles. The difference clearly was Mikhail Gorbachev, who seemed to study closely developments in Hungary and Poland — not to stop them, but in order to learn how change might be introduced in his own country. Moscow's hands-off posture eventually emboldened the democrats, even as it made the communists more accommodating.

Hungary also benefitted from what had become by the 1980s the region's most benign form of communism. During the last decade of the regime, there were no political prisoners. A degree of entrepreneurship and consumerism was allowed, even encouraged. The borders were relatively open, and Hungarians, even known dissidents and critics, were allowed to spend time abroad and then return. In retrospect, it is now clear that some leading figures in the communist establishment were actively and persistently planning to reform the system in a profound way, although they remained nervous about how much deviation from communist orthodoxy would be tolerated by Moscow.

Hungary also benefitted from the relatively homogenous composition of its population. No major separatist or ethnic issues or groups shaped political developments. Indeed, shared interest and concern about Hungarians living in neighboring states, especially Romania, provided a measure of common ground for all political parties. The sizeable Gypsy minority, numbering perhaps 400,000 in a country of 10.5 million, remained almost wholly outside the Hungarian political arena. Though they may one day constitute a substantial political force, to date they do not.

Traditional Hungarian socio-political divisions between urbanists and populists, Budapest and the countryside, internationalists and nationalists, were revived in the context of the re-democratization of politics. Part of the populist community even injected a form of anti-Semitism into the political campaign. Although Western news accounts may have overemphasized issues involving incidents of anti-Semitism, this threat to the strengthening of democratic culture in Hungary remains worrisome for Hungarian democrats. Leaders of all political parties have renounced anti-Semitism, and the effort to establish legitimacy for such destructive sentiments seems to have been thwarted. The marginal status of Gypsies, on the other hand, remains largely ignored — as is the case throughout the region.

By the start of 1991, several factors combined to produce in Hungary the most fully articulated political system in post-communist Europe: the retreating communist establishment did not present a strong enough threat to a democratic opposition for them to fear that the ruling party would win reasonably fair elections; the extended and public nature of the negotiations toward transition provided numerous groups with the opportunity to establish public profiles, to see their popularity reflected in opinion surveys and to articulate specific policy differences with other democrats; and the election system guaranteed that any party attaining 4 percent support nationwide would be represented in the National Assembly, which encouraged a certain proliferation of parties.

Much discussion has centered on the relatively low turnout (66 percent) in Hungary's national elections. This phenomenon may be attributed to several factors. First, within 18 months, Hungary held two referenda, two rounds of legislative elections and two rounds of local elections. Turnout generally fell with each voting exercise. Second, the absence of significant communist political power by the time of the elections may have deprived many people of an overriding motivation to vote. Third, in the November referendum, the communists narrowly lost a vote that was important to them but accepted the result. Thus, the public may have believed that the civil administration would do an honest job and that little danger of manipulation existed. Fourth, with the old regime marginalized, choices about which one of the numerous democratic parties was most attractive or competent may not yet have mattered as much. Finally, Hungary has always demonstrated the lowest turnout among communist states — averaging 92 percent in the 1970s and early 1980s, instead of the familiar 99.9 percent.

In the end, only six parties garnered enough support for National Assembly representation, and three of them formed a coalition government. This situation left not only the former communists in parliamentary opposition, but also two strong democratic parties. While the social democratic portion of the political spectrum familiar in the West remains meager, a full range of viewpoints has largely found representation in the parliament.

The municipal elections in the autumn provided an opportunity for the public to vote against the national government parties, as is frequently the case in many countries. Consequently, many councillors and mayors are now members of SZDSZ and FIDESZ, the parties in opposition at the national level. This process has successfully dispersed political power by decentralizing governmental authority and by allowing different parties to hold offices at various levels. Several parties will therefore have the opportunity to learn the political consequences of governing — a healthy development for a young democracy.

*Chapter 5*

# Slovenia
# April 7 and 21, 1990

## Edward McMahon

*This chapter is based on the observations of a six-member NDI survey mission, which was in Slovenia at the time of the April 7, 1990, elections. Slovenia was the first of the Yugoslav republics to hold multiparty elections and thus set the stage for elections in the other republics. The survey team visited five of Yugoslavia's six republics, with the goal of designing a democratic development program for Yugoslavia. Building on the work of the survey mission, NDI organized a conference in October 1990 on democratic governance in multi-ethnic states. Political leaders of all the republics attended the conference, which was held in Cavtat, Croatia.*

*This chapter was written by NDI Senior Program Officer Edward McMahon, who also was responsible for organizing NDI's October 1990 conference.*

As the 1980s drew to a close, no single electoral process existed throughout Yugoslavia. Rather, there existed seven distinct electoral systems at varying stages of development: one in each of the six republics and one at the federal level. Elections took place in all six republics, but not nationally, during 1990.

During this period, politics in Yugoslavia had become even more complex than before. This was particularly true of the electoral process. Yugoslavia was a country in transition, in which the challenge of replacing traditional communist structures was inextricably linked with nationalist pressures to redefine the relationships among republics. Each republic was confronting this delicate task, wrought with the potential for failure and violence, at its own pace.

This chapter surveys the electoral process in Slovenia, the first republic to hold free elections in 1990, with an emphasis on the republic-wide elections held in April. It highlights the creation of a pluralistic environment, the structuring of electoral laws, the development of political parties, the conduct of the elections and the election results. It concludes with some thoughts about the future of democratic development in the Yugoslav context.

# I

President Josip Broz Tito ruled Yugoslavia for 35 years, largely through force of personality. Tito engineered an ingenious system of checks and balances among republics to deter perceived Serbian hegemonic impulses. In 1971, for example, a collective state presidency was established, and the 1974 constitution emphasized, in theory at least, the devolution of many powers to the republic level. This legalistic emphasis on decentralization, while preserving the power of the Communist Party with Tito as the final arbiter, enabled the republics to maintain their identities and considerable autonomy. It did not, however, extinguish ethnically based nationalist sentiments and desires for greater autonomy, nor did it inculcate a deep-rooted sense of Yugoslav nationalism.

The system Tito established endured throughout the 1980s. That it outlived Tito is not only a testimony to his leadership but is also a result of widespread fear of the consequences of unchecked centrifugal forces. The communist system continued to impose a semblance of unity, but the more developed republics, Slovenia and Croatia, increasingly resented paying a disproportionate share of Yugoslavia's economic bill, and the limited scope of the federal government's powers made centralized economic reform difficult.

Events in the Soviet Union in the 1980s had much less impact for Yugoslavia, which had left the Soviet orbit three decades earlier, than for its Eastern and Central European neighbors. Soviet force had not imposed Yugoslavian communism. In relative terms, Yugoslavs had also for years enjoyed greater freedom of expression.

During the 1980s, several of the republics expressed growing demands for greater autonomy, if not independence. These demands made a fundamental realignment of relationships between Belgrade and the republics seem increasingly likely. The virtual disintegration of the weakened ruling communists was highlighted when the Slovenes and Croats walked out of a January 1990 Extraordinary Congress of the League of Communists of Yugoslavia (LCY). By leaving the congress, the dissenting delegates demonstrated that their loyalties lay with their own republics' nationalist constituencies as opposed to the Yugoslav government.

# II

Slovenia's relatively strong economy and its pre-1989 moves toward democracy contrast sharply with the significantly less developed republics to the south. Slovenia, with 8 percent of Yugoslavia's population, produced 20 percent of Yugoslavia's GNP and 30 percent of its hard currency. Traditionally oriented toward Austria, Italy and Central Europe, Slovenes had long been disillusioned with their status within the Yugoslav federation. As the most affluent republic, Slovenia grew weary of subsidizing the budgets of other republics. Slovenes paid four times more in federal taxes than they received in federal programs and objected to bearing a disproportionate percentage of the nation's fiscal burdens. Slovenes especially resented paying to support an army whose officer corps was predominantly Serbian and that sought to maintain the Yugoslav federation. This situation was aggravated by the fact that conscripts had to serve outside their home republics.

Even before the armed conflict that began in June 1991, there was no love lost between Slovenia and Serbia. In 1989, for example, Serbia imposed an embargo on Slovene goods and services, following Slovenia's refusal to permit a Serbian rights demonstration in Ljubljana, Slovenia's capital.

Slovenia began to move toward political pluralism well before the democratic revolution began in the rest of Eastern Europe. In 1987-88, the ruling League of Communists of Slovenia (LCS) tried to harness popular sentiment by allowing, and to an extent encouraging, the formation of non-communist political movements. At the same time, the LCS leadership assumed an increasingly independent position within the Yugoslav Communist Party debate over inter-republic relations and championed political liberalization at both the republic and federal levels.

In 1989, Slovenia rejected proposed amendments to the federal constitution, which would have consolidated federal powers over the economy, human rights and other divisive issues, on the grounds that they threatened Slovene autonomy. Such changes, Slovenes argued, could only be considered after the adoption of a new Slovene constitution guaranteeing the right to self-determination, including secession.

During this period, the League of Communists of Slovenia became increasingly estranged from the parent LCY. Having asserted its independence by walking out of the Extraordinary LCY Congress in January 1990, the LCS subsequently confronted the issue of just how close it should remain to its origins and whether to keep its name. In a compromise solution, the party decided in early February to become the LCS-Democratic Renewal Party.

# III

Even before political parties were legalized in early 1990, a number of prototype parties formed, beginning in 1987 when the first independent organization, the Small Farmers' Union, was legalized. Other "alliances" followed in 1988. These alternative political organizations included a mixture of traditional and new-style parties, including the Slovenian Democratic Alliance, the Social Democratic Alliance, the Radicals and the Greens. Still, until the end of 1989, any organization applying for registration ostensibly had to become a member of the Socialist Alliance of Slovenia, a government-affiliated omnibus front through which the LCS had long controlled the levers of power.

A number of the new political organizations balked at having to join the Socialist Alliance. The founders of the Social Democratic Union of Slovenia, for example, labeled their organization a political party, although they refused to join the Socialist Alliance. Founded in January 1989, the Slovene Democratic Union successfully conditioned its membership in the Socialist Alliance on the Alliance's agreement to loosen its ties to the Communist Party.

The communist government of Slovenia, searching for popular support and legitimacy, did not discourage the growth of political pluralism. In 1989, more political groupings were legalized, and on December 27 the government enacted laws on "the Election and Recall of the President and Members of the Presidency of the Socialist Republic of Slovenia" and on "Elections to Assemblies." Slovenia adopted a law explicitly legalizing political parties soon thereafter. The electoral law specified how candidates and candidate lists for election to the different offices were to be chosen and how voting was to be conducted. The new, complicated election system was designed to combine freedom of individual expression with a coherent election result that could enable a relatively stable government to emerge. In addition, the laws also set republic-wide elections for April 1990.

The emerging parties included both the old and the new. Perhaps reflecting a Western European political orientation, and unlike in other formerly communist democratizing countries where the word "party" was expunged from democratic political vocabularies because of its historical association with totalitarianism, Slovenes were content to call their "parties" just that. Slovenian parties active before the imposition of the single-party state, such as the Christian Democratic, Social Democratic and Peasant parties, were revived. New parties tended to adopt "radical" platforms encouraging free-market economics and emphasizing ecological concerns. They also were more strident in calling for Slovenian independence and generally enjoyed a younger following, which did not have first-hand exposure to the parties of the pre-communist period.

Six democratic opposition parties from across the ideological spectrum formed DEMOS (Democratic Opposition of Slovenia), a coalition to oppose the Communist/Socialist parties. DEMOS parties included the Social Democratic Union of Slovenia, the Slovene Democratic Union, the Slovene Christian Democratic Union, the Slovene Farmers Union, the Grey Panthers and the Slovene Tradesmen's Party. One significant non-Communist Party, the Liberals, did not join the coalition. DEMOS members agreed that if the coalition won a majority of seats in the Slovene Parliament and created a new government, the party receiving the most votes would select the prime minister.

On January 4, 1990, the DEMOS coalition was strengthened by the addition of the Slovene Peasant Alliance and the Greens of Slovenia. On January 9, the umbrella organization of the communist-affiliated front organizations, the Socialist Alliance of the Working People of Slovenia, constituted itself as a political party.

The Slovene press had been the most liberal in Yugoslavia for some time, and even greater press freedom after 1988 fostered a notably more open climate for the print media and a larger number of media outlets. Freedom of expression was greatest in the print media, which for example, actively covered the case of three journalists arrested by the military. In earlier times, such news would have undoubtedly been suppressed. Irreverent and outspoken publications such as *Mladina* appeared. These publications reflected the political perspectives of a generation of Slovenes who would be exercising a meaningful franchise for the first time in their lives.

# IV

The 240-member Slovenian parliament (*Skupscina*) was divided into three houses, including the Socio-Political Chamber and the Chamber of Municipalities, the lower and upper houses, respectively, and a Chamber of Associated Labor, from which workplace representatives were elected. The latter chamber was a legacy of efforts in Yugoslavia, as elsewhere, to inject the Communist Party into all spheres of life through political organization of the workplace and other social groups. In the April 1990 elections, voters were to select five members of the presidency and 240 members of parliament — 80 seats in the Chamber of Municipalities, 80 seats in the Socio-Political Chamber and 80 seats in the Chamber of Associated Labor. The system was envisioned as being a mixed presidential-parliamentary one, with the strongest powers residing with the governing majority in the legislature.

The president of the republic was to be elected by direct vote, with a run-off required two weeks later for the top two candidates if no one received a majority in the first round. This method was also to be used for election of the remaining four members of the presidency of the republic. The leading political parties all ran candidates for president and for the presidency, but the field also included an eccentric independent who not only enlivened the hustings by campaigning with a monkey on his shoulder but also attracted a surprisingly large following.

In two of the three chambers, elections were held in individual constituencies. A run-off was scheduled two weeks later in constituencies in which no candidate received a majority. The opposition parties and the ruling communists agreed that the Chamber of Municipalities would be contested on a first-past-the-post basis (*i.e.*, without run-off elections). This system encouraged most of the significant opposition parties to unite under common slates throughout the republic in order to compete effectively against the communists.

Candidates from 13 political parties, three civil lists (*i.e.*, groupings of civic associations) and a number of lists of independent candidates contested seats for the Socio-Political Chamber.

# V

By holding multiparty elections in April 1990, Slovenia became the first of the Yugoslav republics to implement democratic reforms and, along with Croatia, the first to seek greater autonomy from Belgrade. With the strongest economy and greatest ethnic homogeneity of the nation's six republics, Slovenia was spared the volatile elements that contributed to political and social instability in the other republics.

Slovenians went to the polls on April 7 and 21, and voting proceeded in a methodical manner. The polls were open from 7 a.m. to 7 p.m. at the 4,135 polling stations. Despite poor weather on April 7, turnout among the nearly 1.5 million registered voters was heavy.

Perhaps because of the overwhelming consensus the republic enjoyed as it embarked on its transition to democracy, there was little sense of drama or exuberance to accompany the first free exercise of the franchise in more than 40 years. Security forces maintained a low profile, and voting progressed smoothly across the republic.

A complicated balloting process caused some confusion with voters. For example, voters on April 7 were confronted with five different ballots, one each for the local council, the Socio-Political Chamber, the Chamber of Municipalities, the members of the collective presidency and the president of the presidency. Despite some voter bewilderment, no significant complaints were raised about the integrity of the process.

A complex balloting process, an absence of computers and an inexperienced election staff combined to produce a painstakingly slow vote count. Officials apparently also wanted to make the process as open as possible, resulting in often-lengthy procedural discussions between election officials and party representatives who were legally permitted to participate on vote tallying teams.

# VI

After the results were counted, DEMOS claimed an overall parliamentary majority, capturing 126 of the 240 total seats. The reform communists, who renamed themselves the Party for Democratic Renewal, fared poorly, winning only 38 seats. The Socialist Alliance received 16 seats, and the independent Liberal Party (Socialist Youth) won 38.

Although DEMOS achieved a majority in two chambers, it fell short of a majority in the Chamber of Associated Labor. This forced DEMOS to negotiate with other parties to form a new government, which ultimately included five independents and three communists among its 27 members. The Christian Democratic Party won the most seats of any party in the DEMOS coalition, and thus it selected Slovenia's new prime minister, Lojze Peterle.

In a run-off election with DEMOS candidate Joze Pucnik, reform communist Milan Kucan was elected president of the republic with 59 percent of the vote. Other candidates elected to the collective presidency were two candidates from DEMOS (one each from the Green Party and the Farmer's Party), one candidate from the Communist Party and one from the Socialist Alliance. Thus, reform communists and allies won a 3-to-2 advantage in the presidency. As a result of the elections, power would be shared between the presidency, controlled by former communists, and the parliament, led by a prime minister from the Christian Democratic Party.

# VII

The Slovenian elections produced a parliament committed to dismantling the communist apparatus, privatizing the economy and beginning measured moves toward independence from the central government in Belgrade. But even as voters ushered out the Communist Party in the parliamentary poll, they elected the communist leader, Kucan, to be president of the presidency. It was widely believed that Kucan's popularity stemmed from his resolute stand against the LCY over the decentralization issue, even while he opposed immediate independence. With only 20 percent of Slovenes favoring outright secession at the time of the elections, the respected Kucan was also seen by many as a check on the power of DEMOS.

DEMOS commanded the authority to set the political agenda. It also benefitted from a prolonged honeymoon period and a general consensus within Slovenia on the over-arching policy question of the country's future relations with the central government of Yugoslavia. After the elections, DEMOS appeared ready to support a confederal structure for Yugoslavia. As inter-republic relations continued to deteriorate, however, during late 1990 and public opinion became more militant, the government felt empowered to move toward a referendum on secession.

Slovenia's relationship with Serbia and the Yugoslav central government grew increasingly tense. Slovenes expressed disgust with what they viewed as Serbian domination of federal affairs and with Serbian leader Slobodan Milosevic's resistance to political and economic reform in favor of a centralized, one-party system. Furthermore, while inter-ethnic conflicts throughout Yugoslavia, and particularly in Kosovo, had become a financial and psychological burden on all of the republics, the Slovenes no longer wished to bear fiscal or moral responsibility for matters in which they felt they had no part. Given the many differences between Slovenia and the other republics, Slovenia sought to withdraw from the Yugoslav federation and to establish closer ties with Western Europe and the European community.

In July 1990, before drafting a new Slovenian constitution, the republican assembly adopted a measure declaring Slovenia a sovereign state and asserting that Slovenian legislation would supersede any conflicting Yugoslavian laws. The republic held a referendum on December 23, 1990 in which 91 percent of the electorate voted in favor of secession. In June 1991, Slovenia survived a Yugoslav army attempt to reimpose federal control.

By the autumn of 1991, it had become clear that the Republic of Slovenia had succeeded in its attempt to disassociate itself from the Yugoslav federation and establish itself as an independent state. The Cold War's demise and the pace of democratization in Central and Eastern Europe had made this possible. But it had begun with the emergence of pluralism in the second half of the 1980s.

*Chapter 6*

# Romania
# May 20, 1990

## Thomas Carothers

*This chapter is based on the election monitoring activities undertaken by NDI in Romania from March through June 1990. In April, NDI helped sponsor a pre-election mission organized by the Washington-based International Human Rights Law Group and conducted an election monitoring training seminar for several newly formed Romanian nongovernmental organizations. For the May 20 elections, NDI, together with National Republican Institute for International Affairs, organized a 60-member international observer delegation led by Senator Joseph Lieberman (D-CT), former Senator Harrison Schmitt (R-NM) and British Labor Party deputy leader Roy Hattersley. Carothers, a Washington, DC attorney, was a member of the delegation.*

*A more comprehensive report on the Romanian elections is contained in **The May 1990 Romanian Elections**, published jointly by NDI and NRIIA. This chapter draws heavily on that report, which* *was written by Carothers and NDI Deputy Program Director Karen Clark.*

Nicolae Ceausescu, a capricious, brutal dictator, controlled Romania as his personal fiefdom from the mid-1960s to the end of the 1980s. In external affairs, Ceausescu was the maverick of the Warsaw Pact, teaming with Yugoslavian President Josip Broz Tito in asserting an independent communist path. In 1967, Romania became the first Warsaw Pact country to establish relations with West Germany. Further, Ceausescu maintained diplomatic relations with Israel after the 1967 Six-Day War and criticized the Warsaw Pact invasion of Czechoslovakia in 1968.

Ceausescu's willingness to break ranks with Moscow won him much favor in the West. Unlike other East European leaders, he was received regularly at the White House, was knighted by the British government and was granted numerous special economic concessions.

Although he conducted an innovative foreign policy, Ceausescu pursued an orthodox communist domestic program of harsh political repression and highly centralized control. He directed the expansion of the secret police, the Securitate, into an all-pervasive network of agents and informers. No dissent was tolerated, and domestic surveillance reached Orwellian proportions. Romanians were required to report all conversations with foreigners to the police, and few Romanians were allowed to travel to the West, or even to other East European countries.

At the same time that he transformed Romania into a political backwater, Ceausescu relentlessly pursued a course of grandiose economic development based on heavy industrial expansion, particularly in the petrochemical sector. Romania borrowed heavily to finance this poorly conceived program, which resulted in a staggering national debt and a standard of living comparable to pre-war conditions. In the 1980s, Ceausescu imposed a punishing austerity program to finance repayment of the foreign debt. Basic elements of everyday life, such as heating oil, electricity and food, were tightly rationed.

Ceausescu consolidated power in a family dictatorship unique in Eastern Europe. Together with his wife Elena and his youngest son Nicu, he fostered a Ceausescu cult and launched massive projects whose only rationale was to serve his increasing megalomania. The most visible undertaking was the House of the Republic, a monstrously excessive and exorbitant palace built on the ruins of a historic neighborhood destroyed to make way for its construction. Ceausescu also implemented a plan to raze more than half the country's villages and to move their residents to "agro-industrial" centers, a program that obliterated the vestiges of traditional Romanian society that had heretofore survived his destructive rule.

# I

As the democratic tide swept through Eastern Europe in the late 1980s, questions arose about how long Ceausescu could resist the regional turn toward pluralism and economic reform. Until the very end, Ceausescu denounced the democratic trend as an anti-socialist plot by the United States and the Soviet Union, and refused to compromise. Nonetheless, in December 1989, change surfaced in Romania with truly revolutionary force.

In the Transylvanian city of Timisoara, the predominantly Hungarian population organized spontaneously in support of an independent-minded minister, Laszlo Tokes, who was threatened with exile. Within two days, the rally grew into a large anti-government movement. Determined to make an example of these protestors, Ceausescu ordered the army and police to crush the demonstration. The resulting "Timisoara massacre" ignited a revolutionary fervor that burned in Bucharest and other cities.

Four days after the events in Timisoara, Ceausescu addressed a large public rally in Bucharest. Without warning, members of the crowd, many of them students, began shouting anti-Ceausescu slogans, and what began as a staged pro-Ceausescu demonstration turned into an anti-Ceausescu riot. Securitate officers fired into the crowd, while military units in the city square held their fire. The army's restraint bolstered the confidence of the rioters, who became convinced that the military was on their side.

The next day, as civil unrest spread through Bucharest and to other cities, Ceausescu attempted to address a crowd of protestors that had formed outside the Central Committee building. He was greeted with a hail of potatoes and stones and was chased to the roof of the building where he and his wife fled in a helicopter.

Within hours of Ceausescu's departure, a small group of people assembled in the Communist Party Central Committee building and declared themselves in control of the country. This group was led by Ion Iliescu, a career party official, marginalized by Ceausescu in 1971, and Silviu Brucan, a high-level party official who had turned against Ceausescu in early 1989. Announcing the formation of the Council for National Salvation, these leaders quickly established friendly relations with the army. The Council formed a transitional government, led by what became known as the National Salvation Front.

Battles continued in Bucharest and some provincial cities for several days, with most of the fighting occurring between army personnel and Securitate members loyal to Ceausescu. The Ceausescus were apprehended by the army shortly after they fled. On Christmas Day, Nicolei and Elena Ceausescu were hastily tried by a military tribunal and executed. With Ceausescu's death, armed resistance by Securitate members dwindled, and by the end of December the National Salvation Front had attained effective control of the country.

Despite the highly visible, dramatic December revolution, considerable uncertainty exists as to its true nature and origins. Two theories dominate.

One theory contends that the revolution occurred as it appeared — a popular revolt born out of deep-seated resentment toward Ceausescu's political and economic repression. According to this view, the Front was a spontaneous, genuinely anti-communist group that formed to fill the power vacuum created by Ceausescu's departure.

The other thesis postulates a widespread conspiracy. According to this premise, anti-Ceausescu elements in the Communist Party, the military and the Securitate were quietly plotting for years against Ceausescu and took advantage of the Timisoara events to stage a choreographed revolution in Bucharest. The Front, in the opinion of these theorists, was neither spontaneous nor anti-communist, but comprised a carefully formulated nucleus of conspirators who sought to institute a new form of one-party rule behind a facade of democratization.

# II

Within a week of taking power, the Front announced an eight-point program to establish basic democratic rights and procedures for Romania. The Front stated that it was just an interim steward whose members would step down once democratic elections were held in April 1990.

Considering the suddenness and violence of the revolution, the political atmosphere in Romania was remarkably open and forward-moving. Political parties formed rapidly. Within a few weeks, however, a political controversy cast a shadow over the transition process: the Front, contrary to its earlier pledges, declared that it would field candidates and compete for power in the national elections. The Front's announcement provoked large, angry demonstrations by leaders of the emerging political parties, representatives of student groups and intellectuals, who now openly questioned the Front's democratic intentions and speculated that the Front aimed to consolidate its own version of one-party rule. The Front ignored these protests.

This reversal of the Front's initial promise to act only as a caretaker government produced doubts about the legitimacy of its exercise of even transitional power. Discontent grew over the prominent role of former high-level Communist Party officials within the Front and the Front's reluctance to confront and prosecute the most odious, still-existing elements of the communist *nomenklatura* and the Securitate. Further, the Front began to display an arrogance of power that raised suspicions about its democratic intentions and fueled the conspiratorial theory of the revolution.

On February 1, the National Salvation Front dissolved the Council and announced the creation of a large multiparty Provisional Council of National Unity (CPUN), dominated by the Front but inclusive of opposition party representatives and independent groups. The CPUN, whose 21-member executive bureau was led by Ion Iliescu as president and Petre Roman as prime minister, was to serve as parliament until after the elections.

# III

In an environment of increasing political tension and distrust, a debate ensued about a new electoral law. Negotiations for an electoral law began in late January, and the final legislation was adopted on March 14.

Setting the election date was a key issue. The opposition parties were torn between two competing desires. On one hand, they wanted to have sufficient time to organize and campaign effectively, and, on the other, they feared that if the Front were allowed to stay in power for too long without elections, it would consolidate irrevocable power.

The Front also wrestled with conflicting interests. A short campaign would relieve growing international pressure for elections and would exploit the poor organization of the opposition parties. By contrast, a long campaign would allow adequate time for administrative preparations, thus making the elections appear more credible to the outside world. The decision to hold elections early reflected the Front's conclusion that the advantage of shortening the campaign period to the detriment of the opposition parties outweighed the dangers of alienating the international community.

The electoral law, which was adopted overwhelmingly by the CPUN, served as a *de facto* provisional constitution since it established the form of Romania's government and the procedures for drafting a new constitution. The electoral law stated that "the basis of Romania's government is a pluralist democracy" with power separated into legal, executive and judicial branches. Under the electoral law, the new parliament was to function both as a law-making body and as a constituent assembly. An 18-month deadline was established for adopting a new constitution. The parliament also was authorized, once the constitution was approved, to make decisions relative to new elections.

Unlike elections in other Eastern European countries, Romania's first post-communist electoral exercise included a direct presidential election. The law stipulated a complex system of proportional representation for the Assembly of Deputies to ensure that small parties would be represented according to the exact percentage of votes they obtained. Such a system was favored by opposition parties, particularly the Liberal Party, that were particularly concerned with the fate of small parties.

The electoral law established a high qualification threshold, 100,001 signatures, for presidential candidates and a low eligibility quota, 251 signatures, for parliamentary candidates. The high threshold for presidential candidates reflected a widespread desire to avoid a fragmented national campaign, while the low threshold for parliamentary candidates demonstrated a keen interest in opening up the new elections to small parties and political neophytes. All candidates and parties were required to submit petitions for candidacy at least one month before the elections.

Article 10 of the electoral law contained perhaps the most notable restriction on candidate qualification. This article prohibited the participation of those people "who have committed abuses in political, judicial and administrative functions, who have infringed upon fundamental human rights, as well as those people who have organized or who have been instruments of repression in the service of the security forces, the former police and militia forces." The Front accepted this stipulation as a moderate alternative to a more extreme provision proposed by some opposition parties that would have barred all former Communist Party officials and some members of the National Salvation Front from competing in the elections. The law did not contain an enforcement mechanism, however, and it was apparently never applied against any candidate.

The electoral law provided that the Central Electoral Bureau (BEC) administer the elections with authority for each district (*judet*) and the Bucharest municipality delegated to provincial electoral bureaus. Both the BEC and the provincial bureaus were composed of judges and party representatives, the latter joining the bureaus only in the final weeks of the campaign due to administrative delays and general disorganization. The judges who composed the BEC and provincial bureaus were suspected of possessing doubtful political independence, given the politicization of the judiciary under communist rule, but political partiality of the bureaus did not prove to be a major pre-election issue.

# IV

The electoral campaign pitted the National Salvation Front against several opposition parties. Led by Iliescu, Roman and dissidents from the Ceausescu era, the Front appeared to be a shadowy, even mysterious, organization throughout the campaign, despite its dominant position in the government. To some, the Front was a heroic organization that had played a crucial role in igniting the December revolution. To others, the Front was a manipulative band of neo-communists determined to reimpose one-party rule in Romania.

During the campaign, the Front did not seek to define itself ideologically other than to wrap itself in the banner of the December revolution. It had a vague platform and did little to clarify speculation about its origins and composition. Iliescu and Roman stated generally that the Front envisioned a mixed economy and a social democratic political system for Romania, but they set forth no specific plans for achieving these goals. The Front effectively played on the deep apprehension felt by many Romanians about the consequences of capitalism by repeatedly raising the specter of foreign buyouts and massive unemployment that could result from opposition plans to implement privatization.

More than 80 political parties opposed the National Salvation Front. The largest of the parties, and the only ones to field presidential candidates, were two historical parties: the Liberal Party and the Peasant Party.

The Liberal Party, originally formed in the 19th century to represent the conservative and monied class, and a major political force in the 1920s and 1930s, disbanded after the communists took over Romania in the late 1940s. In its 1989 incarnation, the Liberal Party had no clearly defined base aside from a loose coalition of professionals, students and intellectuals. The party was led by Radu Campeanu, who returned to Romania shortly after Ceausescu's fall, after having spent more than 10 years in exile in the West.

The Liberals urged a vigorous economic modernization program, including privatization and the reestablishment of property rights. It further sought to establish legal institutions that would guarantee civil and political rights, and to support a multiparty, pluralistic political system.

The Peasant Party, believed to have been the overwhelming victor in the last free elections of 1946, was also prominent in the 1920s and 1930s. The party was associated with the large landlords during the inter-war period and was considered right-wing. It too advocated a transition to a market economy, with an emphasis on the de-collectivization of agriculture and the establishment of a democratic political system. The party chose Ion Ratiu, a wealthy entrepreneur who returned to Romania in March 1990, as its presidential candidate. Ratiu's personal financial contributions supported a significant amount of the Peasant Party's political activities.

All other political parties, except the Social Democratic Party, a marginalized historical party, were created in the immediate wake of Ceausescu's fall. Though a few of these parties, such as the Hungarian and Ecology parties, were visible during the campaign, most of the new political parties were tiny, consisting of no more than one or two leaders and a handful of supporters. Indeed, major opposition leaders believed that a number of the parties were created by the Front to divide the opposition.

# V

The campaign was systematically unfair. The Front enjoyed all the advantages of having assumed the reins of an absolutist state and exploited these advantages to the maximum. The opposition suffered from a lack of every possible resource, including experienced personnel, funds, materials and equipment. It was practically impossible for the opposition parties to move in a period of several months from a state of non-existence to one of formidable contender, able to mount a national electoral campaign.

Access to electronic media was another major area of inequity. The single television station and the few radio stations in Romania were all government-run. Despite electoral-law provisions that guaranteed all parties television and radio time, the opposition suffered from limited access to programming, unpredictable placement and uneven access to recording studios and equipment.

Television news coverage of the campaign was blatantly and consistently biased toward the Front. President Iliescu and Prime Minister Roman were constantly featured on the news in a favorable light. By contrast, the activities of the opposition candidates and parties were barely reported, and then often with a thinly disguised negative tone. Considering that television news is probably the most influential source of information in the country, its bias constituted a major structural advantage for the Front. The same news bias and lack of access afflicted radio, although radio plays a much less important role than television in Romania.

The structure of the newspaper industry also negatively affected opposition parties. Many small independent and opposition newspapers emerged after December 1989, making a significant contribution to the broadened political dialogue in Romania. A number of factors, however, inhibited their efforts during the campaign.

The country's very few printing facilities remained in government hands during the campaign. This government monopoly in effect controlled the printing of independent and opposition newspapers. Efforts by the major opposition parties to establish independent printing facilities were blocked by the government, even when the opposition parties managed to bring in printing equipment from abroad.

Impartial distribution of newspapers was also problematic. While the state-controlled distribution networks distributed pro-Front newspapers throughout the country, independent and opposition newspapers were only sporadically available outside Bucharest and never reached many towns and villages.

In addition, opposition parties provided evidence of systematic government intimidation designed to discourage publication and limit the range of expression. The staff of the Peasant Party newspaper, for example, reported at least one threat of violence per day and alleged that a group of editors had been attacked, leaving one seriously injured. Several opposition papers complained of attacks on their headquarters. This atmosphere made it difficult to recruit staff and to operate effectively.

Difficulties with the electronic and print media were not the only problems facing the opposition parties in attempting to communicate their message to the public. Under Ceausescu, Romania experienced an extraordinary centralization of information and communication. Typewriters were registered with the police, copying machines were impossible to buy or use legally, mimeograph machines were unheard of, and paper and cassettes were difficult to obtain in any significant quantities. Access to foreign newspapers and other publications from abroad was limited to the highest echelons of the Romanian government. Although Romanian society was liberalized after December 1989, the continued centralization of information and means of communication significantly restricted the communication abilities of opposition parties.

The opposition had difficulty obtaining basic materials for the campaign such as paper, newsprint, posters, recording and video cassettes and ink. Established daily papers were forced to reduce circulation during the campaign because their newsprint rations were partially diverted to political parties so that the latter could produce campaign materials. The government controlled the supply of such materials domestically, and buying them from outside the country was laborious and prohibitively expensive. Obtaining equipment from abroad, such as typewriters, computers, video cameras, tape recorders, copying machines, printers and mimeograph machines was nearly impossible. Foreign donation of such material was hindered by bureaucratic customs procedures that often delayed receipt of the goods until just before the elections.

Campaign financing posed another serious problem for opposition parties. The electoral law provided for public campaign financing but little, if any such support, found its way into the coffers of the political parties. Without recourse to state financing, candidates had no money as they were unable to raise significant funds from the impoverished Romanian population.

The electoral law initially prohibited the receipt of financial contributions from foreign sources, although this provision was reportedly amended to permit the practice so long as the transactions were documented. Opposition parties expecting foreign funds complained that such funds were deliberately delayed by waiting-period requirements imposed on foreign currency transfers. Declaration requirements for foreign assistance do not appear to have been followed or enforced, in keeping with the generally lax approach taken by all parties to campaign finance reporting.

# VI

In addition to the structural advantages enjoyed by the Front, the campaign was marred by reports of violence, harassment and intimidation directed at candidates and party members. The victims of these incidents were almost exclusively members of the opposition, while instigators were predominantly police or Front supporters. The Front reported few acts of violence directed against its supporters other than the destruction of windows at some Front campaign offices.

Reports of assassination attempts were frequent among opposition candidates. In April, Ion Ratiu, the Peasant Party candidate, was attacked by Front supporters wielding stones and bottles. After futilely seeking refuge at the local police headquarters, Ratiu escaped the mob only by dispatching decoy cars, which were in turn attacked by the crowd.

In early May, crowds carrying rocks and glass brutally attacked Liberal Party candidate Radu Campeanu during a campaign stop in Bralia. Campeanu was beaten, and one of his top aides — mistaken for Campeanu because of his similar features — was severely assaulted by members of the crowd shouting death threats to Campeanu.

Opposition party headquarters were repeatedly assailed. Written and telephone threats, warning party activists to desist from their political activity, were commonplace. Opposition party rallies and demonstrations were continually disrupted by groups voicing support for the Front. In most cases, opposition members did not bother reporting the incidents to the police, believing such action to be futile and potentially dangerous. Peasant Party representatives from Iasi, whose headquarters was constantly besieged, called the police only to have the police arrive and ransack the building.

President Iliescu made no overt effort to help ensure a safe, tolerant and pluralistic campaign. Worse, Iliescu issued numerous public statements characterizing opposition party rallies and demonstrations as illegal, declaring that the government would tolerate these gatherings but could not protect participants should "others" decide to take action.

The systematic violence directed against opposition parties uncovered two facts that cast doubt on Romania's democratic transition. First, the violence demonstrated that much of the internal structures of repression in Romania were still operational; the December revolution decapitated the Ceausescu regime, but left standing an internal security network that continued to operate against political activists. Second, the Front's participation in, or tolerance of, the violence undermined its stated goals for such fundamental democratic pillars as human rights, freedom of assembly, freedom of speech and pluralistic representation.

# VII

The absence of civil structures external and parallel to government proved devastating to the inculcation of a free democratic process. Almost no civil institutions survived the Ceausescu era as independent, functioning entities representing interest groups other than the state. Several attempts were made to nurture a civil society, yet the lack of supporting structures such as the Church or an entrenched intellectual sub-culture exposed these neophyte institutions to the full brunt of government intimidation and harassment.

The key role played by students in the revolution initially gave them a special voice as the conscience of the 1990 campaign. Yet, while some students advocated the complete "decommunization" of Romania, students generally eschewed partisan politics to concentrate their energies on more self-centered educational issues.

Romanian intellectuals, a small and persecuted sector of society, were represented by the Group for Social Dialogue, formed after the fall of Ceausescu. Though many members of the Group for Social Dialogue were longtime dissidents, highly respected for their democratic opinions, attempts by the Group to use its influence to raise the level of political debate and, on occasion, to mediate between government and anti-government demonstrators were poorly received by the government.

A third nonpartisan group was Fratia, an alternative labor confederation formed after the revolution to compete with the central state-controlled labor confederation. Fratia gained the support of some unions, particularly white-collar unions, yet it did not participate in the campaign as a political party. It advocated a program of transition to a market economy and modernization of management structures.

The formation of these nonpartisan groups, while noteworthy, ultimately represented only a minor feature of the electoral campaign. Iliescu and Roman displayed hostility toward the student groups, especially when a large student-led University Square demonstration developed into a massive anti-government rally. When several student groups joined the Group for Social Dialogue and Fratia to form a National Center for Free Elections, their request to play a monitoring role in the May elections was simply ignored by the Central Electoral Bureau.

A lack of civic education compounded the absence of civil society. Most Romanians knew little of the democratic reforms and the significance of multiparty elections; the need for widespread democratic civic education was glaringly apparent. No civic groups with the requisite resources or skills existed to conduct any large-scale voter education programs.

The government, meanwhile, did almost nothing to improve the situation. Only a few televised advertisements, broadcast just before the elections, explained ballot procedures. Educational tools such as printed sample ballots, when available, depicted an "X" on the Front candidate list. Few voters reported having received any information about election-day procedures, let alone about democracy and the process of democratic transition.

# VIII

Several ethnic minority groups reside within Romania's borders, including Germans, Turks, Hungarians, Bulgarians, Jews and Gypsies. The most numerous and politically organized are the Hungarians, who represent approximately 10 percent of the population. Although cooperation between Romanians and Hungarians in Timisoara initially contributed to the revolution, the subsequent opening of society heightened long-simmering friction between these communities in other parts of the country. Ethnic clashes punctuated an already violent campaign.

On March 20, 1990, these tensions exploded into violent street battles in the Transylvanian city of Tirgu Mures that left at least six dead and 300 wounded. Each side blamed extremists from the other side for the fighting; some attributed the conflict to Securitate provocation. In any event, the incident contributed to the growing perception that the Hungarian minority issue would play a more visible, and possibly conflictive, role in the new Romanian political order.

The structural advantages favoring the Front, the intimidation and harassment of the opposition parties, the lack of any independent civil institutions to support the electoral process and the elevated ethnic tensions resulted in a severely flawed electoral campaign. Furthermore, the campaign was, at root, insubstantial. Campaign activities scarcely reached outside of Bucharest and a few provincial cities. Many Romanians witnessed the campaign only through un-balanced news broadcasts and occasional political advertisements on television.

The campaign took place in a society in which the very concept of politics had uncertain meaning and legitimacy. The presidential candidates fought primarily over who could draw on the most compelling sources of personal and political legitimacy in a society still distrustful of all forms of power and still grappling with how to retreat from 45 years of totalitarianism. The electoral campaign was not a transition to democracy *per se*, yet it symbolized a first step toward more basic goals of establishing a civil society and creating a functioning political system.

# IX

Voting on May 20, 1990 was relatively orderly and peaceful. The National Salvation Front won the elections handily. Ion Iliescu received 85 percent of the presidential votes, while Radu Campeanu obtained 10 percent and Ion Ratiu 4 percent. In the Senate races, the Front captured 67 percent of the vote, the leading Hungarian party and the Liberal Party each garnered 7 percent, and the Peasant Party secured a mere 2.5 percent. In elections for the Assembly of Deputies, the Front won 66 percent of the seats, the leading Hungarian party 7 percent, the Liberals 6 percent, and other parties less than 3 percent. Several parties that received less than 1 percent of the vote were allocated seats in both the Assembly of Deputies and the Senate.

The balloting process was marred by a number of procedural irregularities, virtually all of which favored the Front. At some polling sites, particularly in rural areas, voters confused by complicated procedures were assisted inside the polling booth by election officials. Partisan political paraphernalia, such as campaign buttons, posters and party symbols, were present in some polling stations, and such materials were generally pro-Front. Some observers discovered ballots pre-marked for the Front being handed to voters as they entered the polling places. Polling station administrators were supposed to be politically neutral, but some were openly pro-Front. In addition, ballot paper was relatively transparent, jeopardizing ballot secrecy. Given the tradition of surveillance and political repression in Romania, the lack of secrecy may have had a chilling effect on those contemplating voting for the opposition.

Although these irregularities were numerous and consistently favorable to the Front, there is no indication that the voting process was systematically rigged or that the irregularities significantly affected the results. The Front's overwhelming victory was due, in fact, to more people choosing to vote for the Front than any of the other parties.

In evaluating the elections, an important question to consider is not so much whether the elections themselves were technically fair but whether they were meaningful. The elections represented the final stage of an electoral process that was, as discussed above, systematically biased in favor of the Front. A number of international observers were struck by what seemed to be a sense of purposelessness in the act of voting. Many voters did not appear to understand the concept of choice. Instead, they appeared to be dispassionately carrying out an official duty for the authorities. One observer commented that many voters appeared "pre-programmed," a legacy of the Ceausescu regime.

In retrospect, it is evident that most Romanians possessed little sense of political freedom or choice after 45 years of totalitarianism.

The Front had seized the reins of government by exploiting the wave of anti-Ceausescu sentiment that arose from the December revolution. The opposition was too nascent and fragmented to present any real alternative for the voters. The campaign was a hasty, poorly organized affair that was both unbalanced in favor of the Front and very limited in its ideological and political reach.

The Front treated the election results as a foregone conclusion; they were announced on television with no accompanying analysis or discussion. Images of Iliescu and the Front's party symbol remained fixed on the television monitor. For the Front, the elections were a validation of its commanding position in society, not an actual path to power.

# X

Numerous groups from the United States and Europe observed the Romanian elections. Observers were warmly welcomed by both sides. The government was anxious to secure international validation of the elections and saw the observers as the means to accomplish this goal. The opposition was equally eager to have observers on hand, hoping that they might improve the process. Many opposition party activists held perhaps unrealistically high expectations of what the international observers could accomplish. They saw the observers as saviors who would right the many wrongs perpetrated by the Front and ensure fair elections.

Observer groups were accorded adequate access to the elections. They were allowed to travel to all regions of the country and observe all aspects of the electoral process. Nonetheless, evaluating the elections proved a difficult and challenging task. Technically, voting was relatively fair. But voting is not an adequate indicator of the overall fairness or legitimacy of an electoral process.

Some observer delegations arriving in Romania a day or two before the elections were led astray by what appeared to be technically credible elections and endorsed the process. They did not attempt a comprehensive evaluation, which would have highlighted the complexities, but were content to make sweeping pronouncements based on a single segment of a lengthy sequence of events.

The Front capitalized on these delegations' remarks, publicizing them widely while ignoring the much more balanced assessment of the NDI/NRIIA delegation and other observer groups. Given the government's dominance over the media, the Romanian people were under the impression that all international observers had endorsed the Romanian electoral process. This situation disheartened opposition members and led many to question, in hindsight, the value of international observers.

# XI

In the immediate aftermath of the 1990 electoral campaign, the question confronting Romania's political future was how the Front would behave once it secured power. Would it clamp down and reestablish one-party rule, or would it oversee a process of political liberalization, leading to free and fair multiparty elections in the prescribed 30-month period? The first indication of the Front's intentions was not long in coming. After the elections, the University Square demonstrations diminished in size but nonetheless continued. The protestors, who continued to criticize the Front as an organization dominated by neo-communists, occupied the only visible anti-Front landmark on the Romanian political landscape.

On June 13, police broke up a demonstration and ousted all demonstrators from the Square. Later that day, anti-government protestors clashed with police, and a group of protestors attacked the city police headquarters and the Interior Ministry. These attacks were more violent than any of the previous demonstrations, and some observers believe they may have been the work of pro-government provocateurs who provided the regime with a pretext to call in hard-nosed miners from the countryside.

Early the next morning, thousands of miners arrived in Bucharest and began a two-day rampage during which they terrorized students, members of opposition parties and anyone who looked like a critic of the Front. The miners savagely beat hundreds of people on the streets, tracked down and clubbed student and opposition leaders, and ravaged opposition party headquarters, universities and residences of several opposition party leaders, including Ion Ratiu. The government praised the miners for having arrived in Bucharest to save Romania from "an attempted coup by a force of extremist, rightist elements, a coup of Iron-Guardist and fascist character." After the rampage ended, Iliescu thanked the miners for their "civic awareness."

The events of June were shocking in their violence and brutality. They were disturbing for what they revealed not only about the Front's political intentions, but also about the political character of Romanian society. They demonstrated that a large, powerful element of the working class supported the Front, and that this element would use brute force to attack students, intellectuals and opposition members. In addition, there were many reports that the miners were cheered by Romanians on the streets who urged that the troublemakers be killed.

Two generations of Romanians have grown up knowing only totalitarian rule, and many Romanians reflexively support the government and distrust anyone who dissents. The society is sharply divided along class lines with the dominant working class harboring a deep distrust of students, intellectuals and professionals. From this perspective, the Front is a reflection of mainstream elements of society, and is not merely a political force struggling to maintain control.

Since June 1990, Romanian politics have lapsed again into uncertainty and obscurity. Work on the constitution is underway, although public discussion or debate is almost non-existent. Political space, albeit narrow, exists and some opposition figures as well as some nonpartisan groups are mounting pro-democratic activities.

Democracy remains an articulated but distant goal for Romania. The country made a crucial break from the crippling rule of Nicolae Ceausescu, but has moved only a short distance down the democratic path. Toleration of political opposition is not yet a well-accepted practice by either the government or much of the citizenry. The notion that any political dissent suggests treason and that political debate spells chaos runs deep in the Romanian political consciousness and will not quickly change.

Romania remains a relatively closed society. The means of information and communication are still concentrated in the hands of the government. The government operates in secrecy and has not established any kind of day-to-day accountability for its actions. The structures of repression, in particular the secret police, continue to operate. Romanians do not feel free to exercise basic human rights without fear of retribution.

Romania still lacks a civil society and has taken few tangible steps toward building one. Romania remains a country where the government directly or indirectly controls every major societal institution. Between Romanian citizens and the all-pervasive state, no significant intermediary organizations exist other than student groups, fledgling independent labor federations, the Group for Social Dialogue and a few other small, besieged and isolated groups. The Romanian government has not yet accepted the idea that such institutions are a normal, necessary part of a working democratic society.

Yet, many in the Front, and more generally in Romanian society, want Romania to be part of a democratic and integrated Europe. For this to happen, Romania must adhere to the principles of democratic government and respect for human rights. Given developments since December 1989, Romania's political evolution will be closely scrutinized by its European neighbors for the foreseeable future.

*Chapter 7*

# Poland
# May 27, 1990

## Maya Latynski

*This chapter is based on the observations and research of Maya Latynski, who was present in Poland for both the June 4, 1989 national elections and the May 27, 1990 local elections. In 1989, Latynski was part of a delegation sponsored by the International Human Rights Law Group, which also included NDI President Brian Atwood. Latynski returned to Poland for the local elections with Steven Doyle, a Washington-based attorney who also was a member of the Law Group's 1989 election observer mission.*

*Based on Atwood's visit at the time of the 1989 elections, NDI organized a training seminar for Polish legislators in September 1989 that focused on the role of legislatures in developing national economic policy. Leading the seminar were NDI Chairman Walter Mondale, former U.S. Senate Minority Leader Howard Baker and U.S. Senate Budget Committee Chairman Pete Dominici, along with prominent West European legislators.*

The tide of change that swept the Soviet satellites in 1989 and 1990 came so unexpectedly and brought such a revolutionary transformation that it is often easy to misjudge the complexity of the problems that continue to confront Eastern and Central Europe. The changes have proven extremely difficult to absorb, particularly during what should be one of the most glorious periods of these nations' histories.

This essay looks at the politics of present-day Poland in their national context. The reader is invited to consider whether many of Poland's problems are not already common to the other countries in the region, while others will soon arise. Poland's standing amid these countries is in many respects one of leader, and also of guinea pig. Poland was the first country to renounce its communist regime, to establish a democratic opposition, to hold partly free legislative elections, to elect a democratic government, and finally, to institute radical economic reforms. This does not necessarily mean that Poland has come further in the evolution to democracy than its neighbors or that its chances in the transition to political pluralism and a market economy are the best. Rather it implies that, at least in some respects, the other countries will tread somewhat the same path and have reason to look to Poland to learn from both its successes and its failures.

# I

During the past two years, it has become increasingly apparent that Poland is still a long way from achieving political stability. The population has not gained from the revolutionary change as much as it would have wished, and the political class has not lived up to its early promise. In these circumstances, it is almost with nostalgia that one remembers the moral and political clarity of an earlier time, the period before the June 1989 elections in which a portion of the parliamentary seats were opened to contest by non-communist groups for the first time in more than 40 years.

In 1988, Poland's communist leaders, by negotiating a power-sharing agreement with representatives of the outlawed Solidarity opposition, acknowledged that they could not alone lift the country out of its torpor. The state of Poland's economy, environment, political relations and social health had been declining steadily throughout the years of communist government. The brutal termination of the democratic experiment of 1980-81 following the declaration of martial law in December 1981 served as a grim reminder for much of the population of the challenges involved in curbing communist power.

Roundtable negotiations began in early February 1989 between the government and Solidarity, with the Church's representatives participating as mediators-observers. The discussions took place in plenary sessions as well as specialized subgroups. The best minds from the opposition, both intellectuals and workers, representing a fairly broad political spectrum sat at the various tables with representatives of the government. The talks covered a wide spectrum of public issues, ranging from economic and political reform to the environment, health and youth. The public followed closely the convening of the roundtable, a gripping event after nearly a decade of hopelessness.

In the first days of April, a ground-breaking agreement was reached. The sub-group charged with political reform achieved a consensus on two key issues: Solidarity would again be legalized, regaining the rights it enjoyed in 1980-81; and parliamentary elections — carefully planned to guarantee the Communist Party a substantial share of power — would be held within two months.

By endorsing the agreement, the communists accepted the possibility that their side would be weakened and that the new legislature would no longer reflect their monopoly on political power. The agreement stipulated that in the existing lower chamber (Sejm), one-third of the seats (161) would be open to competition among all parties and candidates, while the remaining two-thirds (299) would be guaranteed to the communist coalition, comprised of the Polish United Workers' Party (PUWP) and its two allies, the United Peasant Party (UPP) and the Democratic Party (DP). In the newly restored Senate, all seats would be open to all qualified candidates. At the same time, Solidarity's concessions to the communists included the creation of a powerful new office of president, with an unspoken agreement that the new legislature would elect General Wojciech Jaruzelski to this office.

# II

The agreement was portrayed by both sides as a great victory for Poland: a nonpartisan attempt to save the country from internal division and economic ruin. The negotiations were especially important vis-à-vis the yet untested Gorbachev leadership. But the reactions of a wing of the opposition as well as of the conservative arm of the PUWP were also significant. The radical faction of Solidarity called for a boycott of the elections, and the hardliners among the communists criticized the reformers in their midst for making too many concessions.

The public beheld the signing of the agreement with a mixture of excitement and unease. While most of the people probably viewed the accord favorably, many were worried and angry that the government had allowed Solidarity barely two months to campaign. This was perceived as a scheme to prevent Solidarity from making any significant electoral gains — after eight years of existence underground the union would be handicapped by a lack of preparation and resources. In fact, Solidarity had very little time to prepare a program and a strategy, to select candidates for all the seats for which it was allowed to compete, or to prepare campaign information for the media and the public.

The life of the democratic opposition changed overnight. Solidarity was once again legal. It began publishing a daily newspaper and revived its weekly for the first time since 1981; its candidates to the National Assembly campaigned freely; and, even though its air time was minimal, it presented campaign programs and advertisements on national radio and television. Despite some well-publicized incidents of illicit government surveillance of Solidarity offices and the censoring of Solidarity's writings and programs, the opposition had effectively been restored to a status nearly equal to that of its political partner, the government.

As the hectic, two-month electoral campaign began, few imagined that Solidarity would win more than a handful of seats. Nonetheless, Solidarity acted with great drive and single-mindedness during this condensed period, matching the spirit of its peaceful national uprising of 1980-81. With the proverbial Polish ability to work harmoniously and dynamically at times of crisis, this organization, which lacked an institutional base and possessed only minimal access to the media, launched an extensive information campaign.

Solidarity's campaign resembled the government's only in that there was no clear-cut presentation of programs. Instead, Solidarity relied on the vague, and yet deeply felt, beliefs of the 10-year-old union/national movement. Omnipresent were photographs of each candidate warmly hugging or shaking hands with Solidarity Chairman Lech Walesa. Vast numbers of volunteers hurled themselves into work at the central and local campaign headquarters, while grade-school children dropped by to ask for posters that they could hang in their apartment buildings or in the streets.

While Solidarity was rejuvenated, the PUWP and its allies virtually did not campaign. Certainly, they appeared on television and displayed slogans on public buildings, and their candidates took part in televised debates, but their efforts seemed half-hearted at best. A few weeks before the elections, for example, a persistent search for a PUWP information booth yielded one in central Warsaw that contained no brochures; two bored, young employees could find only a few posters and flyers devoid of content. Comprehensive lists of PUWP candidates in the various districts were almost non-existent.

This behavior remains a puzzle. The establishment's inability or unwillingness to fight for its survival indicated an arrogance and a lack of imagination in a group that for decades had taken its power for granted. The revealing political memoir of Mieczyslaw Rakowski, the last governing communist prime minister and sub-sequently the last first secretary of the PUWP, sheds some light on this attitude. The predominant tone of the memoirs, published in 1991, is one of bitterness directed at the authorities for selling out to the opposition during the roundtable negotiations, at the Church for siding with Solidarity during the campaign, and at the government for mistakes made in the context of the electoral campaign. But there is also much naïveté. In a mid-May 1989 entry, Rakowski asserts that the reason the communists did not campaign more dynamically was that they were not prepared to fight:

> There are many reasons for this. Forty-five years of exercising power without opposition have made the PUWP lazy. Another reason is the lack of faith in the future and,

actually, in socialism.  The discipline inside the party has
also been weakened.[1]

No one could express it better.  The only sign of initiative shown
on the part of the government was its effort to disguise the background of some of its candidates, in the apparent hope that voters
would naïvely fail to realize that they were communists.  A prime
example of this tactic was the public characterization of Rakowski, an
unpopular life-long establishment figure, simply as "a historian."

# III

A significant concession by Solidarity permitted the communists
to present a "national list" of 35 prominent establishment officials.
This list appeared on a separate ballot and constituted the only
candidates for these reserved seats in the Sejm.  Running unopposed,
they needed only a simple majority to be elected.  The list included
Rakowski, Minister of National Defense Florian Siwicki, Minister of
Internal Affairs Czeslaw Kiszczak, the chief of the pro-government
labor unions Alfred Miodowicz, and the former first secretary of the
PUWP, Stanislaw Kania.  In hindsight, it is striking that the
roundtable negotiators did not provide a contingency plan for the
possibility that any of these candidates might lose, leaving the seats
unoccupied.

To vote for all of the candidates on the list – the decision the
government assumed the voters would make – a voter had to leave
the list untouched; to vote against a candidate, a voter had to cross
out the name.  This unnecessarily complicated method had been used
in all elections since World War II.  In previous elections, most
voters left the ballots unmarked, which yielded winners who received
more than 90 percent of the ballots cast.

Confusion reigned up until voting day about what procedure
constituted the proper method for crossing out the names on the
national list.  Election officials stated that voters would have to cross
out each name individually, while Solidarity leaders argued that voters

---

[1] M. F. Rakowski, *Jak to sie stalo* (*How it Happened*) (Warsaw, 1991),
p. 223.

need only mark a large "X" across the entire ballot. This seemingly banal point gained greater significance in the face of uncertainty about how results would be interpreted and whether the communists might manipulate the vote tally.

A more politically significant controversy developed within Solidarity regarding the national list. Some Solidarity activists declared publicly their plans to cross out all the names on the list. Others, including Solidarity leader Walesa, announced that they would vote for some of the communist officials, specifically those who had actively promoted the roundtable negotiations. Walesa's announcement, which was made on the eve of the elections, was politically motivated and guided by a fear that if the entire list was defeated it would doom the roundtable agreement and compromise Solidarity as a credible partner in the eyes of the authorities. Other Solidarity leaders echoed this apprehension: what if the communists reneged on their word and declared this extremely important election invalid? What if this first step to a brighter future was wasted?

This extreme caution was understandable in view of the apparent enormity of the communist concessions after nearly a decade of intransigence and the uncertainty about Moscow's reaction to these revolutionary developments, even in the Gorbachev era. Poland and Hungary, which was just planning to honor the heroes of the 1956 revolution, had only each other's company on their path to liberalization, while their hard-line neighbors had every reason to demand that Moscow curb these reformist experiments. Still, other Solidarity leaders, and apparently much of the public, considered it misguided and patronizing to ask voters not to express their true preferences in these first meaningful, if not totally free, elections in two generations.

# IV

The Solidarity leadership's method of selecting candidates for the Sejm and Senate, albeit undemocratic, was in large measure responsible for its sweeping success in the June 1989 elections. The Citizens' Committee, the group of intellectuals invited by Walesa in early 1989 to advise him, assumed that only a carefully hand-picked

Solidarity team composed of prominent figures could defeat the communists. The list was produced very quickly by Walesa's inner circle, leading to tensions within the wider opposition who challenged Solidarity's leadership for excluding activists who were not closely allied with it or those whose views lay on the fringes of the opposition. In some districts, Solidarity was criticized for selecting nationally known figures over local Solidarity activists who had proven themselves during the underground years.

Although this policy proved successful in defeating the communist establishment candidates, it greatly contributed to subsequent splits in Solidarity. The problem was that in order to remain a nationwide movement, Solidarity needed to seek alliances and broaden its base, to keep a hand on the pulse of the nation instead of fearing that internal democracy would weaken it vis-à-vis its communist adversary. It needed to have constructive relations with both established opposition organizations and budding new associations and political parties — some of them coming up from the underground, others only just starting out — even if the political beliefs of these organizations were not necessarily consistent with those of Solidarity.

Some of the groups that remained outside Solidarity fielded their own candidates, all of whom were defeated. This outcome can be explained by the maturity of the electorate, which clearly understood the purpose of the elections in the same way that the Solidarity elite did: only a united front could defeat the communists. The electorate was clearly vesting a significant amount of trust in Solidarity and found appealing Solidarity's broad umbrella, which in 1980 had so well encompassed the entire spectrum of popular aspirations and had given people a common bond.

# V

The scale of Solidarity's victory evoked a popular quip that even an ape running on Solidarity's ticket and photographed with Walesa would have won. The elections proved to be a referendum on communism. The population was desperate, and detailed programs did not matter. Solidarity did not need to say much; it was commonly understood that it stood for the opposite of what the communist authorities had been trying to instill into the public consciousness for 45 years.  Its ethic implied listening to what the man-in-the-street had to say, respecting the country's history and its Catholic Church, and speaking the truth.  On the practical level, Solidarity stood for reforming the economy to resemble the Western model.  Simply put, Solidarity represented an instinctive and comprehensive rejection of the rule of lies.

The electorate proved its sophistication further by not becoming confused by the complicated system of voting.  A voter was given anywhere between five and a dozen ballots.  In addition to the national list described above, each party's candidate list was printed on a separate slip of paper, and there were separate lists for the Sejm and Senate.

The extent of Solidarity's victory stunned virtually everyone, most importantly perhaps the government.  Solidarity won 99 out of 100 seats in the Senate; an independent won the other seat.  The national list proved an embarrassment to the authorities; all but two names on it were defeated.  The two who survived the landslide were among the most harmless — the leader of the United Peasant Party, Mikolaj Kozakiewicz, and the chairman of the Association of Lawyers, Adam Zielinski.  They survived, just barely, apparently because their names happened to fall at the bottom of the two columns of names, and as such, they were often not as cleanly crossed off as their 33 colleagues.

The election results were met with euphoria, but also with some reserve, disbelief and fear of the future.  From late night on Sunday, June 3, as the results flooded in from around the country, until the following Wednesday, when they were announced officially, analogies to December 1981 were not far from many people's minds: what if the communists again opted for a hard-line solution?

PUWP's leadership convened a marathon post-election session the next morning during which gloomy accusations and self-reproaches for naïveté and lack of dynamism were aired.  The government's profound lack of understanding of the public mood was exemplified in reflections made by Rakowski, who wrote in his memoirs:

> I don't believe that the voters voted against us because they were guided by a spirit of anti-communism...It wasn't

Solidarity's insistent campaign that did [the PUWP] a disservice...The people simply wanted change. We had not foreseen this.[2]

The election results made clear that those in power would have to accept a genuine power-sharing arrangement or else invalidate the results and opt for the use of force. Some feared that the legislature, now dominated by Solidarity supporters, would become isolated, deprived of real power, transformed into a sort of circus sideshow where courageous and controversial speeches would be made and whose bills would be blocked or overruled by the president, as a helpless population looked on. Others speculated on Moscow's reaction to this further step away from orthodoxy. Few imagined that Moscow might actually welcome this experimental station on its front porch. And even fewer had any inkling of the fate of the Berlin Wall that would fall only a half year after the Poles had begun to depose their old regime.

In the wake of the opposition movement's electoral triumph, many people were surprised by the reactions of Solidarity's leaders. In a televised appearance immediately after the elections, Janusz Onyszkiewicz, Solidarity's spokesman during its outlawed years, seemingly apologized for the scale of Solidarity's success. Other leaders were also cautious, almost embarrassed, in their first public statements following the elections.

This ambivalence was quickly noticed. Asked the writer Wiktor Woroszylski in the Solidarity daily:

Why are you not happy together with us and why are you not allowing us to be happy? Some of your public statements sound like reproaches that when we behaved like free people, like normal voters in a normal world, choosing those we wanted to choose and crossing out those we wanted to cross out, we were behaving thoughtlessly.[3]

---

[2] Ibid. at p. 230.

[3] *Gazeta Wyborcza* (Warsaw), June 6, 1989.

# VI

The largest question looming in Poland that summer was whether the communists, whose bankruptcy the voters had underscored so clearly, should continue to run the country or whether — and this seemed unimaginable — Solidarity should assume the full burden of power and form a government.   In the days and weeks following the elections, the PUWP was unable to form a government, even after reaching out to its former allies and inviting non-communists to join the cabinet.

In response to these overtures, Adam Michnik, an established opposition activist newly elected to the Sejm, publicly promoted the creation of a Solidarity-led government.   On July 3, in an article entitled "Your President, Our Prime Minister," Michnik called for the creation of a government of experts to be headed by a Solidarity prime minister.  He further speculated that Poland's alliances would be best guaranteed by a communist president, whose position had been strengthened in the roundtable agreements.

Michnik's proposal stimulated fiery public debate.  Typical of the criticism voiced by many prominent Solidarity figures was that contained in an article by Karol Modzelewski, another longtime opposition activist.   Modzelewski's arguments reflected widespread fear that the *nomenklatura* would sabotage a Solidarity cabinet.  He hypothesized that Solidarity would hold little power but would nonetheless be held responsible by the desperate population for the worsening economic climate.  Furthermore, in Modzelewski's view, Solidarity had no economic program.  Thus, Solidarity would have no chance of reorienting the country:

> For a large part of the population, the union, as well as the political organization which has emerged from it and which carries the electorate's trust, are the last hope.  If this hope is extinguished, only despair and aggression will be left, and they will close out all chances for a peaceful and democratic evolution.[4]

---

[4] *Gazeta Wyborcza.*

Solidarity faced a grave dilemma. No one seemed to have an alternative to Michnik's daredevil vision. The consensus in the period following the elections was that, for years to come, Poland's economic and political fortunes would not improve. Thus, at worst, the population would revolt; at best, things would drag along. It was even whispered that General Jaruzelski might restore the communists to power, perhaps even reimpose martial law. But few imagined the real obstacles that lay ahead.

# VII

On July 25, Walesa responded to Jaruzelski's proposal of a government coalition that would include Solidarity by asserting "all or nothing." This public ultimatum was followed by behind-the-scenes negotiations on naming a Solidarity prime minister to head a coalition government. On August 17, Walesa announced that Solidarity would form a coalition with the United Peasant Party and the Democratic Party.

Barely three months after the elections, on August 24, the national assembly, with a majority from the communist alliance, approved by a 90 percent majority a coalition government led by Prime Minister Tadeusz Mazowiecki. The new government included ministers from the Polish United Workers' Party and its former allies as well as from Solidarity. Evidently, Michnik was not alone in his belief that Poland's situation was urgent enough to demand nothing less than this courageous and unorthodox solution. The PUWP, lifeless and complacent during the election campaign, had abdicated the bulk of its power.

Mazowiecki's appointment represented an important compromise, one acceptable to Moscow and the Polish communists, the ever-influential Church and a broad section of the population. Mazowiecki had no communist background and was hand-picked by Walesa.

In retrospect, it seems that it might even have been possible to deny Jaruzelski the presidency. The National Assembly elected him on July 19 by a one-vote margin, with some Solidarity deputies either not present or abstaining. Several weeks earlier, Walesa publicly refused to contest the election after the Solidarity faction in the national assembly floated the possibility of fielding its own candidate to run against Jaruzelski.

For a time, the Mazowiecki government enjoyed a crucial honeymoon period. President Jaruzelski remained on perfect behavior, cooperating with the new prime minister. In addition, the two parties for decades in alliance with the PUWP, the Democratic and United Peasant parties, energetically moved to reestablish their democratic credentials, with many of their deputies (as well as PUWP deputies) voting with Solidarity. In January 1990, the PUWP was dissolved, and two smaller parties were formed.

The situation was far from idyllic, and yet the government was succeeding in its effort to transform the country, notwithstanding the constant discovery of obstacles left behind by the years of communist rule. Still, the Mazowiecki government's greatest failing, which ultimately sealed its fate, was its implicit reliance on the assumption that the population's patience and loyalty would last in these extraordinary times. This misguided belief stemmed, in large measure, from Mazowiecki's own nonpolitical approach to governance. The government did little to explain or promote its policies, with the result that the population, accustomed to a government it could not trust, knew little about them. Mazowiecki's massive defeat in the 1990 presidential election left his supporters in shock.

During 1990, as communist power evaporated throughout the former Soviet bloc, and as Mazowiecki appealed for moderation and reason, Poland suddenly appeared to be lagging behind its neighbors: throughout the year, four communist ministers remained in the cabinet, the old *apparachiks* continued to control the enormous bureaucracy and the secret police survived and began destroying their old files. Moreover, as other countries held free elections, the Polish national assembly sat with two-thirds of its deputies having been chosen by a formula devised at the roundtable rather than by popular suffrage.

Walesa's circle, in preparation for the presidential campaign, began calling for an "acceleration" in the pace of change. But the prospects of such an acceleration were an illusion, fed by irresponsible politicians. The other states in the region were beginning to encounter some of the same stumbling blocks that would invariably retard their progress too.

# VIII

From its inception, the Mazowiecki government promoted local government reform and elections as prerequisites for reviving Poland's body politic. The government perceived this need to be both practical and psychological: without the people being mobilized to elect local representatives, their resistance and inertia could slow down the implementation of reforms from the center. Local elections, therefore, were hurriedly scheduled for May 27, 1990.

The local government reform program was ambitious. The new system was built largely on ideas and institutional forms from the pre-World War I and the inter-war periods. The basic administrative district was a "local self-government," not a "local agency of state authority and administration" as in the communist era. The most revolutionary change sought to make the administrative units financially self-sufficient, authorizing them to raise their own taxes to supplement grants from the central government.

The elections were conducted on an enormous scale: a total of 146,281 candidates contested 52,028 seats on 2,500 local councils. Some 1,140 groups, associations, organizations and parties registered to run; fewer than 100 were full-fledged political parties, of which only a few dozen were active nationally. Some formed coalitions. Thirty-two percent of the registered candidates were drawn from the citizens' committees, 8 percent from peasant parties, 16 percent from other political parties, and the remaining 44 percent were independent.

The elections aroused little passion, in part because the population did not believe that they would make any tangible difference in their lives. Many complained that information was difficult to obtain, even though this was not the case. Forty-two percent of the eligible electorate voted, a substantially lower number than the 62 percent who had voted in the previous year's elections, reflecting a growing popular indifference to the Solidarity government and politics in general. The hope that the local elections would stimulate the average voter was not realized, revealing an enormous gap between the political elite and the population at large.

The turnout patterns corresponded to 1989 percentages and reflected historical traditions. The highest turnout figures were recorded in Galicia, the former Austro-Hungarian sector, where political sophistication and civic consciousness run high, and in Greater Poland, where, under the former Prussian partition, there had been more room for local self-government. The lowest voter turnout surfaced in parts of Silesia and in many cities, a sign of disillusionment among industrial workers.

The low turnout nationwide can be explained not only by apathy but also by an exhaustion of people's patience, as the citizenry expressed its alienation from politics in general. The old antagonism toward the communist authorities was now being transferred to the new government, which was seen as equally distant and self-absorbed. This emerging perception foreshadowed the presidential election.

# IX

Poland's political atmosphere deteriorated markedly in the summer and fall of 1990 during the campaign for the presidency. Throughout the campaign, the camps of the two most serious candidates, Walesa and Mazowiecki, engaged in personal attacks that had little to do with differences in their programs. It became clear that substantive differences were few and that it was sheer power that was at stake. A split in Solidarity had been both inevitable and desirable, and yet the bitterness of the fight testified to the political immaturity of the players, contributing significantly to the population's alienation from politics.

The Mazowiecki and Walesa camps joined forces after the first round, when the question was no longer "by how many points will Walesa beat Mazowiecki?" but rather, "how can we prevent Tyminski from winning the presidency?" In the first round, Stanislaw Tyminski, an émigré businessman and demagogue with a record of mental instability and the backing of shady characters from Poland's communist past, finished second with 20 percent of the vote, to Walesa's 39 percent and Mazowiecki's 18 percent. Commentators expressed alarm that the next time around the demagogue would be even worse and command even more votes.

What was it in Tyminski's campaign that brought him such instant success with the electorate? His greatest strength, and his two chief opponents' greatest weakness, seemed to be that he understood the critical importance of the population's economic needs, and that, as an outsider, he was not immersed in the bickering and self-absorption of distant Warsaw. The people who voted for him cannot be easily dismissed as misguided.

# X

It seems, at times, that the Poles, like the other peoples who made the 1989 revolutions, do not fully appreciate the enormity of the challenges that lie ahead and are impatient for their lives to change. Poland's additional handicap is that the events of 1988-89 represented the second time that the population experienced a revolution within a 10-year period. Poland's political elite − comprised in large part of idealists who fought for freedom and democracy for years before 1989, when the political reality was black and white − still must prove themselves capable of governing and of training a new elite.

Public apathy and distrust, resulting from years of communist rule, cannot be underestimated. Most people have not benefitted materially from the great democratic revolution. Freedom of expression affects mostly the intellectual elite, and the lower and middle classes cannot be expected to appreciate it as they struggle with obtaining the basics of daily life, which in some respects have become more difficult than five or 10 years ago. Economic freedom affects only the most enterprising, and weary and inexperienced people can hardly be expected to seize risky business opportunities. Thus, increasing popular alienation followed by an explosion aimed against the new authorities remains a real possibility during the next few years until economic reform begins to yield benefits visible to the average citizen.

It is difficult to speak of political maturity when a nation is stretched to its limit by economic hardship. Popular participation in politics and the emergence of full-fledged political parties can be expected to grow slowly, as the nation becomes more prosperous.

Prosperity will go a long way in establishing mature political structures.

Yet one should not be disappointed with Poland's progress toward democracy, expecting great political sophistication and forgetting just how much has been achieved since 1989. The government, which is often criticized for dragging its feet, has passed important legislation, in two years making a major dent in what had been constructed over 44. After Tyminski's brief rise and fall, no other horrendous figures have emerged on the national political scene. While it is true that voter turnout has been disappointingly low, there may be a healthy side to this popular alienation from politics. Rather than an unfamiliarity with democratic mechanisms, low turnout may be a signal to the national leaders involved in the massive in-fighting in Warsaw that they are out of touch with the needs of the average citizen.

As always in an economic crisis, people are justifiably focusing on their individual interests and doing for themselves what the government has not. Poland's leaders are being challenged to bridge the gap between public policy and private interests, and the success of their efforts will determine Poland's democratic future.

*Chapter 8*

# Czechoslovakia
# June 8 and 9, 1990

## Robin Carnahan and Judith Corley

*This chapter provides an assessment of the electoral process as observed before and during the national elections held in the Czech and Slovak Federal Republic on June 8 and 9, 1990. The chapter is based on information gathered by the 64-member international observer delegation from 12 countries present in Czechoslovakia for the elections, and by representatives of NDI during a series of visits to Czechoslovakia in the period preceding the elections. The international delegation, which was co-sponsored by NDI and the National Republican Institute for International Affairs, was led by Senators Christopher Dodd (D-CT) and John McCain (R-AZ), former Irish Prime Minister Garrett FitzGerald and Honduran first lady, Norma Gaborit de Callejas.*

*In January 1990, a team of election experts visited Czechoslovakia, at the invitation of Czechoslovakia's new president, Vaclav Havel, to advise leaders of Civic Forum regarding possible election*

*systems. Subsequently, NDI sponsored a series of training programs
to help prepare Czechoslovakia's newly emerging political parties for
the June elections.*

*The chapter was written by Robin Carnahan, who was NDI's
representative in Czechoslovakia before the elections, and by Judith
Corley, a Washington, D.C. attorney. The authors relied, to a large
extent, on a pre-election report prepared by Washington, D.C.
attorney Robert Bauer, Anita Dunn of the Democratic Senatorial
Campaign Committee and NDI Senior Counsel Larry Garber.*

On June 8 and 9, 1990, the Czech and Slovak Federal Republic
held its first genuinely competitive elections since 1946. Nearly 45
years after the communists assumed power, the citizens of Czechoslovakia finally were allowed to vote them out. The 1990 elections
marked the culmination of a remarkable series of events that
thoroughly transformed Czechoslovak society.

Until mid-November 1989, Czechoslovakia was a bulwark of
hard-line communist rule. Its leaders steadfastly refused to follow
Eastern-bloc neighbors and the Soviet Union down the path of
economic and political reform. But, on November 17, 1989, one
week after the fall of the Berlin Wall, the "Velvet Revolution" began.
Compared with the experiences of its neighbors, the Czechoslovak
transition was relatively short and painless. After only one week, the
communist leadership acceded to the demands of a group of dissident
writers, actors and students; by December 10, a new non-communist
government was named; and on December 29, longtime dissident and
playwright Vaclav Havel was sworn in as president. Literally within
weeks, the communist regime had relinquished its power and installed
a new government of anti-communist "amateurs" who pledged to
institute sweeping reforms.

On his third day in office, President Havel declared in a New
Year's day address, "My people, your government has returned to
you!" and pledged to make the preparation and administration of free
elections his first priority. The June elections fulfilled this commitment. With more than 95 percent of the electorate voting,
Czechoslovakia demonstrated to the world that its strong democratic
culture had survived 45 years of one-party rule.

The Czechoslovakian experience differed from the other transitions underway in Central and Eastern Europe. First, unlike the

elections held in other Warsaw Pact countries, those in Czechoslovakia were neither organized nor administered by a ruling communist government. Instead, former political dissidents, whose democratic credentials could not be challenged, controlled the election apparatus. Moreover, although the Communist Party retained a core of support, it was not a major contestant or a leading force in the election campaign. The elections clearly confirmed the nation's commitment to democracy, with a huge majority of the electorate participating and little substantive controversy concerning the election process or results.

# I

For centuries, Czechs and Slovaks lived under foreign domination — the Czechs under the Germans, and later the Austrian Hapsburgs, and the Slovaks under the Hungarians. Other than similar languages, the Czechs and Slovaks shared few historical or cultural bonds. Dramatically different levels of economic and political development further divided the two societies. The Czech lands were renowned throughout Europe as an industrial leader and possessed a sophisticated political culture. Slovakia, on the other hand, remained primarily an agricultural region whose people had consistently been denied political rights by the Hungarians.

Czechoslovakia first emerged as a nation in 1918, following the end of World War I and the collapse of the Austro-Hungarian Empire. During the First Republic (1918-38), under the strong leadership of the philosopher-president Tomas Garrigue Masaryk, the two halves of Czechoslovakia co-existed and prospered in a federal, liberal democratic system.

A major blow to Czechoslovakia's freedom and prosperity came in 1938 at a meeting in Munich between Hitler and the leaders of France and the United Kingdom. In the infamous Munich Dictate, Britain and France agreed to Hitler's demand that Germany be allowed to reclaim the Sudentenland (southwestern Bohemia) and its nearly 3 million German inhabitants. Following the Nazi annexation of the Sudentenland, other parts of the country were transferred to Hungary and Poland, and the remainder also soon succumbed to

German control. Rather than stand alone against Hitler's army, the new Czechoslovak president, Eduard Benes, capitulated to this Nazi domination. The Czech lands became the Protectorate of Bohemia and Moravia and were ruled directly by Berlin throughout the remainder of the war. Slovakia was granted an "independent" status for the first time in its history, but was ruled by a puppet fascist regime installed by Hitler.

Sporadic, anti-fascist resistance emerged during the German occupation. In 1942, the acting Nazi commander was assassinated in Prague by Czechoslovak nationalists. The resistance movement eventually reached a climax during the Slovak national uprising of 1944. Czechoslovakia's relatively passive resistance to the Nazis, however, meant the nation was spared the widespread devastation suffered by the more militant Poland during the war.

Following the German takeover in 1938, Benes assumed the presidency of the government-in-exile based in London. Eventually, he shifted his base to Moscow when it became evident that the Soviets would liberate Prague and the bulk of Czechoslovakia, leaving only the western-most part of Bohemia to be liberated by U.S. troops.

In May 1945, Czechoslovakia's pre-war borders were essentially restored and Benes was re-installed as president. A coalition government, which included some Communist Party members, ruled the country until elections in 1946. In contrast to the lingering resentment still harbored against the West for the sell-out of Czechoslovakia at Munich, the public felt deep gratitude toward their Soviet liberators. In this context, the Communist Party won a plurality in the 1946 elections with 38 percent of the vote, leaving Benes' Social Democrats with only 15.6 percent, although Benes was able to organize a coalition government that excluded the communists.

During the next two years, the communists implemented a campaign of subversion to undermine the Benes government. On May 9, 1948, the communists had consolidated enough power to pass a new constitution which formally declared the nation's commitment to building a modern socialist state. Soon Benes followed the path of his other non-communist ministers and resigned.

A united slate of so-called "National Front" candidates selected by the Communist Party contested the May 30, 1948, elections. With no real opposition, this communist-controlled ticket won an overwhelming victory. On June 9, 1948, a people's republic was established, and in July Klement Gottwald became president.

The Gottwald government loyally followed a rigid Stalinist model. During the early 1950s, businesses were nationalized, agricultural land was collectivized and the Communist Party initiated a major purge of its ranks. Following a series of show trials, the government executed Rudolph Slansky, former secretary-general of the party; and the government executed other party leaders, principally of Jewish extraction.

De-Stalinization began in the early 1960s, culminating in the famous Prague Spring of 1968. Communist Party leaders, led by the Slovak reformist Alexander Dubcek, promised "socialism with a human face." The new leadership initiated liberalizing reforms — censorship ended, political prisoners were released and rapid economic decentralization began.

Moscow, however, viewed these new liberal policies as a threat to the unity of the Eastern bloc. When the Dubcek government refused Moscow's requests to halt the reforms, the Soviets stepped in. On the night of August 20, 1968, 250,000 Soviet troops (along with token forces from the other Warsaw Pact nations) invaded and occupied Prague and other major cities in Czechoslovakia.

Although the Dubcek government immediately condemned the invasion, the Czechoslovaks met their new invaders, like the Austro-Hungarians and Germans before them, with relatively little resistance. The Soviets forced Dubcek to recognize the legality of temporarily stationing Soviet troops in Czechoslovakia. Soon after, the Dubcek government resigned, and another Slovak, Dr. Gustav Husak, became general secretary of the Communist Party. The new Soviet-dominated regime, once again, initiated major purges. In the years following 1968, approximately 150,000 Czechoslovaks left the country.

The "normalization" of the 1970s succeeded in reintroducing ideological and cultural orthodoxy. Very little anti-government activity surfaced publicly until 1977, when a group of Czechoslovak dissidents, who were mainly intellectuals and pre-1968 politicians, formed an organization called Charter 77. The Charter sought to publicize violations of the human rights provisions of the Helsinki Accords, which had been signed by the Husak government two years earlier. Despite the arrests and harassment of many of those who signed the Charter, the group survived and, ultimately, spawned other unofficial organizations. In the early 1980s, the plight of the Czechoslovak dissidents gradually began receiving increased international attention, as well-known Charter 77 members Vaclav Havel, Vaclav Benda, Jiri Dienstbier and others went to prison for speaking out on behalf of human rights.

In 1988, Czechoslovak dissidents organized protest rallies to mark the 20th anniversary of the Soviet-led invasion. The regime reacted once again by imprisoning the organizers. In January 1989, on the anniversary of the death of Jan Palach — a university student who set himself on fire in 1969 to protest the Soviet invasion and occupation — government opponents organized another rally. More people were imprisoned, including Havel, who served four months in prison on charges of "incitement."

Meanwhile, profound changes had begun in the rest of the Eastern bloc. Hungary and Poland were moving ahead with dramatic political reforms, and Mikhail Gorbachev was pronouncing *glasnost* and *perestroika* in the Soviet Union. Yet Czechoslovakia, with its proud democratic traditions and strong dissident movement, lagged behind.

But the end of communist domination was near. The Hungarian government's decision to allow East Germans to leave for the West through Hungarian borders placed enormous political and psychological pressures on the Czechoslovak authorities. The mass exodus of East Germans was not just seen on television, it was witnessed in the streets of Prague as hundreds of East Germans flooded into the West German embassy and "freedom trains" packed with jubilant East Germans passed through the city on their journeys west. Then, on November 9, 1989, the Berlin Wall fell.

# II

Before the collapse of the Wall, a group of students at Charles University in Prague had scheduled a demonstration for November 17, 1989, to commemorate the death of Jan Opletal, a student and Czechoslovak nationalist who had been beaten to death by Nazis 50 years before. Following speeches at the university, the students began marching toward Wenceslas Square, the site of momentous events throughout Czechoslovakia's history. Before they reached the Square, however, the students were attacked by riot police wielding shields and truncheons.

News of the brutal police attack spread quickly. The students, long viewed in Czechoslovakia as the "lost generation," provided the necessary spark for a nationwide movement to topple the oppressive regime. In the days and weeks that followed, rumors abounded that the police had beaten a student to death. This November 17 "massacre" incited massive new demonstrations.

On November 19 in Prague, a diverse group of political dissidents from across the ideological spectrum founded the Civic Forum. The following day, Civic Forum's Slovak counterpart Public Against Violence (PAV) formed in Bratislava. Vaclav Havel soon emerged as the leader of these coalitions of opposition groups. Demonstrations grew larger each day, and the Forum called for massive nationwide strikes. After only 10 days, the ruling communists found themselves compelled to sit at the negotiating table with Havel and his fellow dissidents, many of them Charter 77 activists whom the regime had jailed and harassed in the past.

Together, Civic Forum and PAV successfully united the anti-communist opposition and began negotiations with the government. Civic Forum/PAV quickly emerged as the legitimate representative of the hundreds of thousands of demonstrators in the streets of Prague and Bratislava. In just two days of roundtable discussions with the Forum/PAV, the Communist Party agreed to relinquish its monopoly on political power. A new anti-communist government, comprised of a majority of Civic Forum/PAV activists, was installed.

This sequence of events, now known as Czechoslovakia's Velvet Revolution, was both quick and orderly. Havel's leadership, for-tuitous timing and skillful improvisation combined to set the stage for the opposition not only to demand reform from the communists, but to peacefully, systematically and nonviolently depose the ruling elite.

As the last of the Central European countries to challenge the communist's stranglehold on power, Czechoslovakia benefitted from the struggles of neighboring Poland, Hungary and East Germany. A communist establishment weakened by the collapse of its regional collaborators faced a committed, organized internal movement for reform. The crowds that amassed in Wenceslas Square in November were ready to seize the opportunity. Their demands of "Havel to the

Castle" were soon fulfilled when, on December 29, 1989, Vaclav Havel was sworn in as Czechoslovakia's new president. In his inaugural address, President Havel described the his vision of "a republic that is independent, free and democratic; a republic with economic prosperity and also social justice; a humane republic that serves man and, for that reason, also has the hope that man will serve it."

# III

Soon after Havel assumed office, work began on a new law to govern elections for the federal and republic assemblies. Although they were able to dust off an existing, yet almost totally ignored, election law from 1946, those planning the 1990 elections sought changes to address several, sometimes conflicting, goals.

They sought to maintain Czechoslovakia's tradition of proportional representation, while at the same time allowing voters to select individual representatives, rather than be limited to lists prepared by party leaders. (Havel specifically mentioned this point in his New Year's Day address.) They sought to assure that political groups would have access to the political process, while at the same time avoiding a factionalized legislature, in which small parties might hold disproportionate influence. They wanted to set an early election date, but not so early as to preclude political parties from involvement in the administration of the elections at all levels. And they hoped to establish a democratic culture and avoid the afflictions that had gripped some emerging democratic countries, including voter apathy and centralized control of the media.

At the request of Havel, an NDI-sponsored election advisory team met with Civic Forum leaders in mid-January 1990. The election experts, from Great Britain, Hungary, Portugal and the United States, identified several electoral models that met one or more of the above goals. These included:

1) a party primary system;

2) a single transferable vote system;

3) a combined majority and proportional system modeled on the Federal Republic of Germany; and

4) a variant of the personalized preference system, which combined proportional representation with personal preference.

The NDI team further underscored the need to establish an administrative structure that would gain the confidence of the electorate. It reviewed various options for guaranteeing an election campaign in which all contestants competed on relatively equal footing.

The Federal Assembly, which was still dominated by the communists, passed the 1990 Law on Elections on February 27. The new law established procedures for electing not only members of the bicameral Czechoslovak Federal Assembly, but also members of the Czech and Slovak national councils. The Federal Assembly's new House of Nations would comprise 150 members — 75 each for the Czech lands and Slovakia. The new House of People would comprise 150 members (reduced from 200) — 101 from the Czech lands and 49 from Slovakia, based on the relative population of the two republics. The Czech National Council would have 200 members and the Slovak National Council, 150.

The new law outlined a system of proportional representation, modified to allow personalized preference voting within regional party candidate lists. Voters could choose up to four names on a party list. Preference votes would not be counted, however, unless more than 10 percent of the voters in a given region cast preference votes for candidates of a given party. When this threshold was met, any candidate receiving more than 50 percent of the preference votes automatically moved to the top of the party candidate list for the purpose of allocating parliamentary seats.

Only registered political parties or groups could participate in the elections. These included coalitions or "movements" like the Civic Forum/PAV. To register, a party was required to submit a list of 10,000 supporters. Although this requirement was designed to restrict the number of competing parties, 23 separate parties were able to register.

To limit the number of parties ultimately represented in parliament, the law also required parties to receive a threshold number of votes before gaining any seats. In order to win seats in either of the federal legislative bodies or the Czech National Council, a party was required to obtain at least 5 percent of the total valid votes cast in either the Czech or Slovak Republic. A threshold of 3 percent of the vote in Slovakia was needed to gain a seat in the Slovak National Council.

For the federal-level elections, Czechoslovakia was divided into 12 multi-member electoral districts, eight in the Czech Republic and four in Slovakia. The number of valid votes cast in each district, as opposed to the number of residents in that district, determined the number of legislators elected from each district.

Given the transitional nature of the elections, the law specified that the newly elected parliaments would serve only two-year terms, rather than the usual five years. The new law also provided that votes could be cast only within Czechoslovakia; Czechoslovak diplomats and citizens living permanently abroad would have to return to the country in order to vote. Also, the law prohibited publication of the results of public opinion surveys during the week before the elections and required all campaigning to cease 48 hours before the opening of polls. No information about the outcome of the elections could be disclosed until the official election results were available.

Elections were scheduled for two days, June 8 and 9, in order to allow as many people to vote as reasonably possible. The formal election campaign began on April 28, 1990, 40 days before election day and two months after the enactment of the election law. Thus, the new government had three months to prepare for the elections.

# IV

The Federal Election Commission (FEC) was principally responsible for administering the elections, although the Ministry of the Interior, the Bureau of Statistics and municipal town halls also played administrative roles. Subordinate election agencies controlled activities at the ward, district and regional levels. Two regional commissions, 20 district commissions and approximately 20,000 ward polling commissions were established.

Political party representatives participated directly in the commissions. The FEC included two members from each of the 23 registered parties. Each ward commission was required to include designees from at least three parties, although these commissions often had representatives from every party registered in the region.

The FEC instituted extensive training programs designed to ensure that the inexperienced party representatives on these commissions would not be manipulated by more veteran bureaucrats from the former regime. The FEC distributed instructional materials and literature to members of the subordinate commissions. Czechoslovak television broadcast programs to acquaint members of the commissions, as well as the public, with the new election procedures.

The election law permitted citizens 18 years or older to vote and established a system for the compilation of a central voter registry. The registry was drawn from a list of the names and addresses of all citizens supplied by the Ministry of Interior. Ward lists were prepared and posted in municipal halls for public inspection, and people were encouraged to check the list for omissions and errors. The lists could be modified at the municipal hall up until the day before the elections. Complaints about inaccuracies in the voter registry ultimately proved insignificant.

Under the system adopted, each registered voter was to receive a packet of ballots several days before the elections. The packet contained separate ballots listing the candidates for each registered party (17 parties were registered in the Czech lands and 15 in Slovakia) for each of the three parliaments — that is, for the House of People, the House of Nations and either the Czech or the Slovak National Council. As a result, most voters received more than 40 separate ballots.

Both election administrators and party officials expressed concern about the production and distribution of the ballot papers. Despite the use of different colored stripes to distinguish the ballots for each of the parliaments, many feared that the sheer volume of paper would lead to confusion, or worse, to manipulation of the results. In the end, though, a thorough voter education program and the availability of extra ballot packets at all the polling sites minimized confusion. Given the large number of ballot papers required by this system, envelopes signed by the ward commissioners as the voter entered the polling station became the primary means for preventing ballot stuffing and other forms of electoral fraud.

# V

A multitude of political groups participated in the Czechoslovak elections, with many of these groups consciously avoiding a "party" label. In fact, more than half of the original 23 contesting organizations preferred to call themselves a movement, union, coalition, forum, association, organization or group. One campaign poster partly demonstrated how thoroughly the Communist Party had tainted the word "party" by declaring: "Parties are for Party members. Civic Forum is for everybody."

The groups represented a wide spectrum of political views. Some, such as the Social Democratic Party, were revived pre-war parties. Others were new incarnations of the four National Front parties (Socialist Party, People's Party, Democratic Party and Freedom Party), which had collaborated with the communists during the previous 40 years. But most of the contestants were new organizations formed shortly after November 17, 1989. Several represented pre-election alliances of smaller groups hoping to meet the 5 percent threshold for winning seats in the parliaments.

Several significant pre-election coalitions emerged. Civic Forum and Public Against Violence ran coordinated but separate campaigns in the Czech lands and Slovakia respectively. The Christian and Democratic Union united several Christian-based parties, while the Republican Union surfaced as a right-of-center group advocating rapid free-market reforms. Other parties coalesced around specific issues, including the Green Party, which stressed an environmental theme, and the Association of Farmers and Country People, which emphasized the interests of agricultural cooperatives.

A number of political groups formed to protect regional or minority interests. The Romany Party defended the interests of Slovakia's Gypsy population, while the Organization of Independent Romanians, which withdrew before the elections, spoke out for ethnic Romanians in Czechoslovakia. The Slovak National Party, the Democratic Party, the Freedom Party and the Movement for Autonomous Democracy in Moravia and Silesia all promoted forms of separatism. In contrast, other groups, such as the "Coexistence" Party (the name of the party was actually the word "coexistence" in

Hungarian, Slovak, Polish and Czech) and the Movement for Czechoslovak Understanding, emphasized ethnic tolerance and harmony between the two republics.

On the lighter side, the Movement for Civic Freedom represented individuals who rejected all other political parties. And the Party of the Friends of Beer campaigned in the Czech Republic, with significant financial support from several West German breweries, on a platform of promoting distribution, stable pricing, unrestricted availability and consumption of beer.

Participation in the elections by so many parties, even though most had little hope of winning any seats, added to the general atmosphere of openness. At the same time, a few major parties dominated the election debate.

For several months after the emergence of Civic Forum and Public Against Violence in November 1989, virtually all of the non-communist opposition operated under the banner of these two organizations. As elections approached, however, the Social Democrats, Christian Democrats and Greens broke away from under the Civic Forum/PAV umbrella to run independent campaigns.

These divisions were inevitable given the conflicting goals of the organizations. Civic Forum and PAV were concerned about remaining broad movements that could represent the nonpartisan public, while the political parties were more interested in pursuing specific ideological agendas. Eventually, 12 groups remained within Civic Forum, including the Civic Democratic Alliance, Czechoslovak Democratic Initiative, Left Initiative, Movement for Civil Liberty, Rebirth and the Pan-European Union.

Civic Forum and PAV represented a broad spectrum of ideological views. They campaigned on platforms promoting civil rights, multiparty democracy, economic reform and environmental protection. Although Civic Forum and PAV were actually the incumbents in the race, they succeeded in turning the campaign into a referendum on the communists.

Shortly before the official start of the election campaign, the formation of the Christian and Democratic Union (CDU) was announced. The CDU united four groups committed to bringing traditional Christian values, democratic pluralism and free enterprise into the political arena. The small Czech Christian Democratic Party, led by Vaclav Benda, and the much larger Christian Democratic

Movement of Slovakia, led by Jan Carnogursky, possessed strong dissident and anti-communist credentials. Joining them were the People's Party, one of Czechoslovakia's oldest parties and a member of the National Front during the prior 42 years, and the Free Farmers' Party, which vowed to represent the interests of individual (as opposed to cooperative) farmers.

Early in the campaign, buoyed by the April visit of Pope John Paul II to Czechoslovakia, the CDU was viewed as the primary right-of-center alternative to Civic Forum/PAV. The Union was closely tied to and substantially supported by the West German and Austrian Christian Democrats.

The Communist Party, which assumed control of the government in 1948, dominated all aspects of life in the country for 42 years. During the campaign, the party rejected its previous adherence to rigid economic and social policies and adopted a reformist political stance. Unlike its counterparts in the region, though, the Communist Party in Czechoslovakia did not change its name.

Organizationally and financially, the Communist Party enjoyed considerable advantages. Its nationwide political network, which continued to claim between 650,000 and 700,000 members, included many loyalists who remained entrenched in government bureaucracies. The communists emphasized "safety net" issues in the campaign — playing on public uncertainty about job security, prices and living standards under a free market system.

# VI

Czechoslovakia's 40-day election campaign proceeded in a remarkably peaceful manner. None of the contestants was charged with serious campaign violations, and no organized harassment was reported. In spite of the abbreviated campaign period, political groups enjoyed reasonably adequate access to the media to communicate their messages and could do so free from interference by the government, security personnel or the Communist Party.

The campaign reflected the combined anxiety and joy felt by the nation's 20 million citizens. The Velvet Revolution had already swept the communists from power, leaving the government and the election apparatus firmly in the control of the Civic Forum-led interim government. As a result, public confidence about prospects for genuinely free elections in Czechoslovakia was probably greater than that experienced in any other Central European country. But, like their neighbors, Czechoslovaks had endured decades of oppression at the hands of the communists, and lingering fears about manipulation remained. Uncertainty about the nation's economic future added to the electorate's anxiety. Sensing this uneasiness, President Havel spoke repeatedly throughout the campaign about each citizen's responsibility to vote.

During the campaign, each party received four hours of free radio and television time to communicate its message to the voters. The time was divided into segments of varying lengths: one 30-minute spot, eight 10-minute spots, 12 five-minute spots and 70 one-minute spots. The television spots were broadcast in blocks between 5 and 7 p.m. every evening. Placement of the advertisements was based on a computer-generated random schedule agreed upon by all of the contesting parties. This generous access to television was one of the most dramatic indications of Czechoslovakia's new political freedom.

The quality of the television spots varied. Some groups used sophisticated computer images, while others showed a lone speaker talking into the camera. In general, the advertisements focused on the party platforms and featured interviews with party leaders or supporters. Most criticisms of the past regime were limited to satirical and irreverent asides rather than harshly critical attacks.

It is not easy to judge the effectiveness of the political advertisements. Before the campaign period, Czechoslovak television had carried no advertising. In the early days of the campaign, viewership for political commercials was thought to be relatively high. But most political activists agreed that as the campaign progressed, the novelty of the political spots wore off. Broadcasting the advertisements in dense, two-hour marathons, rather than placing the spots more randomly around other programming, probably further reduced their appeal.

The equal access guaranteed to the parties for political advertising did not apply to ordinary news coverage. Immediately following the revolution, control of the state media was removed from the hands of the communists and placed under "independent" jurisdiction, as determined by the new Civic Forum leadership. Not surprisingly, a number of parties charged that the news media favored Civic Forum and Public Against Violence. These claims became more serious when President Havel began appearing at Civic Forum and PAV sponsored events. When several parties lodged formal complaints after live coverage of Havel during a campaign trip in Slovakia and a speech at a Civic Forum rally, all of the other parties were compensated with bonus advertising time.

In addition to using free media time to convey their messages, political groups scheduled rallies, meetings and concerts in an attempt to attract attention. The more established parties also published newspapers and newsletters. Campaign posters were everywhere, and buttons and brochures marked with the group's identifying number on the ballot or symbol were widely distributed. Voters seemed hungry for information, and large crowds often formed around posted issue papers and party platforms.

# VII

Nearly every political group, including the communists, campaigned with identical themes. All the major contestants supported, in varying degrees, democratic pluralism, economic and social reform, cleaning up the environment and European integration. Given the parties', and indeed the nation's, limited experience with these new ideas, however, debate on the issues remained general. The contestants' similar stands on policy issues led to the campaign's strong focus on personalities.

Other than the communists, all of the parties touted their leading personalities in advertisements, posters and rallies. President Havel remained, unquestionably, the country's most popular figure. No other candidate from any party could compete with the impact of his public appearances.

Before the campaign, Havel, arguing that his responsibility was to run the government, had pledged to avoid campaigning directly for any party. During the campaign, however, a number of parties used his image in their advertisements and posters. And most of the leading parties endorsed him for president. As the campaign unfolded, however, Havel's vow not to campaign became increasingly unworkable. Ultimately, he appeared throughout the country at events organized by the Civic Forum and Public Against Violence, all the while taking care to avoid making an explicit endorsement.

Many of the country's other leading political personalities, including Prime Minister Marian Calfa, Foreign Minister Jiri Dienstbier, Finance Minister Vaclav Klaus and President of the Parliament Alexander Dubcek, as well as other leaders from the November revolution, ran for parliament on the Civic Forum or Public Against Violence ballot. The Christian Democratic Union actively promoted its own leading candidates: Interior Minister Richard Sacher, party leader Josef Bartoncik and Deputy Prime Minister Jan Carnogursky.

A dispute about treatment of the communists disrupted the campaign's otherwise cooperative tone. During the campaign, a large demonstration in Wenceslas Square demanded the return of millions of dollars worth of assets accumulated by the Communist Party during its 42-year reign. Several parties sought to capitalize on the public's anger. The People's and Socialist parties, which had collaborated with the Communist Party until 1989, as well as the Social Democrats and the Slovak Democratic Party, repeatedly demanded that the Communist Party be outlawed. President Havel, though, consistently rejected these calls for retribution.

Controversy over the release of information about the relationship between certain candidates and the former communist government surfaced late in the campaign. During the 1970s, the Communist Party claimed a membership of millions. Many thousands of others were alleged to have collaborated as informants for the secret police. In the final weeks of the campaign, allegations surfaced repeatedly that various candidates had served as informants for the secret police. There was no time to determine the truth of such devastating allegations, but several candidates chose to withdraw from the race.

Allegations of undisclosed communist ties and/or connections to the secret police were made against a number of prominent political leaders. Just before election day, for example, officials detained five former government officials for questioning. Among those detained was Milos Jakes, who had been the former Communist Party chief until his ouster in November 1989. The government also announced that it had received evidence that Josef Bartoncik, the leader of the People's Party, which was allied with the Christian Democratic Union, had been a high-level informant during the communist era. Bartoncik withdrew his candidacy. And on the first day of voting, information was disclosed that one of the leading candidates of Public Against Violence, Jan Budaj, had also collaborated with the secret police. Again, the candidate was forced to withdraw.

Nationalism and the future relations among Bohemia, Moravia and Slovakia also emerged as divisive issues in the campaign. Strong nationalistic sentiments appeared, particularly in Slovakia where calls for increased autonomy and economic parity with the Czech Republic dominated the political debate. In April 1990, just before the start of the election campaign, Slovak nationalists succeeded in changing the official name of the country from "Czechoslovakia" to the "Czech and Slovak Federal Republic" to more accurately reflect the country's two-republic structure. The active participation in the campaign of North American expatriates who contributed funds and even returned to the country to vote, also reinforced nationalist sentiments.

Public opinion surveys showed that most voters perceived the elections more as a referendum on communism than a choice among competing party platforms. A lesser number viewed the elections as a referendum on the existing Civic Forum government. Despite the large number of groups contesting the elections, it was clear that much of the electorate considered all but the major parties simply irrelevant.

# VIII

The chair of each ward election commission maintained principal responsibility for ensuring compliance with election-day procedures. In addition to the commission representatives, the election law also authorized the presence of international observers at the polling stations throughout the counting.

In general, citizens were required to vote at the polling station nearest their place of residence. Prisoners were allowed to vote at their place of incarceration, and military personnel voted at their post. Upon request, officials could also take a "sick box" to those unable to visit the polls, as long as two members of the ward polling commission were available to accompany the box.

The 20,000 designated polling stations served an average of 1,000 voters each. In some less populated areas, however, a polling station might serve as few as 50 people. Voting began on Friday, June 8, at 2 p.m. and ended for the day at 10 p.m. Voting resumed the following day, Saturday, June 9, from 7 a.m. until 2 p.m.

Upon entering the polling site, voters surrendered their voting cards, which had been distributed to all eligible voters before the elections, presented national identity cards that were then marked, and had their names crossed off the voter registry. A citizen without a voting card could still vote if he or she was known by members of the commission, presented evidence of identity and residence, or had two people known to the commission members make a positive identification.

Each voter then received an officially marked opaque envelope and, if needed, an extra packet of ballots. Inside the voting booth, the voter selected three of the distinctively colored ballots (one each for the House of Nations, House of People and either the Czech or Slovak National Council) from the multitude of ballots in the packet and placed them inside the official envelope. Once outside the voting booth, the voter placed the sealed envelope into a locked metal ballot box. Unused ballots were discarded in a separate box.

Before election day, many expressed concern about the great potential for confusion about the balloting process. Ultimately, no significant problems were reported. Some voters mistakenly placed their envelopes in the box for discarded ballots, but most seemed to be well informed about the procedures.

The challenges confronting the ward chairs would have been aggravated in a more acrimonious election environment. In a more contentious atmosphere, the multiparty composition of the ward commissions, designed to prevent fraud and manipulation of the results, would likely have complicated the resolution of any serious problems or complaints. No serious conflicts within the ward commissions were reported, however, and a festive atmosphere prevailed. In general, disputes were resolved quickly and congenially among the participating ward commissioners.

At the end of the first day of voting, officials carefully secured each polling place. They sealed windows and doors with packing tape, and the ward commissioners signed the seals. The commissioners similarly signed and sealed the ballot boxes and the boxes for discarding unused ballots. After counting the ballot packets, envelopes and other paper items and sealing them in large envelopes, the commissioners locked and sealed these materials inside locked metal file cabinets.

Members of the police or the military guarded most polling places during the night. In some cases, civilian ward commissioners or other citizens also stayed at the polling sites.

In re-opening the polls on Saturday morning, the officials reversed the process. Commissioners checked and then removed the seals on the windows, ballot boxes and papers. At least two of the commissioners then recounted the materials and verified that everything was in order. Despite this painstaking process, the polls re-opened promptly at 7 a.m.

After the polls closed on the second day, officials counted the ballots at each polling site. While the electoral law set out few substantive vote counting rules, the Bureau of Statistics had established common counting procedures and provided handbooks to the ward commissions. Few problems were reported.

Upon completion of the count, the ward commissioners entered the results, as well as reports about any complaints, on duplicate tally sheets (protocols) and signed those protocols. One copy of the protocol was sent to the district commission office. Personnel from the Federal Bureau of Statistics, working with newly installed computers, checked the protocols and entered the data. District commissions then forwarded the results by computer disk and computer printout to the regional commissions, which transmitted the data via mainframe computers to the Federal Election Commission in Prague.

Despite some apprehensions about how the new computerized system would work, no serious problems arose, and preliminary party results were announced as scheduled on the day after the close of the polls. The Federal Election Commission announced the final results several days later.

# IX

The election law barred publication of results from public opinion polls during the seven days before the elections and prohibited the publication of exit polls during the two days of voting. The Federal Election Commission did, however, sanction the release of exit poll data after the polls closed on the second day. The initial results, released by the West German polling firm INFAS working in conjunction with Czechoslovak Television, showed an overwhelming victory for Civic Forum and Public Against Violence.

Six parties qualified for seats in the parliament by winning more than 5 percent of the vote in the "first scrutiny." The "second scrutiny" proportionally allocated the remaining votes, which were cast for parties receiving less than 5 percent of the vote in either republic.

Civic Forum/PAV won 170 of the 300 seats in the Federal Assembly. The Communist Party placed second, receiving 47 seats, and the Christian and Democratic Union garnered 40 seats. Three nationalist and ethnic groups divided the remaining 43 seats.

On July 5, 1990, the new, democratically elected Federal Assembly chose Vaclav Havel as president of the Czech and Slovak Federal Republic.

# X

Less than seven months elapsed from the start of Czechoslovakia's Velvet Revolution to the conclusion of its first free elections in more than 42 years. Although "too little time" was the most frequent complaint about the nation's new election framework, the process was implemented and administered, at all levels, with remarkable ease. Moreover, there were few serious complaints about the fairness of the process during the campaign, balloting or vote tabulation.

The courage and persistence of a strong dissident community, which maintained the offensive when the communist government was most under siege, made possible the success of Czechoslovakia's revolution. The Czechoslovak opposition, led by Vaclav Havel, skillfully harnessed the revolutionary energy of the people, while at the same time keeping intact the nation's established institutions of government. The military also exercised restraint.

In contrast to the other Central and Eastern European elections of 1990, the Czechoslovak elections were organized by non-communists. Following the Communist Party's abdication of power in late 1989, a well-organized coalition of former dissidents strongly committed to democratic reform assumed the reins of government. As a result, leaders more interested in institutionalizing democratic government than in retaining power controlled the process.

The new leadership's commitment to ensuring free and fair elections inspired public confidence. Czechoslovak citizens understood the significance of the elections for their country's future, and more than 95 percent went to the polls.

The election results reflected both the nation's consensus about the institutionalization of democracy and its uncertainty about economic plans, priorities and philosophies. As democratic reforms evolve, the next round of elections will likely develop as a true competition among ideologies and policies rather than a referendum on democracy.

The election results, like the campaign itself, also provided a preview of some of Czechoslovakia's most difficult post-election problems. Strong nationalistic sentiments were evident during the campaign and in the results. And the government and the newly elected representatives spent most of the remainder of 1990 trying to redefine the distribution of power between the republics and the federal government.

The treatment of communists and their collaborators remained an emotionally charged issue. During the campaign, the issue surfaced repeatedly, and last-minute charges of collaboration against some leading political figures probably affected the election results. Despite the Havel government's attempt to prevent widespread retribution and to adopt a mantle of collective guilt, public animosity toward collaborators and alleged collaborators remained strong. In the spring of 1991, after much speculation and debate, the government published a list of suspected collaborators serving in the new parliaments. In a series of events eerily reminiscent of the past regime, most of those accused resigned from office without trial.

Despite these problems, however, the 1990 elections strongly reaffirmed Czechoslovakia's commitment to rebuilding a democratic system.  The newly elected political leaders thus began the difficult process of institutionalizing the democratic process, even while they confronted  the legacy of 45 years of totalitarian rule.

*Chapter 9*

# Bulgaria
# June 10, 1990

## Larry Garber

*This chapter is based on the election monitoring activities undertaken by NDI in Bulgaria from April 1990 through September 1990. Among these activities, NDI sponsored three pre-election fact-finding missions, co-sponsored with the National Republican Institute for International Affairs a 60-member international observer delegation from 23 countries, and provided material and technical assistance to the Bulgarian Association for Fair Elections, which emerged as a significant, nonpartisan civic organization in the six weeks prior to the elections. The international delegation was led by Prime Minister Steingrimur Hermannsson of Iceland, Senator Robert Hill of Australia, Governor Madeleine Kunin (D-VT) and Representative Robert Lagomarsino (R-CA). A more comprehensive report on the Bulgarian elections is contained in* **The June 1990 Bulgarian Elections***, published by NDI and NRIIA. This chapter draws heavily on that report, which was principally authored by NDI Senior Counsel Larry Garber.*

Commentators frequently refer to the June 1990 Bulgarian elections as a singular example of a reformed Communist Party winning relatively fair elections. By contrast, reformed Communist parties fared poorly in Czechoslovakia, East Germany, Hungary and Poland, all of which held multiparty elections in the spring of 1990.[1] Although the Bulgarian Communist Party (BCP) changed its name in March 1990 to the Bulgarian Socialist Party (BSP), it retained a vast, nationwide party infrastructure. This organizational base, the short time period in which the opposition was able to prepare, and the fear prevalent among the rural population are offered as explanations of this unique outcome.

Negative perceptions of the Bulgarian elections, which many Bulgarians share, overlook the very dramatic political transition that has occurred in Bulgaria since November 1989, when longtime Communist Party leader Todor Zhivkov was removed from power in a "palace coup." Before the coup, Bulgaria was a totalitarian one-party state with no organized dissident movement, an extremely poor human rights record and a wholly state-owned economy. Less than a year later, Zhelu Zhelev, a philosophy professor, author and former dissident, became president; non-communist opposition parties were well-represented and influential in the legislature; the government was a *de facto* coalition, with the opposition controlling the key economic ministries; freedom of expression and association were respected; the human rights situation had greatly improved; and private enterprise was emerging.

The transition in Bulgaria illustrates how an amalgam of peaceful demonstrations, political activism, civic organizing, elections, legislative bargaining and street politics can create the environment for the evolution to a truly democratic society. The Bulgarian transition also highlights the important role played by the international community in promoting political development. Finally, the Bulgarian case suggests the need to view a first election as part of a continuing

---

[1] In Romania, the National Salvation Front purported to be a new coalition that included disparate groups, but most observers inside and outside Romania viewed the Front as comprising primarily former Communist Party members. The Front, too, won an overwhelming victory in national elections, but under conditions that were considerably less fair than those that existed in Bulgaria. See Chapter 6.

process and to avoid premature characterization of a transition as complete or as failed.

# I

In contrast to its Warsaw Pact allies, Bulgaria's relationship with the Soviet Union was based on more than mere military occupation. Bulgarians and Russians share a Slavic heritage, Eastern Orthodox Catholicism, similar languages and the Cyrillic alphabet. Russia assured Bulgarian independence from the Ottoman Empire in 1876, contributing to the amicable relationship between the two countries. Not surprisingly, therefore, throughout the post-World War II era of communist domination, Bulgaria was viewed as among the Soviet Union's most reliable allies.

By 1989, however, when the Soviet Union embarked on political and economic restructuring, Bulgaria began to fall out of step with its traditional role model. The Bulgarian government seemed unable or unwilling to keep pace with Mikhail Gorbachev's experiments with *glasnost* and *perestroika*. This dissonance troubled Zhivkov's younger colleagues in the communist establishment, ultimately paving the way for his removal.

Environmentalists were among the first independent, civic groups to organize in contemporary Bulgaria. Their moment in the international spotlight came in September 1989. The occasion was a long-scheduled meeting in Sofia of the Conference on Security and Cooperation in Europe (CSCE) where official representatives from the 35 signatory states met to discuss international environmental matters. Bulgarian environmentalists, encouraged and protected to an extent by the international presence in the country, organized the first unauthorized, public demonstrations in more than 40 years. Demonstrations became larger and more frequent during October, even after the departure of the CSCE delegates, and the roster of grievances quickly expanded beyond environmental concerns.

On November 10, 1989, the day after the Berlin Wall was breached, the Communist Party Politburo forced Zhivkov, who had assumed power in 1954, to resign. Petar Mladenov, for 18 years Zhivkov's foreign minister, orchestrated the departure of his longtime mentor, reportedly with the explicit support of Gorbachev. Zhivkov's critics believed his uncompromising policies were forcing Bulgaria into international isolation, where its only ally would be "the rotten dictatorial family regime of Ceausescus."

On November 17, the Bulgarian National Assembly abolished a much-hated provision of the criminal code (Article 273) that had been used to prosecute political dissidents. Critics of the government and of the communist system began appearing on television and in the print media; discriminatory decrees directed against the Turkish minority were revoked, although this soon caused a nationalist backlash; and the government promised to eliminate the internal security forces that for decades had been used to repress the Bulgarian population.

The new government blamed the Zhivkov regime for Bulgaria's many problems. In the months that followed, visitors to Bulgaria were bemused to hear longtime Communist Party and government officials proclaim that their entire world view had changed suddenly and completely on "the 10th of November" and that they now rejected all the totalitarian excesses of the previous regime.

The question of holding multiparty elections proved controversial. Mladenov was quoted in November as supporting "free elections and greater pluralism," but other BCP officials explained that this meant "pluralism of opinions, not of parties" and pledged that the Communist Party would remain the nation's "leading force." Then, on December 11, the day after a pro-democracy rally of some 50,000 people in Sofia, Mladenov announced in a major speech that the Communist Party's monopoly on power, hitherto guaranteed by Article 1 of the constitution, would be abolished.

During December, a coalition of groups formed the Union of Democratic Forces (UDF)[2] as an umbrella organization to present a

---

[2] The UDF ultimately included the following constituent groups: Independent Society for the Protection of Human Rights in Bulgaria; Independent Federation of Labor (Podkrepa, or "Support"); Committee for the Protection of Religious Rights, Freedom of  Conscience and Spiritual Values; Citizens' Initiative; Democratic Party; Social Democratic Party; Federation of Independent Student Societies; Bulgarian Radical Democratic Party; Federation of Clubs for Glasnost and Democracy; Eco-Glasnost; Bulgarian Agrarian National Union-Nikola Petkov; Green Party; Club for the

coherent, unified opposition and to negotiate with the communist government. Roundtable negotiations among the BCP, UDF and the Bulgarian Agrarian National Union (BANU), the traditional party that existed as the sole legal "opposition" during the communist era, began on January 3, 1990. The talks proceeded slowly at first, because the UDF, fearing cooptation, rebuffed a BCP offer to form a government of national unity.

The negotiations gained momentum in February, following the 14th BCP Congress and the subsequent resignation of the BCP government. Andrei Lukanov, an economist and former minister of foreign trade, was designated the new prime minister, and he assembled a cabinet that was considered more reform-minded than its predecessor.

Even with these developments, it took two months of difficult negotiations to reach agreement on changes in the constitution and the overall political structure. The agreement covered, *inter alia*, the following matters: recognition of Bulgaria's character as a democratic, pluralist state; acceptance of an economy based upon market competition, with the state responsible for protecting the weaker social strata; the election of a Grand National Assembly — a constituent assembly of the same name formed after liberation from the Turks in 1878; and the adoption of laws governing political parties and elections for the Grand National Assembly. It was agreed that during the 18-month period in which the Grand National Assembly drafted a new constitution, Mladenov would remain as head of state, while the head of government would answer to the Assembly.

# II

The agreement that emerged from the roundtable negotiations reflected compromises made by both the BSP and the UDF, and

---

Illegally Repressed Since 1945; Party of Freedom and Progress; Socialist Party (not the governing party); United Democratic Center; and Democratic Front. The names suggest the varied interests represented under the UDF umbrella.

generally accommodated just these two parties/coalitions and BANU. The UDF, recognizing the need for time to build a national organizational structure and to transmit its message to the public, had initially attempted to schedule elections for November 1990. Indeed, the coalition had threatened to boycott elections that the BSP originally tried to schedule for May 1990, but eventually agreed to the June date. The UDF also accepted Mladenov as head of state for the transition period.

The BSP accepted the concept of a Grand National Assembly, which would be twice the size of an ordinary National Assembly, to exist for the limited period of 18 months. This was a significant concession. The BSP had sought to avoid a series of elections, hoping to obtain an extended mandate in early single elections, for which the opposition forces were not fully prepared. The acceptance of an election system based, in part, on proportional representation, was another concession by the BSP, which believed it would have benefitted from a continuation of the single-member constituency system.

# III

The Grand National Assembly Election Act of 1990 established procedures for electing the 400-member unicameral Grand National Assembly. The law provided for the election of 200 legislators from single-member electoral districts and 200 from multi-member districts under a party list system.

The contours of the 200 single-member electoral districts were based on boundaries used in previous Bulgarian elections, while the 28 multi-member districts corresponded to administrative districts that had been used until mid-1987. The number of legislators elected from the multi-member districts varied, ranging from three in the smallest district to 26 in Sofia.

Not surprisingly, given the lack of either accurate demographic data or a meaningful voting history, none of the participating parties presented any significant objection to the electoral district boundaries before the elections. After the elections, however, the UDF charged that critical variances in the number of voters per single-member constituency benefitted the BSP in the allocation of seats.

In the single-member districts, a candidate needed to obtain 50 percent plus one of the votes to be elected in the first round. If no candidate received such a majority, then the two candidates who acquired the highest number of votes participated in run-off elections on June 17. Also, if voter turnout in a district was less than 50 percent in the first round, a run-off election was required.

In determining the allocation of the proportional representation seats, the Central Election Commission (CEC) relied on its interpretation of the West German election system. Thus, the 200 multi-member seats were allocated in accordance with the proportion of votes received by the party nationwide, subject to one important caveat: a party had to receive at least 4 percent of the national vote to qualify for parliamentary representation. This minimum eligibility threshold was designed to prevent parties with only limited national support from obtaining representation in the legislature. Also, the Political Party Act, adopted in late March, authorized a ban on parties "based on ethnic or religious principles."

The election law established the CEC, 228 district election commissions (one for each of the 200 single-member constituencies and 28 multi-member constituencies) and a sectional election commission for each of the 13,000 authorized polling sites. These commissions included officials from the municipal administration, who were usually identified with the old regime, and representatives designated by the political parties.

The 24-member CEC was formed on April 11. Its chair was Zhivko Stalev, a well-respected professor of law, who was proposed by the UDF, although he was not affiliated with any political party. The BSP, UDF and BANU each designated one of the other three principal CEC officers and apportioned the 20 remaining seats among themselves.

The CEC was responsible for enforcing the election law and adopting procedures and regulations for the elections. With few exceptions, the CEC developed regulations and procedures implementing the election campaign and balloting process in a fair and impartial manner. Moreover, the CEC was responsive to concerns raised by opposition parties and international observers throughout the pre-election period.

# IV

The short time period between the conclusion of the roundtable agreement and the June 10 elections placed enormous burdens on the CEC and the political parties. Local election officials had to be designated and trained, candidates selected, ballots printed, voter registries prepared and a voter education program implemented. At the same time, the government had to overcome public skepticism and demonstrate that it could create conditions for free and fair elections.

The Bulgarian election system was highly decentralized, with considerable responsibility placed in the hands of municipal authorities. These officials facilitated periodic meetings of local contact groups and roundtables to discuss implementation of the national roundtable agreement, including its provisions for the appointment of district and sectional electoral commissions.

District electoral commissions, which formed during mid-April, selected polling-site officials, prepared voter registries and distributed election materials. There appeared to be a good-faith effort to comply with the mandate of the election law by including members of the various parties on the commissions and with the spirit of the law by ensuring that the chairs of the commissions represented different parties and coalitions.

At most of the 13,000 polling sites, representatives of the major parties were designated as polling officials. In approximately 800 sites, however, mostly in rural areas, the UDF was not represented on the sectional electoral commissions, and it was to these sites that the UDF directed the attention of civic organizations and international observers.

Bulgarian citizens who were 18 years or older by June 10 were eligible to vote. According to the law, the national government was responsible for preparing a voter registry with the names of all eligible voters. In addition, a prospective voter needed to present a valid passport or national identification card at the polling site. According to the CEC, there were slightly less than 7 million registered voters.

On May 11, 30 days before the elections, registries were published and posted at every voting section. The lists contained numerous mistakes; names of eligible voters were missing, and the names of those who had died or moved remained on the list. In addition, many members of the Turkish minority were registered according to the Slavic names they were forced to adopt during the 1984-85 assimilation campaign initiated by the Zhivkov regime, resulting in much confusion as some Turks could not recognize their own names on the registries.

Acknowledging that the published lists were unacceptable, the CEC ordered that new lists be prepared by June 5, five days before the elections. However, serious complaints arose regarding the content of those lists as well. To avoid disenfranchising those mistakenly excluded, the CEC issued a decree on June 9 authorizing all Bulgarians to vote at the polling site nearest to their residence as listed on their national identity cards, regardless of whether their names were posted on a list.

The election law provided for the printing of individual ballots for each contesting candidate and party. Ballots, printed according to a pre-assigned color for each political party, contained the name of the candidate(s) contesting a particular seat. Before the elections, parties and candidates were given their ballots for distribution to prospective voters. Ballots also were available at the polling sites. Envelopes were furnished to voters at the polling site to assure a secret vote.

Early in the campaign period, questions were raised about the transparency of the envelopes. It was feared that the use of envelopes through which the color of the ballots could be seen would contribute to a perception that the vote was not secret. In response, the CEC required that the white envelopes be lined with a blue dye to make it virtually impossible to identify the color of the ballots inside.

Given Bulgaria's history of one-party rule and nondemocratic elections, there was a recognized need for effective voter education programs, which would explain the balloting process and reassure the population that their votes would be confidential. The CEC assumed primary responsibility for the government-sponsored effort, while civic organizations developed their own programs.

Throughout the campaign period, television and radio broadcast 10-minute public service announcements that explained and demonstrated the mechanics of voting. The CEC also sought to allay concerns about ballot manipulation involving, for example, the use of special pens to spoil ballots or the use of ballots that would change colors. While the fears sometimes seemed outlandish, they were often heard from UDF supporters in the weeks leading up to the elections.

Critics of the CEC voter education effort claimed that insufficient emphasis was given to the importance of a secret ballot in a country that had experienced 45 years of totalitarian rule. Indeed, some in the opposition charged that this inattention represented a deliberate omission, which benefitted the ruling party whose support was centered predominantly in rural areas where the population was less educated.

Two matters — the question of voting abroad and the handling of complaints — illustrate some of the difficulties encountered by the CEC in developing an election system and campaign environment that was satisfactory to the participants and to the international community.

The CEC decided to limit absentee voting for Bulgarians abroad to government employees, contract employees for Bulgarian enterprises and those who were abroad for less than two months or more than five years. The CEC announced that 60,000 Bulgarians living abroad met these qualifications and were automatically included in the registries.

The principal effect of the five-year requirement, which was endorsed by the three major parties and approved by all but one of the CEC members, was to disenfranchise 250,000 Turkish-Bulgarians who left Bulgaria for Turkey between 1985 and 1989 (*i.e.*, during years of significant repression), unless they returned to Bulgaria to vote in person. To many observers, it seemed anomalous to enfranchise Bulgarians whose ties to the country were quite remote (*e.g.*, those absent from Bulgaria for as many as 50 years), while excluding those who were recently forced from the country.

A second area of difficulty for the CEC involved resolving election-related complaints. The CEC reported that before the elections it had received nearly 1,000 grievances, which ranged from complaints about the formation of sectional election commissions and the destruction of posters to questions about the voter registries. Most of these complaints, according to the CEC members responsible for their review, were resolved at the regional level and usually through local roundtable meetings, although no specific statistics could be provided. The lack of systematic record-keeping on the disposition of grievances reduced confidence in the CEC as a guarantor of fair elections.

# V

The election law contained language that, in principle, permitted a fair campaign, including provisions that guaranteed to the competing parties access to the media and to sources of funding. The CEC and several government ministries were responsible for developing the necessary implementing regulations.

A final evaluation of the fairness of the election campaign in Bulgaria, however, requires analyzing the extent to which all parties were able to communicate their messages and the degree to which the government affirmatively acted to eliminate inequities in the process. On the positive side, the campaign featured a broad spectrum of active parties; no legal or practical impediment prevented any political party from forming or competing in the elections. On the negative side was the disparity in resources available to the parties.

The Political Party Act imposed minimal requirements for the registration of political parties and other organizations. Once registered, a party or organization could nominate candidates simply by registering the candidates' names with the district electoral commissions. An independent candidate was required to obtain signatures of 500 citizens.

More than 1,400 individuals competed in single-member constituencies, and more than 1,700 candidates, representing 30 parties, contested seats in the multi-member constituencies. Many candidates contested seats in both types of constituencies.

Of the more than 45 parties and groups that registered and nominated candidates for the June elections, only four became significant contenders. In part, this outcome reflected the system that evolved from the roundtable negotiations. The smaller parties, which were not represented in the negotiations, were significantly disadvantaged by the institutional benefits (*e.g.*, state revenue, television time, etc.) provided only to the BSP, UDF and BANU. To have treated all parties equally, though, would have diluted the message of the major opposition coalition, providing the BSP with an even greater institutional advantage in the June elections. In large measure, the system accomplished its major purpose: it provided a significant choice among competing parties and it allowed these parties to present distinct messages to the Bulgarian citizenry.

In most parts of the country, a meaningful, if imbalanced, campaign ensued, with the major parties presenting candidates, organizing rallies and distributing party propaganda. Rallies and campaign meetings were held throughout the country, with only a few reported instances of candidates being prevented from speaking. There were, however, reports of damage to opposition party headquarters and the destruction of posters and other campaign paraphernalia. Coupled with other acts of intimidation by BSP supporters, these incidents may have influenced some voters to vote BSP, particularly those living in rural areas, who were less likely to be exposed to the opposition's campaign.

The peaceful nature of the campaign was noteworthy, particularly in a society with no experience in democratic politics. The political parties, in large measure, were responsible for this tolerant climate. Periodic meetings among party leaders at the national and regional levels encouraged most party supporters to respect the rights of their competitors.

The parties presented alternative messages to the electorate. The BSP stressed the reforms the party had made in the months since November, but also emphasized the party's experience in governing and its role in improving the living standards of many Bulgarians over two generations. Throughout the campaign, the BSP, and most notably Prime Minister Lukanov, repeated that it would seek a multi-party coalition, regardless of the election results. According to Lukanov, only a broad-based coalition could address Bulgaria's multiple problems.

The UDF, not surprisingly, emphasized the failings of the communist system and tied the BSP to these shortcomings. The UDF promised a more rapid pace of reform for the political and economic systems, stressing privatization as an immediate goal and a strong orientation toward the Western community.

BANU attempted to distance itself from its former association with the Communist Party and to present itself as a third force capable of mediating between the two major parties. The Movement for Rights and Freedom sought to mobilize ethnic Turks to support a party that would protect their interests.

The BSP, having inherited the spoils of 45 years of Communist Party rule, possessed vastly greater resources and infrastructure than did the UDF and other competing parties. Under these circumstances, it was virtually impossible to balance the political resources during the limited period preceding the campaign. In many instances, the government failed to make a good faith effort to provide, on an expedited basis, materials, including office space and equipment, to the newly formed political parties. The amount of money (US $10,000) authorized by the election law for each of the participating parties was received only days before the elections, too late to make a significant difference in the campaign.

The election law limited the size of political contributions and the amount that a candidate could spend on a campaign, with winning candidates required to file post-election campaign finance reports. Contributions from "foreign corporate bodies" were prohibited. In recognition of the financial difficulties facing the newly formed parties, however, the prohibition was suspended for one year from the enactment date of the Political Party Act. The UDF, and several of its constituent parties, received large amounts of assistance from numerous foreign sources.

The opposition complained that local officials identified with the BSP were guilty of harassment, although overt physical intimidation did not appear to be a serious problem. Likewise, the BSP charged that its activists were similarly threatened. In addition, reports intensified during the later stages of the campaign that local authorities were threatening to terminate public benefits and raise rents if the UDF won. The impact of such incidents, however, was difficult to estimate. At the same time, given Bulgaria's recent history of persecuting ethnic minorities, the fears felt by the general population were heightened in regions heavily populated by minority groups.

# VI

Following the November coup, the media, which for 45 years was strictly controlled by the ruling party, was partially liberalized.

New newspapers and magazines were distributed throughout the country, and the government-controlled electronic media presented perspectives other than the official line on television and radio programs. Nonetheless, given the realities of a transition period, the opposition never achieved full equality with the BSP in their access to the media.

From the last week in April through the end of the campaign, the BSP and the UDF were allotted 20 minutes of free television time, three days a week, while BANU was accorded 15 minutes. This complimentary television time allowed the principal political forces to communicate their messages to the people, most of whom owned televisions. Smaller parties were assigned more limited television access, perpetuating the view that the election was a two- (or at most three-) party contest. No restrictions were placed on the content of the broadcasts, and criticism of the government and ruling party was often quite bitter.

The BSP maintained an advantage in the promotion of its views through tacit control of Bulgarian television. Most independent observers characterized television news coverage as pro-BSP, although no systematic content analysis was conducted. On the other hand, some diversity in programming was offered. For example, the most popular television program was "Every Sunday," a two-and-a-half hour news and variety show hosted by Kevork Kevorkian, a prominent television journalist and vice president of Bulgarian television. Throughout the campaign period, BSP leaders and the ruling party newspaper attacked the "Every Sunday" program, and Kevorkian personally, for unduly favoring the opposition. The program made a concerted effort to include interviews with government and ruling party representatives. In addition, Kevorkian refused to identify himself with any particular party, serving instead as president of the nonpartisan Bulgarian Association for Fair Elections (BAFE).

The print media was quite partisan. *Duma*, the BSP newspaper, boasted the largest circulation. BSP-affiliated regional newspapers were published throughout the country. While strongly oriented toward the BSP, *Duma* and the regional newspapers covered some opposition activities and included stories that under the previous regime would not have been printed because they would have been deemed embarrassing.

Opposition parties published national and regional newspapers, which like the ruling-party counterparts, were notably partisan. These papers proved quite popular, usually selling out quickly, but their circulation was arbitrarily limited: opposition leaders complained that their press run at state-owned printing houses was approximately 10 percent of that for BSP newspapers. In addition, the opposition charged that its newspapers were unavailable in smaller villages because of interference by the government-controlled distribution networks and government manipulation of paper and print stocks.

Both the BSP and UDF held their final rallies on June 7 in Sofia. The rally sites were within one mile of each another, but, despite the large crowds, no confrontations were reported. The UDF rally, attended by an estimated 500,000 people, was considered the largest demonstration in the country's history and provided the opposition with a sense of optimism as election day approached.

# VII

More than 6.3 million Bulgarians, or approximately 90 percent of the eligible electorate, participated in the first round of elections on June 10. This high turnout, in the first contest in more than 40 years where Bulgarians were not obligated to vote, reflected an apparent recognition by the citizenry that the elections were a significant civic exercise.

Representatives of at least two parties monitored the balloting at virtually all polling stations. Also present at most sites were representatives of the Bulgarian Association for Fair Elections (BAFE), which formed in mid-April as a nonpartisan, civic organization to monitor the conduct of the elections. Modeled after similar groups in the Philippines and Chile, BAFE sought to promote confidence in the electoral process by developing voter education programs, mobilizing pollwatchers and conducting an independent, parallel vote tabulation.

Bulgarian and international observers witnessed irregularities in some regions and heard about irregularities in many others. However, the problems, for the most part, involved isolated incidents, which were not considered sufficient to invalidate the overall electoral process.

Several complaints centered on the extent to which the secrecy of the ballot was guaranteed. In addition to questions about the transparency of the envelopes, at some polling sites the voting booth was made of sheer cotton fabric, which allowed the voters to be seen inside. In other sites, the booth was situated so that the members of the sectional election commission could look inside. In most places, however, the booths provided an adequate degree of privacy to assure a secret ballot.

Little political campaigning or obvious coercion occurred at polling sites, although observers noted the possibility of more subtle forms of pressure. In many towns and villages, for example, the mayor or other officials were present in or around the polling sites, contributing to fears that local BSP authorities would retaliate against those voting against the BSP by denying them such necessities as winter heating oil.

Ballots were counted at the polling sites, after which the results were transmitted to and ultimately released by the CEC. Most of the results from the single-member constituencies were officially announced on Tuesday, June 12, two days after the polls closed. In 120 constituencies, winning candidates received a majority. The BSP won 75 seats, the UDF gained 32 seats, the MRF received nine seats, four seats were captured by candidates representing small parties, and BANU failed to win any of the single-member constituencies. In the remaining 80 constituencies, a second round of voting was scheduled for the following week.

Tabulating the results for the multi-member constituencies took slightly longer than anticipated; the official results were not announced until Thursday, June 14. The BSP garnered 47 percent of the total ballots, entitling it to 97 of the 200 multi-member seats. The UDF trailed with 36 percent and 75 seats; BANU won 8 percent and 16 seats; and the MRF obtained 6 percent and 12 seats. While some suspicions were raised concerning the late announcement of these results, the delay appeared attributable to the novelty of the election system and the careful scrutiny with which each tally sheet was reviewed by the CEC.

Notwithstanding the delay in announcing the multi-member results, concern over possible manipulation was greatly alleviated by the election-night release of unofficial results generated by two parallel vote tabulations, one organized by BAFE and a second by INFAS, a West German polling firm.   These efforts deserve considerable credit for calming tensions during the days following the elections.

From the outset, BAFE viewed the parallel vote tabulation as a critical component of its activities.  Similar systems have been used recently in other countries experiencing transition elections to deter fraud and to provide an independent basis for verifying the results. The BAFE system relied on volunteers to observe the count at approximately 10 percent of the polling sites (1,302 were included in the sample) selected randomly.  By tabulating the actual results from the sample polling sites, the national results in the multi-member constituencies were projected with a relatively small margin of error.

Originally, Bulgarian television commissioned INFAS to conduct an exit poll similar to those conducted in other countries in the region.   The UDF objected to exit polls on three grounds: the possibility that questioning voters regarding their party preferences in the context of these elections could be perceived as intimidating; suspicions regarding the political orientation of the interviewers; and a fear that the exit-poll results would be publicized on election day thus possibly influencing those voters who would cast their ballots late in the day.  The CEC accepted the UDF position and proscribed the use of exit polls.

Soon after midnight on election night, BAFE and INFAS representatives appeared on television to offer their preliminary results, which, notwithstanding the differing methodologies, indicated virtually identical BSP pluralities.  The fact that the results released that night on television were accurate to within less than 1 percentage point of the official results announced four days later testifies to the quality of the methodologies utilized.

In Bulgaria, the parallel vote tabulation played a quite different role than originally envisioned, at least by BAFE organizers.  Unlike in the Philippines and Panama, the parallel vote tabulation did not reveal that the ruling party was stealing the elections.  Unlike in Chile and Nicaragua, the parallel vote tabulation was not used to pressure the government to recognize an opposition victory.   Rather, the BAFE parallel vote tabulation proved critical in convincing UDF supporters that the BSP had in fact won the elections.  The UDF knew that BAFE was not another BSP-front organization; in fact, most BAFE activists and leaders were UDF supporters.

Given the suspicions that existed after more than 45 years of totalitarian rule, it is questionable whether the results would have been accepted by the opposition without BAFE's timely independent results. Moreover, election-night tensions might have increased, and a deterioration in the situation, in a manner similar to Romania, could have developed. Instead, a second round of voting occurred a week later with the participation of all eligible parties.

After several days of indecision, on June 14, the UDF formally conceded defeat and committed itself to participating in the second round of elections. The June 17 run-off elections were conducted peacefully. Turnout was again high, this time in the 85 percent range. Pollwatchers from political parties and civic organizations were present at all polling sites.

The counting process for the second round was conducted more expeditiously than for the first round. On Monday the results were announced. The BSP received the most votes in 39 of the constituencies, giving the party 211 of the 400 seats in the Grand National Assembly. The UDF won in 37 constituencies, allotting it 144 seats total. The MRF won seats in two constituencies, and independents took the remaining two seats.

# VIII

The BSP's overall success in the elections was noteworthy, but perhaps not all that surprising. Historically, the Bulgarian Communist Party enjoyed a higher membership per capita than did Communist parties in the neighboring Soviet bloc countries. Unlike post-Communist parties elsewhere in Eastern Europe, the renamed BSP remained well-organized and cohesive, with few members defecting from the ranks. In rural areas in particular, the BSP was usually the most powerful social force in a town or village. In the major cities, where the BSP's policies were subject to greater public criticism and its grip on the lives of the population seemed somewhat less certain, the party was weaker.

During the campaign, the BSP used its considerable control over the news media to dramatize discord within the ranks of UDF, characterizing the latter as an incoherent amalgam of conflicting interests unable to rule. The BSP also stressed the experience of its leaders and members.

Still, the elections highlighted certain trends evident among the Bulgarian electorate. For example, an extreme divergence of party choice existed between the large cities and the countryside. In Sofia, the UDF was successful in 24 of the 26 single-member constituencies and 53 percent of the party-list vote. Likewise, in Plovdiv and Varna, Bulgaria's second- and third-largest cities, the UDF obtained majorities in all of the single-member constituencies. In rural areas, however, the BSP dominated.

In the weeks following the elections, some UDF supporters claimed that the distribution of seats demonstrated that the boundaries for constituencies used for the June elections had been drawn to guarantee a BSP victory. Critics pointed to the difference between the 114 seats won in single-member constituencies and the 97 seats won under the proportional system; according to the argument, this difference represented a "bonus" of 17 seats, reflecting a bias in the drawing of constituency lines that favored the rural areas where the BSP was strongest.

The above numbers, however, do not establish a deliberate attempt to manipulate the results by creating unequal constituencies. In most countries where it is used, the single-member system provides such a bonus to the party obtaining the most votes. Moreover, the fact that there was a strong rural bias in the drawing of Bulgarian constituencies should not be surprising, particularly because the constituencies had been drawn more than 45 years before; it is only in recent years that established democratic countries have attempted to redress the historical bias favoring rural areas.

A second phenomenon concerned the defeat of several leading BSP candidates in the single-member constituencies. Because individuals could be nominated as candidates for both single-member constituencies and on the proportional lists, these prominent BSP figures were nonetheless elected to the Grand National Assembly from the latter category. Indeed, in order to capitalize on the rule permitting dual listings, the BSP may have purposely designated some of its more visible candidates in hotly contested districts, as opposed to providing them with safe seats.

Notwithstanding the disappointment within the UDF regarding the election results, its leaders realized that the coalition's strong showing represented a major accomplishment. Zhelev, as leader of the UDF, demonstrated considerable skill in maintaining a united UDF through difficult negotiations and an intense campaign. The fact that the political parties in the coalition were not well developed as discrete organizations before joining the coalition also may have helped maintain unity in the weeks before the elections.

The success of the Movement for Rights and Freedom (MRF) was the source of considerable discussion. Although nominally open to all Bulgarians interested in promoting civil liberties and human rights, MRF was essentially the party of the Turkish minority, which constitutes approximately 10 percent of the population. The Movement presented candidates in constituencies with significant Turkish populations. It remained on generally uneasy terms with the UDF, having been rebuffed by UDF leaders when it sought to join forces early in the transition process. Indeed, all parties contesting the elections attempted to avoid identifying too closely with the Turkish minority for fear of a nationalist backlash from the majority of Bulgarian voters.

MRF was not included in the roundtable and did not receive much infrastructural support or access to the media. Despite the disenfranchisement of Turkish-Bulgarians abroad, the limits placed on some MRF campaign activities, and the looming threat that the MRF could be proscribed as an ethnic party, the Movement obtained the overwhelming support of the electorate in regions with large ethnic-Turkish populations. It thus became the only group that did not participate in the roundtable negotiations to enter the Grand National Assembly (GNA) with a significant bloc. After the elections, a small but vociferous nationalist group organized demonstrations to protest the seating of the MRF members in the Assembly, and GNA members from the BSP and the UDF publicly supported proscribing the MRF from participating in future elections.

BANU failed to win any single-member constituency seats and fared considerably more poorly in the proportional representation elections than party leaders expected. Since November 1989, BANU leaders had attempted to re-establish their *bona fides* as the successor to the Agrarian Party of the pre-communist period, which in the minds of many was identified with Bulgaria's early independence and as a genuine political alternative to the BSP. BANU had withdrawn from the BSP-dominated government and sought to portray itself as a true opposition party. However, the electorate apparently did not agree with BANU's portrayal of itself as a third force, and BANU obviously failed to translate its institutional and historical advantages into voter support.

# IX

On the day after the June 10 elections, students at Sofia University went on strike to protest alleged irregularities in the election process. The walkout later spread to universities in other cities. While these actions disrupted some traffic, they were for the most part confined to the universities. The strikes, however, increased moral pressure that in the weeks after the elections produced several significant consequences.

In addition to demanding an investigation of election irregularities, student activists sought the resignation of President Mladenov for his videotaped remarks suggesting a willingness to call in tanks to quell a peaceful demonstration in December, at a time when the transition was just underway. In response to the student demands, the government appointed a committee of experts to determine the authenticity of the videotape made at the time of the December demonstration. The experts concluded that the tape was genuine. Thus, on July 5, Mladenov, the man who had led the internal coup against Zhivkov, launching the process of political reform, and whose tenure as president for the duration of the Grand National Assembly was guaranteed by the roundtable agreement, was forced to resign.

With Mladenov's departure, the student strikes ended only to be replaced by the establishment of a "City of Truth" directly across from the BSP headquarters in downtown Sofia. The organizers of this effort sought to pressure BSP leaders to assume moral responsibility for the repression of the previous communist regime. One specific demand called for the removal of the body of Georgi Dimitrov, the leading figure in the Bulgarian Communist Party during the 1930s and 1940s and the first communist head of government in the 1940s, from a memorial mausoleum in the center of the city. To the surprise of many, the government acceded to the demand and, in the middle of the night, removed and cremated Dimitrov's remains.

With Cities of Truth in place around the country, the Grand National Assembly met for the first time on July 10 in the city of Veliko Turnovo, Bulgaria's historic capital. Returning to Sofia, the Assembly elected officers and began the task of electing a new president to replace Mladenov. The first four votes for a new president, conducted by secret ballot, failed to produce the requisite two-thirds majority. Both the BSP and UDF possessed sufficient votes to block candidates proposed by the other side.

Finally, following protracted negotiations among the major parties, Zhelu Zhelev, the UDF coalition leader, was elected president by a vote of 270 to 100. After taking the oath of office, Zhelev nominated Antas Samerzhiev, a BSP member who had been minister of interior until the previous week, as vice president, and Samerzhiev was overwhelmingly elected.

# X

The Bulgarian elections highlight the difficulty in evaluating the fairness of an election process in a country emerging from decades of repressive rule. The ruling party in Bulgaria had the advantages of incumbency, more developed organizational expertise and infra-structure, control of the electronic media, and easy access to, and great leverage over, the rural segments of the population. At the same time, the leading opposition groups were united, were able to campaign freely, had significant access to the media and could blame the ruling party for Bulgaria's many failures.

Absolute equality of opportunities for political parties and movements, or even relative balance, is seldom possible. The matter is complicated further when a ruling party, whose democratic credentials are viewed with suspicion by a large segment of the population, wins an election it administers. When the opposition prevails in these types of transition elections, as in Chile and Nicaragua, alleged irregularities committed by the ruling party become moot, because they obviously did not affect the overall outcome. In the case of Bulgaria, the flaws in the process cannot be dismissed, but they also do not automatically invalidate the entire process.

Still, the question lingers as to why Bulgaria was, at the time, the only country where a reforming Communist Party succeeded in scoring a victory in multiparty elections. A few impressions are offered.

Time was a critical factor. The elections occurred just seven months after the political opening in Bulgaria began. Unlike Czechoslovakia, in Bulgaria no opposition movement or even an organized dissident community existed before the November coup. Given this lack of a democratic political culture, the brevity of the campaign period was insufficient to eliminate the effects of a totalitarian society that developed during 45 years of communist rule.

The election system itself was a factor. The BSP benefitted from its insistence that at least half the Grand National Assembly be elected from single-member constituencies. This is not to say that such a system is flawed and should not be maintained. The allocation of seats as a result of these elections — with two large national parties, a minor national party and a strong regional party obtaining significant representation — suggests that the system worked reasonably well, and serious consideration should be given to retaining, perhaps with minor modifications, this type of system for future elections.

Fear was also a factor. Feelings of uncertainty, fear of losing jobs or pensions, and anxieties about suffering rent increases were often-heard concerns, especially among the elderly and those living in rural areas.

More perniciously, intimidation played a role. Threats, some overt and others psychological, were reported in many regions, although, in the absence of large-scale violence or corroborated reports of a concerted conspiracy, the confirmed incidents were insufficient to call into question the overall election results.

Finally, the role played by international observers in the Bulgarian election process is worth noting. The election law that emerged from the roundtable negotiations included provisions that allowed "guests" inside polling sites during the balloting and counting processes. Initially, the government sought to define the term "guest" as applying only to a group of officially invited legislators from a limited number of countries. However, pressure from opposition political parties, BAFE and the international community convinced the government that it was not in the country's best interests to impose restrictions on individuals visiting Bulgaria at the time of the elections. In the end, the government and the CEC cooperated fully with the many observer groups.

The observation efforts did not begin on election day. Several organizations such as NDI sponsored pre-election fact-finding teams to report on different aspects of the campaign period and preparations for the elections. In several instances, authorities adopted the recommendations of these groups. More important perhaps, the periodic presence of these pre-election missions reassured the Bulgarian public that the fairness of the elections was a matter of international concern.

# XI

Regardless of how the election process is ultimately evaluated, it is fair to say that Bulgarian political life underwent a radical transformation after the November 10, 1989, coup. Through a hectic but condensed political process, Bulgaria moved quickly from a repressive one-party state to a society where different political tendencies were openly expressed and could influence public policy.

Still, as demonstrated during the weeks following the elections, the strategies for institutionalizing a transition process are not always clear. Although the opposition obtained significant representation in the Grand National Assembly, it was street politics that instigated Mladenov's resignation and the removal of Dimitrov's body from the mausoleum. The environment created by the protestors also contributed to Zhelev's election.

Yet, reliance on street politics poses dangers. First, as occurred in August when a mob burned and ransacked BSP headquarters, the situation can simply run out of control, creating a real possibility of violent confrontation. Second, while street politics may reflect extreme discontent with current conditions, promoting a realistic vision of what is workable within a constitutional framework represents a far greater challenge.

A dilemma also arises for an opposition when it is offered the opportunity to join a coalition government. The BSP sought from the beginning of the transition process to entice the UDF, or at least parts of the UDF, into the government. The UDF feared cooptation and blame for the difficult choices that a new government would have to make in order to implement an effective economic recovery program. On the other hand, remaining on the outside during this critical, post-election period might result in a further deterioration of the economic situation, creating long-term burdens for Bulgaria even if the political consequences for the opposition prove beneficial.

In Bulgaria, the opposition finally relented in December 1990 when it agreed to the formation of a government comprising representatives of the major parties and independents. A political agreement setting forth the specific objectives of the government was signed by the principal parties, but the timetable for implementing the agreement could not be kept.

Another dilemma relates to the need for opposition unity during a transition period. The UDF's ability to maintain internal unity among disparate groups contributed significantly to its relative success in the elections and to its ability to determine the new president. However, at some point, the Bulgarian polity will have to determine whether to develop a variety of ideologically oriented parties, as is true in most of Europe, or to promote the emergence of relatively nonideological amalgams, with the United States as the model. The type of election system adopted in Bulgaria will contribute to a resolution of this matter, as will the future evolution of the BSP.

Finally, promoting minority rights poses another dilemma. The contemporary ideal, as it emerged in the Copenhagen document adopted by the CSCE countries in June 1990, imposes a positive obligation on governments to promote minority rights. Under this ideal, minorities should be granted the right to use their own languages to educate their children in separate schools and to express themselves politically through voluntary associations and even political parties.

A majority of Bulgarians from across the political spectrum are troubled by such a vision. They fear that it will create an irredentist movement among Turkish Bulgarians, perhaps encouraged by their large neighbor and former colonial ruler to the east. Thus, it is not surprising that Bulgaria's delegation to the Copenhagen meeting presented an interpretive statement to the effect that the applicability of the provisions pertaining to minorities is a matter that falls exclusively within the domestic jurisdiction of each state.

The political dilemmas facing Bulgaria must be confronted in the context of an economy buffeted by a series of shocks, including negative economic fallout from the collapse of the Soviet Union's economy, the Persian Gulf War and the debts assumed from the previous regime. A gloomy short-term forecast is a safe assumption, but the vibrancy of the democratic transition process suggests that a return to totalitarianism is unlikely.

*Chapter 10*

# Parties, Mediation and the Role of Civil Society

## Shlomo Avineri

The recent experiences of Eastern and Central Europe demonstrate that it is the presence of social and institutional infrastructures that makes possible a genuine transition to democracy. These infrastructures must be provided by what might be called "civil society," which includes social institutions such as the church and the arts, advocacy groups such as human rights organizations and, of course, political parties. Such an infrastructure is necessary for the emergence of "democracy" in its most fundamental sense, to translate a mere formality into a viable social and political process. By contrast, neither fair elections nor good intentions necessarily creates the conditions required to anchor democracy and to establish the processes of a free society in the consciousness and behavior of the citizenry.

The experiences of Western democracies have proven that the presence of such networks make the emergence of democratic forms of government possible. A simple transfer of Western constitutions to societies that lack these mechanisms, however, will not guarantee the success of democracy. Both the Latin American and African experiences suggest — despite the obvious differences between these two sets of examples — the limits of the formal adoption of purely legal measures. Moreover, the sincerity and commitment of a small, educated elite — which existed, for example, in most countries before decolonization — does not guarantee that they, by themselves, can make democracy work.

In post-communist societies, this reality is compounded by the heritage of totalitarianism. As a concept, totalitarianism suggests an attempt by a ruling party to not only arrogate total control of the political mechanisms of society, but also to ensure that no alternative ideology or institutional structure can challenge the party's monopoly of power in the fields of education, social ideas and belief systems. On paper at least, communist regimes have historically strived to maintain this monopoly of control over all areas of society.

A society emerging from decades of totalitarian control cannot succeed if its citizens are disorganized, alienated and lacking a network of societal structures that can mobilize and articulate a general political will into an effective instrument of governance. The democratization process in Eastern and Central Europe is illustrative. The existence of mediating structures within some of the societies contributed to the success of their transition processes. Conversely, the absence or weakness of such mediating structures made the transitions in other societies more problematic.

# I

While the mediating structures may differ in every country undergoing a transition, a close examination suggests their usefulness and centrality in understanding the process of democratization. Because Poland was the first country in the region to establish a non-communist government in the summer of 1989, developments there are instructive.

The emergence of Solidarity in the early 1980s became the crucial vehicle for transformation in Poland. Yet, Solidarity did not appear out of thin air. The impressive coalition between workers and intellectuals took advantage of specific Polish conditions, particularly a pre-existing civil infrastructure.

For historical reasons, and in contrast to the situation in other countries, the communist regime in Poland always allowed, especially after 1956, a relatively wide scope of activity to the Catholic Church. Despite constant persecution of the Church, a Catholic university in Lublin was allowed to train not only priests but a highly sophisticated lay intelligentsia. PAX, an organization originally intended by the communist government to be an alternative lay Catholic organization, became a breeding ground for another species of lay Catholic intelligentsia hostile to the regime.

The Polish episcopate shrewdly used these niches within the system to establish a trained priesthood sustained by a lay leadership whose intellectual horizons, paradoxically, were far wider than those of the Polish Catholic intelligentsia before World War II. Polish nationalists also identified with the Church, adding an anti-Russian legitimacy to these islands of relative autonomy within the Polish communist system.

The Church, with its autonomy and identification with Polish nationalism, proved the perfect institutional vehicle for the "spontaneous" appearance of Solidarity. The Church infrastructure provided a sanctuary for political gatherings, resolving the often mundane question faced by any opposition group in a totalitarian system of where to hold a meeting.

The communist government realized that cracking down on the Church would only alienate the citizenry even further. But the catastrophic murder of Father Popieluszko in October 1984 testified to the desperation of the Polish authorities.

The emergence of Solidarity was also a training ground for a further important condition for a successful transition to democracy: coalition-building. The post-transition rifts in Solidarity highlight the heterogenous nature of its original composition. Only the common goals of bringing down communism and reasserting Polish independence vis-à-vis Soviet (and not only communist) hegemony could keep such disparate groups together. But coalition-making is not a given, and in many other instances opposition groups have found themselves divided and atomized. Several years of effort were required to bring together the working-class element of Solidarity, with its sometimes not-too-sophisticated piety and anti-Russian sentiments, with the intellectuals, both lay Catholics and former communists who had been the nucleus of the Committee for the Defense of Workers (KOR).

Coalition-making required the burying of hidden — and not-so-hidden — differences and enmities and advancing by the slow process of discussion and consensus rather than by quick majoritarian decisions. The leadership qualities of certain individuals, undoubtedly, made this possible. Leaders recognized the need for patience and compromise and relied on a traditional Polish propensity to value consensus as symbolic of national unity.

The roundtable discussions of 1988-89, which dragged on in a desultory fashion for months, represented perhaps the most crucial stage in Poland's transition process. These discussions confronted the communist government and Solidarity with the stark reality that neither of the two major groups could proceed without the help and concurrence of the other. The jailers and their prisoners found that they were both captives in a unique political situation. The government, while still nominally in control of the instruments of power, was totally devoid of popular legitimacy and did not possess even a workable Communist Party anymore. Solidarity recognized the government's weakness, but also understood that the government could not be toppled without the government's consent.

These extraordinary circumstances produced an historic agreement concerning the June 1989 elections. Solidarity was allowed to contest a specified quota of seats in the Sejm (lower House), with a majority of the seats reserved for the Communist Party and its satellite parties. The agreement also permitted Solidarity to contest of all the seats in the newly created Senate.

Each partner's expectations about the election outcome are now irrelevant. What is relevant is the remarkable patience and readiness to compromise demonstrated by both sides; ultimately, this mutual cooperation made possible the development of a formula for power-sharing. Little in the backgrounds of either the communist government or Solidarity, however, indicated that they would be ready for such a far-reaching compromise. Undoubtedly, though, the years of coalition-building within Solidarity, the emergence of an entire network of civil society that publicly debated political issues, and the pressures under which both the government and Solidarity labored resulted in an outcome that hastened the formation of the first non-communist government in a Warsaw Pact country.

A further element should be added here: the roundtable talks provided the Communist Party and its satellites a guaranteed majority in the Sejm. Until this time, the satellite parties — mainly the Peasant Party — were considered nothing more than communist front organizations. Yet, the astounding outcome of the elections created a dynamic of its own. The satellite parties, which had been subservient to the Communist Party for decades, realized that the future of the country would be in their hands. Emboldened, they decided not to follow the communists blindly, but instead opted to forge an independent policy, ultimately allying with Solidarity. This development made possible power-sharing between a communist president and a Solidarity prime minister.

While focusing here on political coalition-building, it should be recalled that this process was accompanied by the slow emergence of an unusual kind of parallel society that characterized Poland during the 1980s. Beginning with the crackdown on Solidarity and the introduction of martial law, society in Poland developed a degree of autonomy and freedom unknown in most other Soviet-bloc countries. Large sectors of the intelligentsia — artists, writers, poets, film-makers, scholars — operated in a civil society that paid little attention to official pronouncements. This environment legitimized an institutional network for an alternative body politic. These developments received much attention in the unofficial media, forcing the government media to be more open and accessible. Thus, the monopoly of information was assaulted at the same time as the monopoly of power was disintegrating.

The Polish example also suggests that in processes of post-totalitarian democratization, the historical parties may be ill-equipped for successful re-entry into the political arena. This unreadiness may be due to their elitist nature, their having been tainted in some cases with semi-fascist ideologies, and the success of the communist regimes in delegitimizing them in the eyes of the population — a delegitimization that survives even the demise of communism. But most importantly, the failure of these historical parties results from the fact that in most cases they have not been part of the process of creating the alternative, civil society.

# II

In a different mode, and with varying intensity, the elements apparent in the Polish transition can be seen operating in the other countries of the region as well. In Hungary, while no organization emerged that directly parallelled Solidarity (nor did the Church serve this role), the formation of the Democratic Forum in 1987 created the necessary infrastructure for the initiation of a public discourse not monopolized by the Communist Party. The economic liberalization, which was undertaken by the communist government, created islands of relative autonomy, further eroding the Communist Party's totalitarian grip on the country.

While Solidarity kept under its wings some very disparate elements (at least so long as it was in opposition), in Hungary a split developed within the Forum soon after its formation. The Democratic Forum and the Free Democrats emerged not only as two distinct parties, but as representatives of two Hungarian political traditions: nationalist and liberal. They thus introduced an element of pluralism into the political debate, and simple anti-communism ceased to be an umbrella under which all disparate elements of society could unify. Consequently, Hungarian civil society appeared, on the eve of the March 1990 elections, far less nationalistic and unitary than did Polish society a year earlier.

The debate about the election of the president and the ensuing referendum, as well as the roundtable discussions about the modalities of the election law, also created a context in which communists and their protagonists and former victims had to coalesce in order to reach consensus decisions. The complexity — and fairness — of the Hungarian election law, balancing proportionality and regional representation, is such a finely tuned compromise that it suggests by itself a profound commitment to pluralism.

The 1989 by-elections focused public attention on the procedures of electoral politics. They received wide media coverage, thus assuring their educational effect on the Hungarian public and sensitizing society to the fact that elections require a culture of debate and civility. The public debate within the ruling Hungarian Socialist Workers Party, which led to its split before the general elections, was another element in bringing the political discourse closer to the surface of social concerns.

The elections in Hungary thus were the culmination of a series of developments that gradually opened up society by stages, with each interval accompanied by the emergence of new social and political structures. These developments created a society that paralleled the official, communist society.

# III

Developments in Czechoslovakia were much more dramatic and less deliberative, although ingredients similar to those described above existed there. Notwithstanding the extremely repressive nature of the post-1968 Czechoslovakian regime, the emergence of Charter 77 created a rallying point and an organizational network of far-reaching efficiency that welded together various individuals and groups. Anti-communists, veterans of the 1968 reform communism movement, former communist intellectuals, individuals with links to the Church − a medley of people with apparently contradictory persuasions − found in Charter 77 a vehicle for expressing a common agenda. Because of the range of opinions involved, and the underlying threats facing all participants, an effective organization required consensus-building and mutual compromise.

When the surprising events of November 1989 unfolded, the nucleus of Charter 77 offered a solid foundation for the emergence of Civic Forum, which by its very name gave testimony to the importance of the pre-existing civil society. The coalition-building and negotiating skills, so masterfully wielded by Vaclav Havel and his colleagues in days and nights of negotiations with the beaten and frightened communist leadership, stemmed from years of activism within Charter 77 − activism that stressed the virtues of patience, mediation, consensus and compromise.

During the course of the transition process, Civic Forum relied on the party headquarters and organizing talents of the small Socialist Party for holding and arranging the crucial meetings on Wenceslas Square, highlighting again the role of the erstwhile satellite parties in the transformation of the system. The Socialist Party disappeared in the elections of June 1990, but its very existence and its decision to jump from the sinking ship of the communist regime were of incalculable help to the democratic forces.

There were like-developments in the case of East Germany, and only two will be briefly mentioned here. In most instances, the Lutheran Church filled the mediating role of the parallel civil society. The Church provided places for meetings immune from direct police action, especially in Leipzig and Dresden, and served as an effective network for the dissemination of information and the provision of legitimacy. The satellite parties, long subservient to Communist Party leadership, also exhibited their independence, which caused some of the difficulties involved in the transformation of society. That the outcome of the democratization process in the GDR led inexorably to German unification − contrary to what the original reformers intended − illustrates another element in the nature of the recent transitions: the strength of historical structures and belief systems, be they national or religious, cannot be ignored.

# IV

The lack of mediating structures and the virtual absence of a parallel society helps explain the problematic nature of the transition in Romania and to a lesser degree in Bulgaria. The Ceausescu regime was unique in Eastern Europe in that its power did not rest on Soviet military and political presence, but paradoxically derived its legitimacy in part from its decision to stand up to the Soviet Union in the name of historical Romanian nationalism (with its strong anti-Russian undercurrents). Because of the regime's extreme, repressive nature, no organized opposition existed, nor could any parallel civil society greet the fall of the dictatorship when it did occur. The Orthodox Church in Romania, for example, remained subservient to the powers-that-be and thus could not assume the role played by the Catholic Church in Poland and by the Lutheran churches in East Germany. While individual intellectuals and artists were persecuted under Ceausescu, no critical mass emerged parallel to that which gave rise to Charter 77 in Czechoslovakia or the lay Catholic and former communist intellectuals in Poland.

When the coup occurred in Romania, a vacuum resulted. There was obvious mass support for a new order, but no institutional structures existed to take over from either the discredited party or the Securitate. The National Salvation Front thus filled the void, but it could never speak for an alternative, parallel civil society. It basically remained a *junta*, with most of its leaders tarred — whether justly or unjustly is for the purpose of this analysis immaterial — with the communist brush.

The lack of parallel structures also expressed itself in the elections, where the only alternative parties to the Front were the historical parties — mainly the Liberals and the Peasant Party. Their aging leaders returned from exile burdened by associations with a pre-communist regime that was anything but democratic. The failure of the historical parties in the elections was testimony to the need for alternative mediating structures to mobilize support, which these historical parties, with their Rip van Winkle characteristics, lacked. The viability of the Hungarian Democratic Union in Transylvania, which emerged as the second largest party in parliament, underscored the fact that the cultural structures of the Hungarian minority, with their foundation in the various ethnically based Protestant churches, represented the only effective vehicle for mobilization.

The Bulgarian situation, while less extreme, showed similar traits of a weak civil society, again including the characteristic subservience of the Orthodox Church to state power. Similarly, the Turkish minority's ethnic structures helped a predominantly Turkish movement obtain a significant number of seats in the Grand National Assembly, although their overall influence was more limited than that of the Hungarians in Romania because there a strong opposition party emerged from the elections.

# V

The mediating role of civil society structures is connected with the historical experience of every society. Powerful democratic traditions, as in Czechoslovakia, or even incomplete ones, as in Poland and Hungary, greatly facilitated the rise of civil societies. An historical lack of democratic institutions and traditions, as in Romania and Bulgaria, greatly inhibited the growth of such meditating institutions during the communist era.

Lastly, some consequences may be drawn from this about processes of democratization in the former Soviet Union. Disregarding the former Soviet Union itself (which was never a nation-state, as the Eastern and Central European countries more or less were), and concentrating on Russia, the prognosis may not be very encouraging. There is no doubt that the prolonged process of reform initiated by Gorbachev has created islands of autonomy in Russian society. But whether they are strong enough to overcome the historical dead weight of Russian (and Soviet) traditions remains to be seen, and a degree of skepticism may be advisable. The scope of civil society in Russia appears limited, and some of this space is inhabited by resurrected nationalistic and xenophobic organizations.

All this may remind one, paradoxically, of Karl Marx's comments about the differentiated course of revolutionary developments. When asked whether he envisaged the proletarian revolution to be violent or gradual, Marx responded in an 1872 speech in Amsterdam, that there may be differences between countries. He distinguished between countries with parliamentary and partially democratic traditions and those without such traditions, adding:

> We know that one has to take into consideration the institutions, mores, and traditions of the different countries ...and we do not assert that the attainment of our end requires identical means.

Marx might have been wrong about communist revolutions, but, ironically, he appears to have been right about the dismantling of communist dictatorships.

## Chapter 11

# Models of Transition

## Antonio Vitorino

During the 1970s, democratic transitions occurred in the southern European countries of Portugal, Spain and Greece. These transitions ended authoritarian right-wing regimes that, in the cases of the Iberian peninsula, had lasted for almost 50 years. After the re-establishment of democracy, these countries became full members of the European community.

In the 1980s, authoritarian regimes were progressively dismantled in Latin America and replaced by new democratic systems, most of them characterized by remarkable instability and enormous economic problems.

Now, during the 1990s, transitions to democracy are occurring in "old" Europe, in the Central and Eastern European countries.

Comparative analyses of these three successive waves of democratic transition highlight the difficulty of adopting rigid models of classification. This is due to the particular characteristics of each country and also to the changes that have occurred in the international political and economic environment.

# I

Economic characteristics provide one point of comparison among the countries experiencing transitions, the implications of which can only be analyzed now in the medium term. In southern Europe and some Latin American countries, there were always free-market economies; thus the transitions were exclusively political. At the beginning of the transitions in Eastern and Central Europe — with the exception, in specific and restricted areas, of Hungary — the countries did not have free-market economies. The former communist regimes relied on centrally planned economies and were extremely dependent upon the USSR. These countries now face the challenge of implementing simultaneously a political and an economic transformation. This considerable hurdle makes the affiliation of former communist countries to the European Economic Community a much more problematic issue.

A second comparison contrasts transitions from an authoritarian regime as a result of violence with transitions by means of negotiated agreement. The Portuguese case was one of rupture through a revolutionary movement, a bloodless *coup d'état* led by a faction of the army. The Spanish case was an example of a negotiated transition (*la rotura pactada*) led by the reformist faction of Franco's regime under the stabilizing leadership of King Juan Carlos.

Romania was a typical example of violent rupture. Curiously, it also represents the only Eastern and Central European case where the genuineness of the transition is open to question. The other cases involved negotiated transitions to democracy, from the pioneering events in Poland and Hungary to the exceptional case of transition in Czechoslovakia.

Again, comparative analysis must be employed carefully. For example, the similarity of a violent rupture in the cases of Portugal and Romania is merely formal. The Spanish transition, meanwhile, was dominated by the role of the king, who controlled the right-wing sectors of the army. This situation had no parallel in Eastern and Central Europe.

A third point of comparison is the outcome of the transition from the perspective of those who initiated it: were they able to control the transition's evolution? It is clear that in Eastern and Central Europe different causes and different elements accelerated the transitions. In Poland and Hungary, for example, the Communist parties, to some extent, started down the path to democracy as they tried to shape the transitions according to their own interests. Hoping to secure the survival of their power, the communists in these countries attempted to keep the evolution of events within "acceptable" limits.

In both Poland and Hungary, ruptures in the Communist parties substantially weakened them. The Hungarian Socialist Workers Party divided into two factions, both of which were badly defeated in the March 1990 elections. The Polish United Workers' Party (PUWP) suffered two splits at its 1990 Congress. Although the PUWP remained in parliament (under a social-democratic label), it lost almost all influence during the transition period. In these cases, where reformist factions of the Communist parties controlled and promoted the transitions from the outset, the outcome for the parties was fatal.

By contrast, in the German Democratic Republic (GDR) and in Czechoslovakia, the Communist parties initiated democratic reforms only at a very late stage and under significant pressure from mass demonstrations. In both the GDR and in Czechoslovakia, the transition began from below, with help from international pressures. The Communist parties quickly lost control and subsequently lost the elections, thus forfeiting completely any further influence or power.

Lastly, in Bulgaria and Romania, popular demonstrations emboldened the reformist factions within the communist establishments to remove from power Todor Zhivkov and Nicolae Ceausescu, respectively. In Bulgaria, the "conversion" of the Communist Party into a so-called "socialist party," though arousing serious internal divisions, represents the only case where the reformists who initiated the transition retained control of the government after free elections (although a leading figure in the party, Petar Mladenov, was forced to resign from the presidency soon after the elections and was replaced by the leader of the opposition). In Romania, the Communist Party was replaced by the National Salvation Front. The communist structure survived under of the National Salvation Front's umbrella, and many democratic goals have yet to be met.

## II

Three main political currents influenced the transition to democracy in Central and Eastern European countries.

First, the new foreign policy of the Soviet Union, adopted by Mikhail Gorbachev after 1988, rejected the Brezhnev Doctrine of the limited sovereignty of socialist states and postulated that the people should be free to choose their own political and social systems.

Second, after 1988 it became clear that the Soviet Union, due in part to increasing internal problems of its own, would not undertake any new military interference in its satellite countries. The Soviet Union's unwillingness to support the old satellite regimes significantly undermined the capability of national Communist parties to respond to popular demands with repression, as they could have in the past. This new arrangement generated growing pressures, which fueled the dynamics of the democratic transitions and accelerated the internal divisions of the Communist parties, which split among reformist, hard-line and opportunist factions.

Third, opposition organizations and cultural movements arose in response to the communist system's perceived vulnerability. Eventually, new democratic forces emerged, in many cases as outgrowths of previously existing cultural and dissident organizations that had fought for the protection of human rights and respect for the Helsinki Accords. Soon, the communist authorities urged these poorly organized groups to share political responsibilities. Consequently, these groups were able to exert a substantial influence during the 1989 transitions and to obtain significant popular support in the first free elections, held in the spring of 1990.

## III

In each of the Eastern and Central European transitions, even in the most controversial one, Romania, at least some faction of the Communist Party perceived the need to find its own solutions, without relying on the protective shield of the Soviet Union. Thus,

Communist parties promoted roundtable discussions, envisioning them as forums to negotiate the evolution of new systems. The roundtables gathered the declining leadership of the Communist parties, who were frequently controversial even within their own parties, and individuals representing opposition organizations. With the exception of Solidarity, the latter group held no specific institutional legitimacy.

The roundtable idea originated in Poland in January 1989 during negotiations promoted by the Rakowski government. In addition to the Polish communists, this first roundtable included representatives of Solidarity, which was still illegal at the time, and several prominent individuals affiliated with the Polish Catholic Church. The negotiations were, above all, a direct consequence of the total failure of the government's economic reform program, which was initiated in 1987-88.

The roundtable legalized Solidarity as an opposition force and initiated political reforms at a time when it was already clear that the Soviet Union would no longer protect the Polish communist establishment. The roundtable negotiations also resulted in an agreement to elect, by direct and free vote, an upper legislative chamber (Senate) and 35 percent of the members of the lower chamber (Sejm). In the elections that followed, Solidarity candidates won 99 out of the 100 seats in the Senate and all of the seats contested in the Sejm. Thanks to this overwhelming victory, Tadeusz Mazowiecki became the first non-communist prime minister of an Eastern European country.

A faction of the Hungarian Socialist Workers Party (MSZMP), which had gained power during the reformist period of the Janos Kadar regime, initiated the Hungarian transition. Imre Poszgay, Mathias Szuros and Miklos Nemeth were the leaders of this faction. The dynamics of transition led the MSZMP to change its name to the Socialist Party of Hungary, which assumed the role of liquidator of the communist system under the pressure of the democratic forces represented at the roundtable.

The transition to democracy in Czechoslovakia was the most remarkable example of a peaceful disintegration of the communist apparatus. Spontaneous popular pressure, combined with ethical and political guidance provided by cultural and dissident organizations, sped the denouement of communist rule. This accelerated process, which caught everyone by surprise, culminated in the election of playwright Vaclav Havel as president.

In Romania, after the events of December 1989 drove Ceausescu from power, democratic forces pressured the National Salvation Front to negotiate the modalities of the transition period with opposition organizations. Nonetheless, the Front raised questions about its ultimate intentions when it reversed a pledge not to compete in elections.

In Bulgaria, the initial transition events took place within the Communist Party: a reformist wing replaced longtime party leader Todor Zhivkov in a palace coup. After some hesitation, the "reconstructed" Communist Party began negotiations on the pace of transition in a roundtable setting, with 17 opposition organizations that formed the Union of Democratic Forces. Unlike their counterparts elsewhere, the communist leadership in Bulgaria, whose reformist positions resembled those of Gorbachev, kept control of the transition. While the June 1990 Bulgarian elections seemed to reward the reforming communists, the economic crisis, popular discontent and government instability made clear that the situation in Bulgaria was far from settled.

The transition in the German Democratic Republic was unique. There, the reformist elements inside the Unified Socialist Party (SED) emerged at a very late stage; the replacement of Erich Honeker by Egon Krenz was a mere provisional solution. The escape of GDR citizens to the Federal Republic of Germany through Hungary and Czechoslovakia, combined with popular demonstrations in September and October 1989, forced the SED to negotiate with democratic forces in a roundtable setting. Negotiators very soon confronted the major issue of German unification. Originally, the communists and some opposition forces, such as the New Forum, wanted to negotiate the democratization of the GDR, but they clearly opposed unification. The attraction of unification, however, overwhelmed them. Soon, the political parties of the Federal Republic, especially Chancellor Helmut Kohl's Christian Democrats, were at the center of the GDR's political debate, promoting their East German counterparts. After January 1990, transition to democracy in the GDR became only a vehicle to accelerate the real goal: the integration of the GDR into a newly unified Germany.

# IV

The participation of democratic forces in the roundtables was mainly a consequence of the transition process itself. In many cases, the communist leadership, eager to use negotiations to maintain power, invited opposition forces to the roundtable. As they saw their position threatened, the communists increasingly sought assurances that they would not be outlawed after the transition and that there would be no persecution of their members.

Both sides came to the roundtables in pursuit of their own ends. The communists accepted the roundtables as a safety valve to alleviate growing popular pressure for democratic reforms. Opposition forces, which had limited government experience and which lacked effective organizations, used the roundtables to dismantle the communist power structure and to promote free elections.

As time went on, the roundtables became the real center of power, where the political agenda of the transition process was settled. Significantly, the roundtables agreed on constitutional changes that were adopted by the relevant legislative bodies, even though the legislatures were still controlled by the communists. Most important among the constitutional changes was the removal of the clauses enshrining the leading role of the Communist Party in society. Constitutional amendments were also necessary to provide a juridical legitimacy to the opposition forces represented at the roundtables and to create conditions for multiparty elections.

The roundtable negotiators accepted the legitimacy of constitutions that had been imposed by the Communist parties after 1945. The negotiators made clear that their priority was to promote free and fair elections. The newly elected legislatures would develop new, democratic constitutions.

Some constitutional changes immediately affected the structure of power. In some cases, to facilitate approval of the agreed upon constitutional amendments and legislation, the roundtables empowered the opposition forces to replace members of the existing legislatures. In other cases, the roundtables formed new governments that included opposition representatives.

In addition to proposing constitutional amendments, the roundtables also proposed legislation necessary to implement the transition processes. This legislation covered the formation of political parties, freedom of the press and the abolition of censorship, the repeal of laws that repressed democratic activities, and the creation of an adequate legal environment for free elections. The roundtables also sought to dismember, or at least the neutralize, the repressive apparatus of the communist state, including the secret police and the security establishment the popular militias, and the party structures in the work place.

Much of the work of the roundtables involved the preparation of new electoral laws. The elections were designed to legitimize the transition process, controlled by a communist leadership without democratic legitimacy and opposition forces whose leaders had not been elected themselves. The participants debated the critical choice of electoral systems, which have shaped these emerging democracies.

In many places, there were also local roundtables, which helped to promote democratization at the local level, to implement the decisions adopted at the national roundtables and to exert the greatest possible control over local communist administrations. Moreover, local roundtables provided confidence to the population and offered opposition forces an opportunity to gather local support and to organize as political parties.

# V

The roundtable processes proved successful in providing forums for resolving difficult issues before the elections in each of the Eastern and Central European countries. With the exception of Romania, they also established a level of confidence that permitted the occurrence of credible elections   Freely elected legislatures then assumed roles previously played by the roundtable negotiators. As debate over legislation has become more strident, some legislators have expressed nostalgia for the seemingly uncomplicated roundtable format. But now, if the transitions are to be sustained, these newly elected legislators must cope with the more complicated realities of a democratic polity.

*Chapter 12*

# Reflections on Recent Elections in Latin America and Eastern and Central Europe

## Genaro Arriagada

Comparisons between Latin American and Eastern European countries must be guided by prudence, because rather different political, social, cultural and geopolitical contexts are involved. With this caveat, however, such comparisons are relevant, and this essay considers several assertions about the recent experiences of free elections in Latin America and Europe.

## I

How did the idea of free elections become a reality? My thesis is that people in countries such as Chile, Poland, Nicaragua and

Hungary perceived free elections as a way to overcome a "stalemate" or, more precisely, a "catastrophic balance." This term describes the condition of a given society where two antagonistic forces achieve a similar amount of power, neither of them being able to impose their will on the other or willing to negotiate and compromise. Such equilibrium is catastrophic for the society in question, for it ends by destroying the political system and the social fabric.

In a 1987 book, I described the Chilean reality two years before the historic 1988 presidential plebiscite as a situation of catastrophic balance.[1] Remarkably enough, that very year Joseph Rothschild described the overall situation in Europe as a precarious stalemate.[2] Rothschild depicted the state of affairs in Poland in the following terms:

> Poland, in short, was in the grip of a civil-political stalemate. On the one hand, the regime could not obtain legitimation from a defeated, resentful, yet contemptuous and still defiantly "self-organizing" society that stubbornly insisted (in Adam Michnik's resonant phrase) "on living as if we were free." On the other hand, this society could neither obtain access to the forums of political decision-making nor convert its potency into power.[3]

Poland, Nicaragua, Hungary and Chile — to mention just four very different countries — were not totalitarian regimes at the start of their free-election experiences. They were rigid, at times brutal, dictatorial systems. Within them, there existed an essential contradiction, reflected in the clash between the state-supported authoritarian regimes and the democratic opposition movements supported by their civil societies.[4]

---

[1] G. Arriagada, *Pinochet, the Politics of Power* (Allen and Unwin, Boston, 1987).

[2] S. Rothschild, *Return to Diversity*, (Oxford University Press, New York, 1989), p. 119.

[3] Id. at p. 203.

[4] Similarly, in Panama Noriega's dictatorial regime struggled against an opposition movement. Unfortunately, many of those who attempted to make a contribution to democratic development in Panama — in my case, such an

The power of Pinochet, Jaruzelski and also, to a lesser extent, the Sandinista commanders was overwhelmingly military and almost exclusively state-based. At its core was the concentration of very strong executive and absolute military powers in the hands of one person, or a small group of people. To counter such powerful, highly militarized states, opposition movements relied on social, political and international influences.

In this regard, the cases of Poland and Chile were remarkable, because in both countries the opposition movements were uniquely successful almost from the beginning. The term "opposition" is used here in its broadest sense, involving not only the political parties, but also other components: moral forces, such as the Catholic Church and the vast movement of human rights activists; the world of intellectuals and artists; and the labor, professional and student movements. These opposition movements rescued the basic social and political fabric of their countries. They rescued and took control of the civil societies, *i.e.*, the thousands of non-state entities through which men and women organize to achieve ethical and ideological goals, defend and represent economic or social interests, and launch political projects. Finally, a fundamental power weapon for the opposition movement was derived from the solidarity of international public opinion and the support received from governments in Western Europe, Latin America and North America.

Obviously, there were important differences among the countries. Internationally, Pinochet was the weakest target, isolated from virtually the entire international community. In contrast, Jaruzelski initially enjoyed the support of the Warsaw Pact countries and the USSR; cracks in the communist bloc thus played a critical role in weakening his position. The Sandinistas, representing a third situation, were supported for a long time by important European social democratic parties, but once the USSR's support wavered the Sandinistas became as isolated as Pinochet.

In some respects then, governments and opposition movements enjoyed similar amounts of political power, even though the sources

---

endeavor resulted in my arrest and expulsion from the country — were profoundly frustrated by the United States invasion, which many in Latin America considered an unacceptable outrage against fundamental principles of international law.

of that power differed enormously. Governments were extremely strong at the state level, the military providing the main source of their power. Opposition movements, meanwhile, were empowered by civil society.

Such realities were the framework of the catastrophic balance: on the one hand, the dictatorial regimes were strong enough to remain in power; on the other hand, their strength did not suffice to crush the opposition movements. The opposition movements, in turn, were powerful enough to maintain, against all pressures, their overwhelming influence in the student, worker, professional and party organizations, but not to overthrow the dictatorial systems.

This balance gradually turned into a genuine catastrophe for the countries involved. Political wars of attrition ensued, where conflicts escalated and became more profound, and no solutions seemed conceivable. In this context, both governments and opposition movements began considering free elections as the sole way out of a situation that was becoming increasingly unbearable.

# II

From the point of view of Pinochet, Jaruzelski, the Sandinista commanders and the other communist regimes that launched electoral processes during 1989 and 1990, the possibility of losing elections suggested serious, but not fatal, consequences. Previous experiences demonstrated that, even after an electoral defeat, the regimes, and the forces supporting them, would retain a significant amount of power. At the very least, and distinct from a scenario of a violent end to a dictatorial system, the price of political defeat would not be death, torture or exile.

As far as the opposition movements were concerned, free elections represented risks and opportunities. The most perilous risk was that such elections would be neither free nor fair, but would instead provide a new set of mechanisms and institutions that would entrench dictatorial regimes. The opportunities — besides, obviously, that of winning the elections — derived from the fact that even in case of fraud or effective electoral defeat, the mere existence of the campaign would open new and wider freedoms, and strengthen opposition political parties and the institutions of civil society. These conditions, in turn, would create circumstances more favorable than those existing before the start of the election process. Indeed, this was the message conveyed by international observers to the young leaders of the Bulgarian Association for Free Elections (BAFE) the night that the Bulgarian opposition was defeated in the 1990 parliamentarian elections.

As a model of political confrontation, free elections designed to defeat a dictatorial system are very different from normal democratic elections. In firmly established democracies, elections are contests between ideas and programs. Elections to end dictatorships, however, are struggles for dignity and against fear.

For an opposition movement confronting elections under a dictatorial regime — be it communist, or a left- or right-wing military regime — it is not a question of challenging a government or head of state who enjoys a certain level of public support. Jaruzelski, Pinochet and Noriega were not popular among the populace. On the contrary, the overwhelming majority of citizens believed that their regimes were inefficient, dictatorial and abusive. Moreover, the criticism presented by opposition forces was deeply rooted in people's minds. Still, the problem was how to achieve a victory.

Wherever the opposition tried to use free elections to defeat a ruling dictatorial system, the starting point was an acute sense of futility and failure. Hope seemed to be at an end. In a number of instances, people had mistakenly believed so many times before that the regimes had been weakened and could be defeated that they seemed unable to believe again. In other cases, past failures had been so harsh and the dictators' reactions so brutal — like in Hungary in 1956, Czechoslovakia in 1968, or during "protests" in Chile — that people had been taught to accept that attempts to change the political system were counterproductive. No approach had succeeded in the past. Nobody could be trusted in the present, certainly not those deluded individuals contending that brutal dictatorships could be overthrown by elections.

This skepticism merged with an acute feeling of impotence. The series of defeats not only had taught people to despair but — maybe worse — had strengthened the notion that the regimes were invincible. Nothing could change the situation. All sacrifices were useless. Governments were omnipresent and almighty. Dictatorships might be — and certainly were — bad, but at least they were also efficient, just as the opposition was inefficient.

Fear was the predominant feeling among the majority of those who had lived under authoritarian regimes without ever belonging to parties, trade unions or human rights organizations. As such, fear was the most serious obstacle to be overcome if the regime was to be defeated. Fear stemmed from a wide variety of sources, and affected people of all groups and political leanings. For some, fear was a consequence of the political repression; for others, there existed a fear of the unknown; and still others feared the social and economic instability that might result from challenging the regime.

On the other hand, the main feature of all societies subjected to dictatorial regimes is a feeling of humiliation, particularly prevalent among adults. These citizens have witnessed or have become the victims of economic discrimination, police brutality, abuse by the oligarchies (be they formed by the military, the upper classes, or the *nomenklatura*), lost rights and the dismantling of civil organizations. They feel deprived, and they lack commitment to their work. Those living in a long-standing dictatorial regime also suffer from a lack of respect and, more frequently, experience abuse, suspicion and harassment. They fear submitting claims to anyone and remain silent in the presence of crime and abuse. Obviously, such humiliations erode people's self-esteem, which, in turn, undermines their potential to respond.

Hence, wherever I had the opportunity to talk with leaders of opposition forces seeking to defeat their authoritarian regimes through electoral processes − in Paraguay, Bulgaria or Nicaragua − I remarked that they did not need to win people's minds; they had to recover people's dignity and self-esteem, which, politically speaking, was tantamount to regaining their willingness to fight.

# III

If the larger public had to be encouraged to retrieve its dignity, opposition leaders had to be convinced of the need for moderation. Long dictatorial periods produce divisions and stifle communication between opposition leaders and their supporters. During the years of harsh repression, belonging to the opposition was not only a political option but also, for some, a higher moral calling. It was an option for courage and generosity. In extreme cases, one's life, freedom and right to live in one's country were at risk; but even when such risks were not so serious, members of the opposition defied the absolute might of regimes.

The price of criticism or challenge often involved being isolated from the job market; being excluded from the civil service, the universities and the mass media; and, usually, being condemned to serious economic mediocrity. Never were politics more generous and noble than among opponents to Poland's or Czechoslovakia's communist regimes, or to Pinochet's right-wing dictatorship. Their distinctive trait was decency, and the main reward they sought was unity among men and women who, even while supporting different philosophies and political projects, joined forces to expose crime and torture and demand justice and more freedom.

Such was the experiences of many in Chile. This was also noticed by Timothy Garton Ash in Eastern Europe:

> travelling through this region over the last decade, I found treasures: examples of great moral courage and intellectual integrity; comradeship, deep friendship, family life...more broadly, qualities of relations between men and women of very different backgrounds, and once bitterly opposed faiths — an ethos of solidarity.[5]

This was the noble side of the opposition to dictatorial systems.

However, the borderline between this kind of pride and a smugness is as tenuous and dangerous as a razor's edge. Those opposed to strong authoritarian regimes risked isolating themselves from the needs and aspirations of the broad masses. In the framework of repression, these opposition leaders often become isolated in closed circles, where tactics and strategies are unceasingly discussed and passionate speeches are delivered about the need to confront the dictators through forms of protest entailing growing levels of risk. The greater the repression, the more courage was required of the opposition. However, there also was a greater tendency to make political meetings bear a heavy burden of moral indignation, ending in an endless series of tales of horror and abuse by the regime.

---

[5] T. Garton Ash, *The Magic Lantern* (Random House, New York, 1990), p. 154.

The overwhelming majority of people admire and respect the bravery of those who challenge dictatorships; very seldom, however, are they able to emulate these courageous individuals. The people merely request from their leaders sensible, balanced solutions. They do not want their husbands, wives or children participating in a world of violent clashes and endless sacrifices.

Still, the opposition's isolation was, above all, the result of the authoritarian regime's deliberate policies. In fact, what is a dictatorial regime but an attempt to isolate the masses and, sever their communication channels with those who effectively invoke freedom, justice and respect for human rights? Each dictatorial regime, particularly when possessing clear-cut goals and efficient methods, is an attempt to teach people conformity, to feed them with banal concerns and to try to make them impervious to injustice and their neighbor's sufferings.

# IV

From the moment an opposition movement decides to challenge a dictatorial regime in elections or in a plebiscite, the gap between leaders and the masses has to narrow. Leaders must be ready to moderate their tactics while simultaneously encouraging people to become more committed. Where this gap is not closed, opposition movements will be defeated.

This is what happened to the Polish opposition movement in 1981, when a radicalization process resulted in the severing of communications between the leaders and their base. Likewise, the Chilean opposition fizzled in 1984-85, when protests ran out of control and led to increasingly radical patterns of resistance. In contrast, the Polish and the Chilean opposition movements succeeded — in 1989 and 1988, respectively — when leaders and people found not only a common goal but a mutual means to accomplish it.

A brief reference to the Chilean scenario might help further illustrate this point. From the beginning, public opinion polls showed that the overwhelming majority of Chileans were concerned with order, safety and better living conditions. To succeed, opposition leaders had to respond to these demands. The human rights issue, by contrast, attracted a surprisingly low level of interest. Thus, a platform of moral indignation was not sufficient. The human rights issue could not be disregarded, however, since it formed an essential part of the opposition's denunciation of the dictatorial system.

Throughout the campaign, a sensible handling of the human rights issue — not emphasizing horror tales or trying to provoke hatred or resentment among the public — succeeded in increasing the profile of this issue for the great majority of voters. The Chilean opposition uttered condemnations, but it also sought to promote reconciliation rather than fear. Eventually, the general population began to accept the truth of the charges of tortures and disappearances, and to firmly condemn such acts. By the end of the campaign, the human rights issue, initially a matter of secondary importance, had become a primary concern for most Chileans.

# V

In the Central and Eastern European struggles, intellectuals repeatedly played a fundamental role. In Latin America, the Chilean opposition to Pinochet provides a remarkable parallel. Visitors to Chile during 1988 were surprised by the important role being played by an outstanding group of intellectuals within the "No Campaign" and within its constituent parties.

The relationship between the intellectuals and politics did not merely involve political and social scientists providing useful ideas. Rather, the contribution of intellectuals to politics was more direct. In Chile, for example, intellectuals actively participated in the campaign against Pinochet. They belonged, almost without exception, to the same generation, and despite heterogeneous political affiliations, shared similar experiences in the country's recent past.

This generation was the last to experience democracy. It comprised young people whose careers blossomed during the administrations of Presidents Eduardo Frei (1964-70) and Salvador Allende (1970-73). The leaders of this generation considered themselves chosen to transform ideas into reality, thus establishing a new political, economic and social order. The 1973 military coup smashed these hopes.

In 1984, Eugenio Tironi described, from a leftist perspective, the moral climate within which this generation developed:

History itself was for us a continuous advance..., free from violent or irreversible backslides whatsoever. We felt the world was in our hands....[By the end of the '60s], our generation came to the foreground. We did not request permission: we were the country's masters...We were the engine of a historic, progressive, ascendent, multifaceted, total movement....During Salvador Allende's admin- istration, this experience or culture of our generation reached its climax...[and] in September 1973, suddenly, overnight, this all was put to an end, and the historic trend supporting the universe of our generation was liquidated. All of a sudden, we became groundless, adrift. We were abruptly banished from this Chile that was so ours and so safe; we were deprived of any chance to make a con- tribution.[6]

In 1980, I described this phenomenon in similar terms:

the people of my generation — by [1973], 30-year-old individuals — had survived over a long period bearing the burden of utopian-suggesting words, and proclaimed [without too much conviction of our own] that such utopia was about to be fulfilled: all that was needed was a rapid, drastic and massive "structural change" that we were called upon to trigger from the heights of political power. However, on having reached the bottom of the crisis (*i.e.*, a brutal military coup) this all turned into rubbish and we turned to be persuaded by simple values.[7]

While our political initiation — during the years of Frei and Allende — had been characterized by "enormous words" — one of which was "revolution" — and by the idea that we were creating a progressive, ascending and historic movement, the military coup led us to adjust of our outlook:

---

[6] E. Tironi, *La Torre de Babel* (*The Tower of Babel*) (Ediciones Sur, 1984), pp. 17-18.

[7] G. Arriagada, *10 Años, Visión Crítica* (*10 Years, Critical Vision*) (Editorial Aconcagua, Santiago, 1980), p. 15.

during the harshest days [of Pinochet's regime], when we heard tales of atrocious events... we were moved by the preaching of priests who invoked terms as simple as charity, love for one's neighbor, reconciliation, peace, forgiveness, the value of the human being, the superiority of the moral good.[8]

In an important manner, the campaign that defeated Pinochet resulted from the work and the inspiration of the people of this generation — the people who were, at the most, 30-year-olds at the time of the military coup that overthrew Salvador Allende and were in their mid-forties by the time of the 1988 plebiscite. During the hard struggle against the dictatorial regime, this generation learned respect for political approaches focusing on tolerance, the idea of justice, the sense of proportion and fairness, and the profound respect for the feelings of all people.

These former revolutionaries became moderates, accumulated basic values and principles, united despite political party differences, and viewed ideologically tainted schemes with skepticism. They put aside all types of violence while promoting active mobilizations, whereby the people, in huge demonstrations, gained control of the streets and squares. A burst of idealism and hope was achieved by means of a platform of moderation.

---

[8] Ibid.

*Chapter 13*

# Choice of Electoral Systems

## Antonio Nadais

A multitude of factors shaped the choice of electoral systems for the 1990 elections in Eastern and Central Europe. Foremost among them, at least as implicitly identified in roundtable discussions, were the need, first, to confer legitimacy on the democratic transition by ensuring the broadest possible representation of the population, and, second, to establish mechanisms that could solve the numerous economic, social and political problems that formed communism's legacy.

Solving these problems requires political stability. To achieve a certain level of stability, a majoritarian-oriented electoral system, with a strong and credible executive branch of government, seemed preferable. Interest in creating a closer relationship between the electors and the elected also argued for the adoption of a majoritarian system. On the other hand, proportional representation systems provided greater assurance that all sectors of the population, including minority groups, would be represented in the new legislatures, an important consideration after years of one-party rule.

In short, the classic dilemmas regarding the choice of an electoral system — between representativeness and stability and between a strong legislature and a strong executive — were apparent in Eastern and Central Europe. The critical challenge was to achieve both representativeness and stability, especially given that the prior regimes had been not only politically repressive but also grossly inefficient. Each country faced this quandary, however, according to its own particular conditions and priorities.


# I

In addition to these general factors, other considerations also influenced the choice of electoral systems. Of particular importance were the communist electoral traditions and, where it existed, the memory of a democratic period before the arrival of communism.

Two contradictory reactions to the communist electoral tradition emerged. The natural first response was one of rejection: everything inherited from the communist regime was bad and, therefore, should be replaced. The second reaction, albeit subconscious or for reasons of convenience, was acceptance of previous practices, at least as a starting point.

As for past experiences with democracy, again two competing reactions were apparent. On the one hand, the new decision-makers looked, with understandable nostalgia, to the pre-communist era as a model. On the other hand, they recognized the mistakes made during this earlier period — mistakes that often translated into political and governmental instability, which facilitated the overthrow of democratic regimes by fascism before the war and by communism afterward.

Each country also had to consider how to structure its party system. During the transition period, large numbers of parties emerged in all the countries, in addition to the Communist and satellite parties that already existed. The new parties suffered from an understandable lack of structure and resources, especially at the local level. These circumstances argued for the creation of rules to encourage some form of party consolidation, by benefitting large umbrella coalitions that could better compete with the well-organized Communist parties. Consequently, several countries introduced refinements to the proportional system that established threshold clauses for parliamentary representation: 5 percent in the case of Czechoslovakia, 4 percent in Hungary and Bulgaria. These clauses were designed to discourage small parties from contesting the elections independently and thus undermining an opposition coalition to the benefit of the Communist Party. Similarly, Bulgaria, Hungary and Poland chose a two-round version of the majoritarian system because it would be more likely to encourage party coalitions and consolidation than would the one-round version.

The interests of the Communist Party, and the extent to which it still enjoyed a relatively strong position in the country, also played a role. In Bulgaria, for instance, many saw the decision to elect one-half of the parliament by the majority system in single-member constituencies as benefiting the Communist Party, whose candidates, in principle, were better known. This was somewhat offset by the decision to use a two-round system, which permitted the opposition parties to unite in the second round behind a single candidate, who would then stand a better chance of defeating the Communist Party candidate.

# II

Not surprisingly, considering the competing considerations involved, the countries of Eastern and Central Europe adopted diverse electoral systems. Broadly speaking, there were three groups: 1) Czechoslovakia, Romania and the GDR, which chose proportional systems, 2) Poland, which kept the two-round majority system inherited from the communist regime, and 3) Bulgaria and Hungary, which adopted mixed systems − or to be more precise, systems with two (or more) components, one being proportional and one using the majority principle. Actually, Romania, at the same time as it held legislative elections using a proportional system, held a direct presidential election using a two-round majoritarian system.

In Bulgaria, half of the 400 deputies to the Grand National Assembly were elected by a two-round majority system in single-member constituencies. The other 200 were elected proportionally, according to the so-called d'Hondt method, in relatively small constituencies (normally electing between four and 11 deputies, with one electing 17 and Sofia, the capital, electing 26). There was no connection whatsoever between the two parts of the system.

In the GDR, elections to the 400-seat Chamber of the People (*Volkskammer*) were held under an electoral law that established a pure proportional system, with no threshold clause, within the framework of 15 rather large electoral constituencies, each of which elected an average of 27 deputies. The GDR made this choice for a number of reasons. First, the system had historical roots in the Weimar Republic. Second, the GDR was influenced by the Federal Republic of Germany, which has a system that, apart from establishing a threshold of 5 percent, is strictly proportional. Finally, the electoral system structure was influenced by the inclusion in the roundtable negotiations of many small groups, such as New Forum and Democratic Awakening. These groups, so influential in the downfall of the communist regime, would have lost all their leverage at the polls had a threshold clause been adopted.

In Czechoslovakia, the electoral law for the two houses of parliament, the Chamber of the People (200 seats) and the Chamber of the Nations (150 seats: 75 each drawn from the Czech Republic and the Slovak Republic), resulted from negotiations among the different parties. The Communist Party, which dominated the parliament, and Civic Forum, whose Vaclav Havel occupied the office of the presidency and that dominated the coalition government, played the leading roles. The communist members of the government were generally unorthodox and acted more or less independently of the party, which was already in disarray. Respecting Czechoslovakia's tradition, the electoral system was a proportional one, with 12 electoral constituencies and a threshold clause requiring a party to obtain 5 percent of the vote in at least one of the two republics in order to obtain seats in parliament.

To allow voters some choice with respect to individual candidates, the law provided that if more than 10 percent of those voting for a party exercised their right to make individual selections from among the candidates presented by that party, they could effectuate a reordering of the party list. Thus, candidates obtaining more than 50 percent of the preferences would be ranked according to the order of the number of votes cast for them, regardless of their place in the list. In the elections, there was no reordering of lists, even with an educated electorate and a high turnout.

The method used for allocating seats among the different parties worked as follows. The total number of valid votes cast in each constituency was divided by the number of deputies to be elected in that same constituency plus one (the "electoral quota"). The number of votes received by a list in a constituency was then divided by the electoral quota for that constituency, which determined how many seats a list received in a given constituency. The votes that were not used (the "rests"), as well as the seats that were not filled, were considered at the republic level, using the same procedure, except that the seats that were still not filled were allocated to the parties with the largest "rests" (and not, transferred to the national level).

In Hungary, the system adopted was particularly complex and yielded rather unpredictable results. Of the 386 deputies to the parliament, 176 were elected by a two-round majority system in single-member constituencies, 152 were elected by the proportional system in 20 relatively small electoral constituencies and 58 were elected at the national level by a proportional system applied to the votes that were "not used" (as defined by law) at the other two levels.

To be elected from a single-member constituency, a candidate was required to obtain more than half of the valid votes, provided that a majority of the registered voters participated in the elections. If these conditions were not met, a second round was held. Where less than the requisite number of voters participated in the first round, all the candidates were eligible to contest the second round. If no candidate received a majority in the first round, the three leading vote recipients, plus all candidates that received more than 15 percent, competed in a second round.

At the regional level, a system of electoral quotients was used for each constituency. The electoral quotient was found by dividing the total number of valid votes cast in the constituency by the number of seats to be filled plus one. As many candidates from each list were elected as the number of times the electoral quotient was contained in its result. If some deputies of the constituency remained un-elected after this process, the vacancies were transferred to the national constituency. At the national constituency level, all the votes that were not used to elect a deputy in any of the other two levels were collected. A coalition or union of lists was allowed, and a threshold clause of 4 percent at the national level was established.

In Poland, the roundtable negotiations occurred at a time when expectations about the possibility of a truly democratic outcome were less sanguine, and this more limited view is reflected in the electoral system accepted by the Solidarity-led opposition. A two-round majority system, inherited from the communist regime, was retained. The opposition agreed that the freedom to present candidates would apply to all 100 seats in the Senate and to 35 percent (161) of the 460 seats in the Sejm. The other 65 percent of the seats in this lower house were reserved for candidates endorsed by the ruling party and its satellite parties. To be elected outright in the first round, a candidate had to obtain more than half of the votes cast. If no candidate obtained a first-round majority, the two front-runners competed in a second round. As in Hungary, for the election to be valid, at least half of the registered voters in a constituency had to cast their ballots.

In Romania, the Provisional Council of National Unity chose a proportional electoral system for the two houses of parliament. The House of Deputies had, in principle, 387 deputies, but the total could increase. If a party representing a national minority and registered before the enactment of the law did not elect any deputies by the normal procedures, it was automatically granted one seat. The Senate had 119 seats, two to four for each constituency and 14 for Bucharest.

The Council was completely under the control of the National Salvation Front, but other parties, including the Liberal, Peasant and Social Democratic parties, argued for electoral changes. It was the opposition, and particularly the Liberal Party, that, for obvious reasons, insisted on the adoption of the proportional system.

# III

As is often the case in developing regulations for elections after a period of dictatorship, added care was taken to ensure that the elections were genuinely democratic. This need was heightened in Eastern and Central Europe by the fact that the dominant party of the old regime survived, in one form or another, and contested the elections.

From the opposition point of view, it was thus imperative to secure two essential points: to prevent the remnants of the old regime from subverting the fairness of the elections, especially in the administration of the process, and to counter the advantages acquired by the Communist parties through their long tenure in power. Still, somewhat surprisingly, many communist-era practices with respect to election administration were maintained for reasons ranging from inertia to the seeming political neutrality of those practices to the sheer practical impossibility of substituting other systems.

In some countries, the transition period also influenced the organization and development of the elections in a peculiar way. Groups that played leading roles in their country's transition processes — a small number — inevitably gained significant control over such essential aspects of the electoral process as electoral administration, access to the mass media and campaign financing. An exception was the GDR, where the groups that led the movement to overthrow the communist regime were soon pushed aside. The decisive role belonged to the West German parties, which, by giving their Eastern counterparts material support and respectability, completely altered the character of the transition process.

# IV

In all the countries under consideration, local authorities prepared electoral registries on the basis of existing lists of citizens maintained either by local or by central authorities. In theory, citizens were not required to take any action to be included on the voter registries. In some countries, such as Bulgaria and Romania, commanders of military units conducted registration of military personnel. In Czechoslovakia, by contrast, it was strictly forbidden to create polling places — and therefore registries — that included only military personnel. The decision-makers felt the need to prevent imposing any kind of pressure on military personnel, especially in the form of collective sanctions, that might have been attempted if the results from the military vote could have been easily distinguished from that of the general population.

The registries were publicly displayed, and in some cases written notification was delivered to every registered citizen. Following publication of the registries, citizens could present grievances about the accuracy of the lists to the responsible authorities. The decisions made by these authorities could be appealed before the local courts. The possibility of appeal, which would be of great importance in countries with long-standing democratic traditions, was rather less relevant in Eastern Europe given the character of the judiciary under the communist regimes. Nonetheless, the judiciary represented at least some form of check on a local administration that was still largely under communist control.

A common feature of the registration procedures was the provision for absentee ballots. In several countries, local authorities issued certificates of registration to electors who would be unable to vote in the place where they were registered, thus enabling them to vote elsewhere. This process usually entailed eliminating the name from the original register and entering the name in a special section of the register at the place where the individual sought to vote. The rationale was to allow the greatest possible participation on election day. At the same time, these liberal provisions could have opened the way for double voting and other types of fraud. In Bulgaria, authorities stamped national identity cards explicitly as a safeguard against this form of fraud.

# V

Each country established a central commission to administer the elections, a necessary measure to promote confidence in the fairness and freedom of the electoral process. Typically, there was a three-tier system of electoral commissions, comprising a central or national commission, constituency commissions and polling-station commissions. The systems granted the possibility of appeal to a higher level commission. There were four different systems used to determine the membership of the electoral commissions.

The first system of selecting a national electoral commission involved creating commissions comprising an equal number of representatives of the parties contesting the elections. This system represented a complete break with the communist legacy. It was used in Czechoslovakia and the GDR.

The second system was similar, except that it added to the party representatives some members elected by parliament or by local authorities, after consultations with the parties. In spite of the fact that there were fewer of these government-selected members than of the party representatives, this system presented some risks, because the bodies that elected them were still under communist control. This system was used in Hungary.

The third system provided for commissions that included a fixed number of party representatives (one seat each allocated to the parties presenting the largest lists of candidates) and a smaller number of judges (or, in the lowest tier, jurists or other people of outstanding reputation) selected by lot. This system had obvious risks, due to the close relationship under the communist regime between the judiciary and the ruling party. In Romania, where this system was used, these risks were exacerbated by the fact that the commissions were allowed to function before the party representatives were nominated, with the sole presence of the judges. In fact, the party representatives were able to begin working only one or two weeks before the elections.

The fourth system established commissions that included individuals designated by the major parties that participated in the roundtable negotiations. In addition, the same parties recommended several nonpartisan members. In Bulgaria, where this system was used, the president of the republic and local authorities formally nominated the commissions.

# VI

Establishing mechanisms for ensuring a fair campaign was of paramount concern to those negotiating the election laws. Especially critical was the issue of access to the mass media or, more broadly, the role of the mass media in the campaign. The state or the Communist Party (or affiliated organizations, such as trade unions) owned and controlled all radio and television station and essentially all other media.

General rules were established granting parties and candidates free and equal access to the mass media. Implementation of these rules, however, differed widely. In Hungary and Czechoslovakia, political parties were granted time on radio and television for political advertising. In Czechoslovakia, all parties received equal time, while in Hungary part of the available time was allocated to the parties in proportion to the number of candidates they presented.

In Bulgaria, parties were also granted time on radio and television. With respect to television, during three nights a week the ruling party and the leading opposition coalition were each granted 20 minutes; the third major party was granted 15 minutes and the remaining parties split five minutes. Radio and television also were required to provide coverage of the campaigns of the different parties in proportion to their numbers of candidates.

It is no surprise that the problems relating to media access were greatest in Romania: the law stated the principle of equality and freedom of access but provided no specific implementation rules, and so in practice the principle was not respected. The National Salvation Front retained tight control over radio and television and therefore enjoyed much more prominent coverage of its campaign. Some other peculiar legacies of the Ceausescu regime, such as the need to register typewriters and other materials with the authorities, also remained in effect. The government also refused to allow the opposition to use printing presses offered by foreign entities, while at the same time printers at the government presses refused to print some opposition materials. These problems certainly hindered the electoral campaigns of the opposition parties.

Campaign financing was also a major issue in all of the countries. The Communist parties enjoyed considerable advantages in terms of resources, and therefore the opposition parties insisted on mechanisms to create a modicum of balance. In some cases, opposition parties faced the prospect of not being able to campaign effectively, or at all, without some form of financial assistance.

Funding for the parties and candidates consisted principally of subsidies from the state budget. These subsidies existed in Bulgaria, Hungary and Romania (although in Romania the criteria for the allocation of the subsidies were far from clear). In Czechoslovakia, on the other hand, the law specifically required that the parties themselves finance the campaign. But the law also created a procedure that allowed parties to obtain bank loans to finance their campaigns. And after the elections, all parties that received more than 2 percent of the valid votes for any of the houses of parliament in either of the republics were provided a "refund" from the state budget at the rate of 10 crowns for each vote.

In addition to subsidies, the government sometimes offered the use of buildings and equipment to the opposition parties, but these gestures were never enough to offset the wide disparity of resources between those parties and the communists. Given the generally dire economic situations in these countries, parties could not rely heavily on private donations from individuals. In many cases, financial assistance from abroad, whether by individuals or by organizations, helped reduce the gap. Laws governing foreign assistance ranged from implicit permission to a complete prohibition. In Bulgaria, the electoral law exempted the 1990 elections from the general rule that parties accept no foreign assistance.

# VII

Secrecy of the ballot constitutes a fundamental element of a truly democratic electoral system. And so, the electoral legislation of all the countries under consideration not only guaranteed the possibility of ballot secrecy, but deemed it mandatory. Voting outside the booth was sometimes expressly forbidden (as in Bulgaria), and assistance to the voter inside the booth was allowed only in very narrowly defined cases. An exception was Romania, where relatives of the voter or election officials received liberal permission to lend assistance inside the polling booth.

The importance of explicit provisions regarding the secret ballot was a legacy of elections under the communist regimes. Under these regimes, while the possibility of a secret ballot was normally written into the law, it was common practice for the vote to be public. Voting in secret was often viewed with suspicion. Moreover, during the transition period the communist apparatus was still in place. Consequently, forms of intimidation or pressure over the voters were still clearly possible and had to be reduced. Mandating a secret ballot and publicizing this fact was considered necessary to counter the population's fears.

The concern for secrecy and openness was reversed when it came to the counting of the votes: what was secret during the communist regime (and helped produce extraordinary majorities) now had to be as open as possible to ensure the fairness of, and confidence in, the electoral process. One way of opening the work of the electoral administration, as discussed earlier, was to include representatives of different parties on the electoral commissions. Another was to allow people other than the commission members to witness the counting and tabulation processes. In Bulgaria, candidates and their aides, party workers, reporters and guests (*i.e.*, members of nonpartisan organizations and international observers) could be present during the counting of the votes at all levels. In the GDR and Hungary, the activities of the electoral administration were characterized in the law as "public," thus assuring that every citizen and especially the media could monitor all aspects of the process. By contrast, in Czechoslovakia, where fear of electoral malpractice was considerably less, only members of the higher commissions or people authorized by the Central Electoral Commission could be present inside the polling stations during the counting process.

Generally speaking, the electoral laws of Eastern European countries did not explicitly address the issue of ballot security after the votes were counted. Still, it was an important issue, particularly in the case of a recount, as occurred in several instances in Bulgaria.

Despite the continued domination of local authorities by the communist status quo, several countries saw no problem in entrusting them with the task of keeping the election materials following the elections. In the GDR, however, these materials were delivered to the National Electoral Commission. In Hungary also, in the event of a protest, local officials sent election materials to the competent electoral committee for review as opposed to the local council.

The issue of judicial review during the electoral process was rather complex. Whereas judicial review is an important guarantee in democratic countries where the rule of law is well established, it created special problems in Eastern and Central Europe. The complicity of the judiciary in communist rule, and its consequences for the recruitment and training of judges, meant that the courts could not be fully trusted to ensure fairness. As a result, opposition parties generally did not want judicial interference in the electoral process. Nonetheless, in certain circumstances — particularly in less sensitive areas such as electoral registration, as discussed above — the courts represented an additional check.

As for the review of actions by the electoral administrators, particularly with respect to the counting of votes, all the countries relied primarily on the electoral administrators themselves: any decision made by an electoral commission could always be challenged before a superior commission. But the courts were not totally absent from the process. In Czechoslovakia and Hungary, decisions of the central or national electoral commission were subject to judicial review by the Supreme Court, whose decision was final. In Hungary, it was also possible to appeal to the local or municipal courts decisions made by lower electoral commissions; the decisions of these courts were final. Meanwhile, in Bulgaria and Romania, the relevant house of parliament determined whether to validate or invalidate the parliamentary mandates, but the courts could review issues relating to the nomination of candidates.

# VIII

In conclusion, and with some hindsight, we can ask whether the electoral systems that were chosen for the 1990 elections in Eastern and Central Europe effectively achieved their aims. With respect to ensuring the broadest possible representation of the population, we can fairly say that this goal generally was met: the voters were able to cast their ballots relatively freely, and the electoral systems did not distort their will in an unacceptable way.

According to public opinion polls shortly after the elections, it seemed that the parliaments of Eastern and Central Europe already failed to represent broadly the opinions of the electors. This phenomenon, to some extent, is common everywhere, albeit to a lesser degree. And if it occurred in Eastern and Central Europe with greater intensity, this was due less to the electoral systems than to the fact that the elections were held during a period of rapid transition. The parliaments that faced the greatest problems of legitimacy, however, were those in countries where the elections took place during an earlier stage of the transition process, such as Bulgaria and Romania, and where, consequently, the communists or former communists maintained greater control.

The problem, generally speaking, was not in the expression of the electors' will, but in its formation.  And there, the electoral legislation had only limited reach, namely when regulating electoral campaigns.  Legislation did what it could, and only in Romania were widespread, serious problems reported with respect to the openness and fairness of the campaign.

As for the aim of establishing mechanisms that could solve the problems inherited from the communist regimes, reaching a verdict is somewhat more difficult.  Political stability has not been easy to find among the countries of the region.  Yet political instability is, almost by definition, an inherent part of any transition process. There was not much the electoral systems could do to counter the existing deep political causes of instability.

At the same time, the countries of Eastern and Central Europe have managed reasonably well to contain their instabilities, even by Western standards.  Instability only seems of such great concern because of the severity of the problems facing these countries. Nonetheless, the alternatives in the choice of electoral systems could certainly have been more fully explored, in the light of the peculiar conditions of the countries involved and the need to encourage more fully the participation of all sectors of the population in the transition process.

In short, legitimacy prevailed over stability.  From a longer-term perspective, the democratization of Eastern and Central Europe is well under way.  In this context, the choices of electoral systems have been, all things considered, of relatively minor importance.  The really important choices concern the issues of policy that confront the newly elected executive and legislative bodies in each of the countries of the region.

*Chapter 14*

# Political Parties and the Rebirth of History

## Andrew Ellis

Before 1989, people generally thought of the countries of Central and Eastern Europe, perhaps with the exception of Yugoslavia, as one large, monolithic block behind the Iron Curtain. These countries were not very accessible, they were subject to centrally directed economies that snuffed out individual initiative, and they were dominated by the USSR next door. The diversity that exists among the different nations and peoples of the region was, for the most part, repressed.

The 1989-90 democratic revolution has brought with it the joy of rediscovering the region's diversity. In this context, the task of finding the perfect revolutionary, model political party and electoral system is — if posed in such terms — quite rightly unachievable. Still, many common threads have emerged even as we celebrate pluralism.

The history of Central and Eastern Europe differs dramatically from that of the countries farther west. While the western regions of Europe were developing the nation-state and resolving the problems of nationalism, Central and Eastern Europe remained firmly in the grip of hegemonic empires. Some of these empires — Prussia and Austria — were active participants in the Industrial Revolution; others — Russia and the Ottoman — were not.

For Bulgarians, for example, the legacy of Vasil Levski's unsuccessful insurrection against the Turks in 1873 stands as a potent political symbol. For Poles, the partition of Poland by the empires in 1795 commands a similar significance. And it is impossible to hold a sustained political discussion with Serbs without hearing references to the last stand of the medieval Serbian Empire against the Ottomans at the Battle of Kosovo Polje in 1389.

This historical perspective sets a major part of the stage for debate, particularly since the last 45 years have been frozen in time, a period in which history has not happened. The process of awakening is thus Rip van Winkle-like, with debate owing as much to the issues of former centuries as to those of the recent transition from communism and the difficulties of economic restructuring.

Political parties and movements have been forced to deal with these historical and current agendas simultaneously. They have been forced to do so in the context of the destruction of civil society, where the process of people coming together to discuss issues, reach a decision by consensus or by vote, and take the necessary action to implement the decision, has been retarded. Consequently, many people have had to learn the most basic skills of living in a democratic society.

As political parties have formed, even those that have stood against the previous regimes, they have had to move from a posture of permanent opposition to one where it is necessary, at times, to assume responsibility. No doubt, tremendous progress has been made, but the process also has seen many failures. These have resulted from a lack of organizational skills, from clashes of personalities and, perhaps above all, from the fact that the personalities most suited to clandestine operation are often least ready for the open communications and negotiations required in a successful government.

These problems have been common to both new and re-established historical parties. Meanwhile, the Communist parties, with or without new names, have faced very different issues. While the loathing of the Communist Party appears to have been more strongly rooted in some countries than in others, the key determinant of the survival and relative success of the party has been its ability to react and adapt to events. The Communist parties in Bulgaria and Slovenia, for example, were controlled eventually by leaders who anticipated change. As a result, they were able to remain significant players on the new political stage. The Czechoslovak communists, however, reacted slowly to political developments and were soundly defeated in the June 1990 elections. If the communists opened the floodgates themselves, they stood a better chance of riding the wave of reform.

While some Communist parties were able to maintain a significant role in their countries' political affairs, the same did not hold true of the former "bloc parties," which were aligned with the Communist parties during the post-World War II era. This is hardly surprising. Once the force of change was liberated — whether unleashed by internal coup or by revolution — it was impossible for those who were tainted by the old system to successfully claim a new identity and separate themselves from the communists. Thus, the bloc parties polled badly and were, in most cases, politically decimated. After all, with the communists competing in elections, "why vote for the monkey when you can vote for the organ grinder?"

One important exception to this phenomenon was the Christian Democratic Union (CDU) in East Germany, a bloc party that led the coalition that won the March 1990 elections. But it did not do so strictly on its own strengths. By the time elections were held, the political system in East Germany was no longer indigenous but rather was largely an extension of the alignment in the Federal Republic, whose CDU leader and chancellor, Helmut Kohl, promised immediate reunification.

Ironically, political parties that were the reincarnation of pre-communist-era parties, even those that had resisted becoming bloc parties, also did not perform well in the 1990 elections. Some such parties — the Slovak Democratic Party, the Hungarian Smallholders' Party (FKgP) and the Romanian Peasant and Liberal parties, for example — re-established a significant minority presence at best. The Fkgp's position, as a difficult junior coalition partner, is currently the most influential of any of the historical parties.

This relative lack of success appears paradoxical until one looks at the almost inevitable legacy of 40 years without any significant political activity. The historical parties tended to resume their activities with open power struggles between the 80-year-old former leaders and younger recruits not prepared to accept a supporting role. This hindered the ability of these parties to contest elections against entrenched Communist parties and broad-based democratic coalitions.

Successful parties have offered some notion of direction and vision, have produced leaders who would appear to make credible government ministers and have understood that success requires a degree of unity and discipline as well as unrestrained debate. Parties that voters distrusted — because their leadership lacked credibility or because of their factiousness and disunity — have failed at the polls, even where they were seen as serious contenders for political power during the early stages of the transition. And parties that were established by isolated groups, a natural course of events given poor communications and the legacy of suspicion, have not succeeded at all in the electoral contests in the region.

But the unusual nature of the transition has also clearly brought with it some rules of its own, the most important being that a successful move to democracy from totalitarianism is a two-stage process. In stage one, all major opposition groups unite to challenge the communists. In stage two, distinct factions of the unified opposition separate from the movement, and the real debate of a pluralist system begins.

All successful changes followed this pattern. The New Forum in East Germany and Civic Forum and Public against Violence in Czechoslovakia formed as mass street movements. Solidarity in Poland developed as a popular free trade union movement. The opposition parties in Hungary cooperated until the completion of the roundtable talks. And the UDF in Bulgaria, despite great pressures to fragment, waged a united campaign in 1990 against the incumbent Bulgarian Socialist Party.

Parties in Romania, not surprisingly given the evolution of the transition in that country, demonstrated the opposite tendency. The National Salvation Front (NSF), in the view of many observers, represented a reincarnation of the Communist Party under non-Ceausescu management. The NSF's overwhelming success in the elections was amplified by the inability of the opposition parties to unify.

It was perhaps inevitable that large numbers of parties would form for the first free elections in more than a generation.  Almost any group of individuals with opinions, however hazy, had incentives to constitute themselves into a party.  In the early phase of the transition, there was much concern about this tendency toward balkanization.  Upon reflection, however, an initial proliferation of parties can be seen as natural, especially in societies where access to media is restricted, the availability of publicity material and the money to produce it is limited, and internal communication networks − in particular telecommunications − are neither well-developed nor reliable.  After the winnowing process of the first elections, there are now a more reasonable number of distinct parties in each of the countries, with obvious exception of Poland.

The availability of resources for use by political parties plays a crucial role in democratic elections.  With the old economic systems in place, the 1990 elections in Central and Eastern Europe were contested within a structure of a centralized distribution of resources.  Thus, the communists or their successors could always be sure of paper or newsprint or broadcast time, whereas the opposition parties struggled to obtain similar perquisites.  The situation was particularly dire in countries, such as Bulgaria, that were not producing newsprint domestically, but relied on imports from other countries.

Opposition parties that formed links with Western parties or political groupings (*i.e.*, Liberal, Socialist or Christian Democratic internationals) could to some extent rely on their new friends not only for expertise but also for the provision of material assistance.  Among the Western Europeans, the West Germans, in particular, made a noticeable contribution.  In addition, parties like the Croatian Democratic Union were able to draw on donations from exiles and expatriates.  These ties, however, were not guarantors of success.  The Hungarian Social Democrats, for example, received substantial help from members of the Socialist International, but were unable to overcome internal divisions and other problems.

Demographics also affected party development in the region.  The party-building experience, as well as the election results, differed between the cities and the countryside.  For the most part, the major cites of Central and Eastern Europe, and especially the capitals, were home to the intelligentsia and the youth. These groups were the engines of change, incorporating those who not only rejected the old regime but sought something concrete to replace it. The large cities were places, too, where it was physically easier for people to communicate and organize. Thus, the foundation for new political parties was largely city-based. Likewise, most members of the Communist Party *nomenklatura* lived in the capital cities; at times, as in East Berlin, these urban areas also provided a base for the communists.

The countryside, on the other hand, had a more elderly population. In those areas where the Russians and Ottomans held sway – eastern Poland, Bulgaria, southern Romania, and Serbia and Macedonia – the structure of society, despite formal collectivization, is still peasant oriented. In these rural areas, new parties, even the various agrarian groups, were not nearly as successful in recruiting active supporters. These difficulties were reflected in the election results. In Hungary, local elections in cities produced support for the more radical parties, while independent village figures were successful in rural local elections, despite the fact they had held the same positions under the communists. In Bulgaria, the general election results showed an almost perfect correlation between urban areas and UDF victories, and between rural areas and communist wins.

At the beginning of the democratic reform process, nobody knew what to expect. In Europe, Spain and Portugal offered the most recent examples of building new democratic institutions. But economic freedom existed to a significant extent under the fascist regimes, and these countries did not have to cope with consequences of a destroyed civil society.

The fact that democratic elections have taken place with relatively few significant problems and that resulting pluralist parliaments have functioned without collapse, despite the magnitude of the changes and the inexperience of their members, is remarkable in itself. What is also remarkable is the way in which the interplay of political forces follows patterns that already established democracies will recognize: the way in which personalities and policies interact, the impact of radio and television, and the judgment of voters based on issues of competence and of unity as much as of policies. Each new democracy is developing its own special political culture; electoral systems, political and economic historical experiences, personalities and a wide range of other questions are all playing a part. But equally, all are contributing to the growth of democratic institutions as a single universal process. And the examples and lessons are there for all of those embarking on the same road throughout the former Soviet republics.

*Chapter 15*

# The Role of International Observers

**Larry Garber**

International observers[1] were present for all of the 1990 elections in Eastern and Central Europe. Their collective efforts highlight the growing acceptance and understanding of the roles that international observers can play in supporting free and fair election processes, especially in transition elections following years of nondemocratic rule. Moreover, these election observation experiences led to an institutionalization of the process among the countries party to the Conference on Security and Cooperation in Europe (CSCE) as reflected in the Copenhagen declaration adopted

---

[1] Defining the term "international observer" is not always easy. Generally, an individual's self-definition is accepted by both the domestic authorities and by the international community, including the media. Of course, such self-definition ignores the *bona fides* of an individual or group as a neutral and objective observer of the process.

on June 29, 1990, less than two weeks after the elections in Bulgaria marked the conclusion of the spring 1990 election season.

This chapter describes the attitudes exhibited toward observers in the different countries of the region and evaluates the contribution that the observers made to the election processes. The final sections comment on the lessons to be learned from the observers' experiences in 1990 and on the future direction of observation efforts in the region.

# I

The different governments in the region all accepted the presence of international observers for the 1990 elections. For those who have worked hard to convince reluctant governments in other regions of the world to permit international observers, the warm welcome afforded international observers marked a surprising and positive development in Eastern and Central Europe. In some countries (*e.g.*, East Germany, Hungary, Poland and Czechoslovakia), the presence of observers was not seen as necessary to ensure a fair campaign environment or to deter fraud; indeed, for the 1989 Polish legislative elections, Solidarity and other groups discouraged the presence of large observer delegations because they believed that it would be more beneficial in the long term to develop and rely on local monitoring initiatives.

The Central European countries welcomed observers principally as a means of demonstrating international support for the dramatic changes occurring in these countries. In Hungary and Czechoslovakia, the National Democratic and Republican Institutes for International Affairs jointly sponsored large-scale international delegations that not only observed the elections, but also participated in post-election seminars, respectively, on "Mechanisms for Promoting a Transition Process" and a "Symposium on Democracy." The observation process became a learning experience, which was particularly relevant for delegation members who were seeking to initiate democratic transitions in their own countries.[2]

In Romania and Bulgaria, where democratic traditions are much weaker, observers played the more traditional roles of encouraging a fair campaign and of deterring election-day fraud. No barriers were encountered by observation efforts in either country, although expectations varied as to the significance of their presence in encouraging fair elections. The quality of the evaluations issued by different observer groups also varied. Still, there can be no doubt that observers in both countries gave added confidence to populations participating in multiparty elections for the first time in more than a generation. Moreover, in several instances, the observers, during pre-election surveys, were able to suggest administrative reforms that improved the quality of the process.

In Romania, the government initially invited the United Nations to observe the May elections. The Secretary General declined the invitation, ostensibly because the election was occurring in a sovereign country and no regional security threat was at issue.[3] The government then encouraged the presence of observers sponsored by governments and nongovernmental organizations. A far-reaching decree was adopted providing observers with free and unimpeded access to the observation process, from the beginning of the election campaign until the announcement of the election results.[4] The

---

[2] The delegations in Hungary and Czechoslovakia included nationals from Bangladesh, Kenya, Liberia, Nigeria and South Africa.

[3] The United Nations' attitude on the question of observers has been undergoing some evolution in recent years. Until recently, the U.N. would observe elections only in a decolonization situation. The February 1990 elections in Nicaragua represented the organization's first foray into observing elections in a sovereign country. The Secretary General explained the decision to observe the Nicaraguan elections as fulfilling the U.N. mandate to contribute to regional security. This rationale was more attenuated in Haiti, where again the U.N. decided to observe elections in a sovereign nation.

[4] The decree provided observers unhampered access to information and documentation on the legal framework concerning the elections and on the norms governing basic human rights and freedoms, uninhibited travel and

Romanian government maintained this open attitude even after observers conducting pre-election missions issued statements critical of the campaign environment.[5]

Opposition supporters also encouraged the presence of observers, even while they discounted the possibility of fair elections. At times, opposition leaders and activists held quite unrealistic expectations about the contribution that international observers could make to a fair process. These activists, and also prospective voters, noted that observers would be present only for a short time and expressed fears regarding what might happen after the observers left the country. Indeed, the Romanian experience underscored the limited role that observers can play, particularly in a society where domestic groups are not well-organized.

In Bulgaria, the government's attitude toward observers was initially more ambivalent. While the election law adopted in April 1990, two months before the elections, authorized the presence of "guests," the government sought to confine the definition to a discrete group of legislators from neighboring countries. Under pressure from a variety of sources, the government ultimately acceded to permitting free access to all those who sought to be present for the elections.

The observers in Bulgaria benefitted from the emergence of a nationwide civic organization, the Bulgarian Association for Fair Elections (BAFE) (see Chapter 8). Both in the pre-election period and on election day, BAFE facilitated the activities of the observers, without linking the observers to a particular contestant in the election process. Moreover, BAFE's network and its successful implementation of a parallel vote tabulation provided observers with reliable and immediate information regarding the overall process, thus

---

contacts with the leaders of any political group,...and unconditional access to electoral meetings and to monitoring the electoral process in any of the country's localities. The decree also provided that observers abide by their neutrality status and not interfere with the electoral process, and that the observers could convene press conferences at the end of their mission and request to be received by the Romanian authorities.

[5] See, *e.g.*, International Human Rights Law Group, *Report on the Romanian Campaign for President and Parliament* (May 9, 1990).

assisting the delegation's ability to issue a statement soon after the elections.

Bulgaria offers a good example of how observers contributed to the election process by more than just their presence on election day. During the pre-election period, observers from NDI and other organizations encouraged reforms in the administrative process relating to the tally sheets and the voter registration lists. On election day, the leaders of the NDI/NRIIA international observer delegation, building upon the goodwill established between government officials and participants in the pre-election missions, played a critical role in ensuring that the parallel vote tabulation was implemented as planned. And following the elections, some of the observers investigated complaints registered by the opposition, demonstrating a seriousness of purpose and adding substantive weight to their overall assessment of the process.

# II

The Romanian and Bulgarian experiences highlight the difficulties that observers face in evaluating controversial elections. In Romania, observers confronted a situation in which the ruling National Salvation Front scored an overwhelming victory, following an election campaign marked by Front abuses of the perquisites of incumbency and serious acts of intimidation. In addition, the elections were fraught with administrative problems and in some cases outright fraud in the balloting process.

Some observers, most notably members of a British parliamentary group and an official delegation sponsored by the United States government, visited the country for only a few days and directed their attention primarily to the balloting process. Failing to observe systematic fraud, these delegations issued generally favorable statements.

Other observers were more skeptical. In its statement, the 60-member NDI/NRIIA international delegation stressed the problems that existed during the campaign as well as on election day. While recognizing that some democratic progress had been made, the delegation emphasized that the elections had not demonstrated the democratic *bona fides* of the Front.

In Bulgaria, the situation was equally complicated. Here too, there was a serious imbalance in resources available to the contesting parties, although a much more meaningful campaign took place than in Romania. Moreover, pre-election and election-day visits throughout the country reported on the existence of a climate of fear, caused in large measure by the legacy of 45 years of totalitarian rule. Nonetheless, few administrative problems occurred on election day, and very few incidents of outright fraud were alleged. The parallel vote tabulations conducted by BAFE and by a West German polling firm detected no fraud in the tabulation of results.

In Bulgaria, as in Romania, some observers sought to emphasize the positive aspects of the process. For its part, the NDI/NRIIA international observer delegation drew a more subtle distinction, highlighting the existence of fear and its impact on the process but also recognizing that this factor in and of itself did not provide a basis for invalidating the elections. The delegation recognized that, despite the imperfections, the elections provided Bulgarians an opportunity to participate in a meaningful process and that the results reflected the will of the voters as expressed at the ballot box on election day.

## III

Several lessons can be drawn from observing the 1990 elections in the countries of the region. Recognition was given to the different roles that observer missions can play in transition elections, ranging from demonstrating support for a democratic process (East Germany and Hungary) and celebrating the rebirth of democracy (Poland and Czechoslovakia) to evaluating elections occurring under difficult circumstances (Romania and Bulgaria).

The elections, particularly in Romania and Bulgaria, also highlighted the importance of adopting sound methodology in assessing election processes. Such a methodology includes conducting pre-election missions to identify problems and facilitate solutions; establishing contacts and informing the population of observer presence; maintaining a neutral and objective point of view; working with local, nonpartisan organizations; and being prepared to conduct post-election follow-up investigations. Encouraging parties and other organizations to conduct parallel vote tabulations can also significantly enhance the observation process.

# IV

On June 29, 1990, the 35 countries then party to the Conference on Security and Cooperation in Europe (CSCE) approved a lengthy document concerning the "human dimension" of the CSCE process. Influenced by the events of the previous months, the CSCE countries declared "that the will of the people, freely and fairly expressed through periodic and genuine elections, is the basis of the authority and legitimacy of all government."

The document sets forth standards for free and fair elections in CSCE countries. The standards require that CSCE countries: hold free elections at reasonable intervals; permit all seats in at least one chamber of the national legislature to be freely contested; guarantee universal and equal suffrage to all adult citizens; ensure that votes are cast by secret ballot or by equivalent free voting procedure; ensure that the votes are counted and reported honestly; respect the rights of citizens to seek political office, individually or as representatives of political parties; ensure that law and public policy permit a free campaign environment; provide for unimpeded access to the media; and guarantee that the candidates who obtain the necessary number of votes are duly installed in office. These standards reflect a broad consensus on what constitutes free and fair elections and should serve as a model for the development of similar standards by other inter-governmental organizations.

With respect to international observers, the CSCE document provides:

> The participating States consider that the presence of observers, both domestic and foreign, can enhance the electoral process for States in which elections are taking place. They therefore *invite* observers from any other CSCE participating States and any appropriate private institutions and organizations who may wish to do so to

> observe the course of their national election proceedings, to the extent permitted by law. They will also endeavor to facilitate similar access for election proceedings held below the national level. Such observers will undertake not to interfere in the electoral proceedings.

This is the first international document to recognize the status of international observers. By virtue of its very explicit language, the document should help deflect arguments that election observing constitutes interference in the internal affairs of CSCE countries. This provision also may help overcome the resentment felt in some countries regarding the willingness of developed countries, which are advocates of election observing, to welcome observers for elections in their own countries.

Several questions remain to be addressed in order to determine the future role of observers in CSCE countries. First, the CSCE must decide whether to establish a mechanism for observing elections itself rather than simply encouraging member states to do so. The advantage of CSCE observer missions would be their ability to formally represent the entire CSCE community, thereby adding international encouragement for free and fair elections.

Establishing such a mechanism, however, would raise a host of additional questions. Are all CSCE states eligible for representation on an observer mission? Which elections would be observed by CSCE observer missions? How long would an observer team be authorized to spend in the country (and who would pay for the mission)? Would the observer missions be limited to a reporting role or would they be instructed to facilitate the resolution of difficult legal, administrative and political issues? Finally, what weight would CSCE observer missions have on the issue of government recognition and bilateral relations in the case of a critical evaluation of the election process? Similar questions are currently under consideration by other intergovernmental organizations, including the United Nations,[6] the Organization of American States and the Commonwealth nations.

---

[6] See, G.A. Resolution 45/150 (adopted December 18, 1990). See also, *Response of the National Democratic Institute for International Affairs to United Nations General Assembly Resolution 45/150: Developing a United Nations Elections Assistance Capability* (submitted to the Secretary General, June 15, 1991).

Assuming CSCE observer missions prove impossible to organize, at least in the short term, government and nongovernmental organization observer missions will continue to play key roles. The CSCE document assures such delegations access to the election process but does not spell out in detail what that access entails. In keeping with the trend exhibited in Eastern and Central Europe during the spring of 1990, and in other parts of the world during the past five years, observer missions, at a minimum, should be authorized: to monitor all aspects of the election process from the beginning of the campaign through the installation of a new government; to travel and communicate freely within the country; to visit polling sites on election day and vote tabulation centers after the polls close; and to issue public statements before and after the elections. The decree adopted by the Romanian government before the May 20, 1990 elections could serve as a model in this regard. The observers, of course, would be obliged to abide by all domestic laws and regulations and to avoid interfering in the domestic political process.

Governments and nongovernmental organizations sponsoring observer missions should comprehensively brief their designees on what is expected of them and should set forth terms of reference reflecting the complexities involved in evaluating an election process. At the very least, the terms of reference should require objective standards and the requirement that the observers evaluate the three critical phases of an election process: 1) the election campaign; 2) the balloting and counting processes; and 3) the post-election disposition of complaints.

Observer groups sponsored by different organizations should be prepared to share information regarding the process, although it will be difficult to coordinate the post-election statements issued by various observer groups. The domestic and international media, which serve as the principal vehicles for disseminating the views of international observers, should be selective in their reliance on information from observer groups, relying, to the extent possible, on those groups that are observing elections in a manner consistent with evolving international standards.[7]

---

[7] See, L. Garber, *Guidelines for International Election Observing* (International Human Rights Law Group, 1984).

# V

Given the role that observers played in Eastern and Central Europe in 1990, it is not surprising that there are high expectations for continued observer involvement in future elections. While the allocation of resources for observer missions can almost always be justified for transition elections, the direct benefits become less obvious as elections become more institutionalized and fears of fraud and intimidation become less severe. In such circumstances, other forms of political development assistance — directed at newly established legislatures, independent judicial systems, free media outlets, local governments and other institutions — become more relevant.

Still, a trustworthy election system is critical to ensuring the existence of a democratic form of government. When questions arise regarding the quality of the election system, governments and nongovernmental organizations should be prepared to sponsor international observer delegations that can then determine whether a commitment to free and fair elections exists and, where appropriate, encourage ways to improve the electoral process.

*Chapter 16*

# Reflections on the Transition in Eastern and Central Europe

## J. Brian Atwood

History was made in Eastern and Central Europe in 1989 and 1990. Societies transformed themselves in a seemingly revolutionary manner. An ideology that dominated the region and transfixed the world collapsed as communism finally succumbed dramatically to human nature. But the story of this transformation still unfolds as these societies proceed through critical transitions to democracy.

This volume focuses on the elections that formed an integral part of these transitions. Although elections are only part of the story, they provide important benchmarks for retrospective analysis. The first genuine elections held in the region in 40 years forced these societies to focus on their past, present and future unlike any other events in their national histories.

The first elections of the new era in Eastern and Central Europe provided the essential prologue to the history that is now being made. The legal and administrative systems used for these elections grew out of negotiations among the most powerful sectors of yet-to-be democratic societies, including the then-ruling communists. They drew on limited past democratic epochs, outside counsel and traditional models. The electoral laws embodied the collective desire for democratic legitimacy and the urgent need to break with the past.

The election campaigns were vigorous as well as cathartic. Nations previously dominated by single-party propaganda now experienced multiparty competition. In most cases, the first elections provided a referendum on the past, an opportunity to nail the communist coffin shut. As in all election campaigns, parties, movements and coalitions proposed new ideas and tested the transformed political terrain for the limits of acceptable engagement. Battling a common enemy, these prototype parties also began to discern differences of ideology and temperament within their own ranks, distinctions that would soon divide them and form the basis for more cohesive party structures.

Most of all, these elections were social tests. How would ordinary people react to an open political environment? Would they participate actively by competing themselves or by supporting candidates and parties? Would they choose wisely among parties, policies and candidates? The answers to these questions are found elsewhere in this book and reveal much about how each of these countries started the transition to democracy.

It is hardly the role of an institute whose mission is to assist those building democracy to assess objectively the prospects of democracy succeeding in particular countries. Yet, the work of the National Democratic Institute has inspired reflection. We have learned much about the development process because we have worked side by side with the people of the region. Their commitment and courage, despite tremendous obstacles, are cause for optimism.

This book chronicles the crucial transitional prelude, embodied in the initial electoral phase. This concluding chapter, written in early 1992, analyzes the progress made in institutionalizing democracy since those first elections. It presents the personal perspective of a political development institute director deeply engaged in the democratization process.

The National Democratic Institute has adopted a development approach based on its work with transitional societies around the world. Our principal resource is people — hundreds of gifted people with real life experience in the practice of building democratic institutions under difficult circumstances. Our method is to introduce these political professionals at critical moments of transition to fellow democrats in need of information, guidance and encouragement. Since the first inkling of change in Eastern and Central Europe, NDI has worked with the region's talented new political leaders, expanding their horizons and encouraging their desire for positive change.

Identifying the particular needs that exist in a transition situation requires a framework for examining political processes — a method to gauge the state of democratic development. This framework can be defined, in NDI's parlance, as a "hierarchy of democratization needs." Using the region's first elections as benchmarks for the beginning of democratic transitions, this hierarchy provides a useful way to measure the progress of the nations of Eastern and Central Europe.

# I

The first and most basic development need is a civic culture, a prerequisite for a successful transition to democracy and the foundation on which democracy rests. Developing a strong civic culture means promoting the concept of citizenship. It means creating an appropriate relationship between the responsibilities of the state to the citizen and the responsibilities of individual citizens to the nation and to each other.

The command approach of the communist system attempted to destroy civic culture, and it nearly succeeded. It produced populations in Eastern and Central Europe that were exceedingly passive. In most of these societies, people had little awareness of how they could participate in government to change their lives and those of their neighbors. And on the government side, there was little knowledge of, or even concern for, the need to encourage citizen participation.

The development of a civic culture requires both grassroots education, to increase understanding of citizens' rights, responsibilities and opportunities, and high-level political work, to stimulate parties, parliaments and executives to communicate, consult and enhance citizen confidence in the democratic process. This mutually reinforcing effort will, over time, produce full-scale participatory democracy and citizens who will be:

- capable of assimilating political arguments and making political choices;
- committed to the inherent legitimacy of society, their political leadership and institutions;
- confident that their rights will be respected;
- prepared to take economic risks or, if necessary, to make economic sacrifices for the good of the community; and
- perhaps most important, tolerant and respectful of fellow citizens whatever their ethnic background, gender or religious belief.

Quite obviously, ideal democracies do not exist. No nation has ever met this highest standard of full-scale participatory democracy. These conditions certainly do not exist in the United States where democratic practice is more than 200 years old. But the American democracy is no longer fragile precisely because there is a consensus that defines the ideal. The American civic culture, like that of many other stable democracies, is capable of rejecting political appeals that contradict its fundamental democratic nature.

Such a civic culture was not yet present in any of the Eastern and Central European nations at the time of their first elections. And for this reason, all of these democracies were fragile and subject to potentially fatal manipulation, particularly by those seeking political power through the electoral process.

This, of course, is not to say that the conditions in these seven states were identical when they held their first elections. Clearly, the three nations of Central Europe — Poland, Hungary and the Czech and Slovak Federal Republic — started the transition at a more advanced level. Their modern democratic culture was popularized in the 19th century with active engagement in European affairs. They benefitted from the degree to which democracy developed institutionally in the inter-war period and to the strength of organized resistance throughout the communist period. And the communist governments of these countries were forced to liberalize to avoid the prospect of a violent upheaval that posed a constant threat to their survival.

Parenthetically, it is interesting to note that the three Central European countries supported a much stronger civic culture than did East Germany at the beginning of the transition process. This was a consequence of the lack of democratic experience of any living East German at the time the Berlin Wall came down and the harshness of the totalitarian regime. The same could be said of Albania, Bulgaria, Romania and parts of Yugoslavia, which bear the legacy of their historical ties to the Ottoman Empire, where notions of individual rights and participatory democracy were never part of the political culture. Yet, Bulgaria has made greater progress in creating a civic culture than have the other Balkan nations. The new Bulgarian government — including the leaders of the Union of Democratic Forces and some in the Bulgarian Socialist Party who had accommodated the changes — and the Bulgarian Association for Fair Elections and Civil Rights deserve great credit for accelerating the pace of development.

In Romania, the challenge was greater than elsewhere in Eastern Europe. Ceausescu's government was easily the most brutal and cynically manipulative in the region. While other Eastern European countries produced effective anti-communist groups or were led by reform-minded communists, the December 1989 Romanian revolution was triggered by a chain of chance events. It did not produce an opposition capable of filling the political vacuum. It was no wonder that so little trust existed in Romania when that country went to the polls. The first elections held there clearly failed to produce a government whose legitimacy was beyond doubt.

In Albania, the transition period had not yet begun when the elections that are the subject of this book were conducted. The isolation of this small mountain nation and the severity of the communist regime were difficult to overcome, as was reflected in the conduct of the March 31, 1991 elections. The collapse of the ruling party following the elections provides a good indication that the electoral process failed to generate a minimum level of popular support and legitimacy.

The disintegration of the federal state of Yugoslavia and the outbreak of war between Serbia and Croatia in 1991 alarmed Western governments. Nationalism in some of the Yugoslav republics ran amok precisely because civic culture was not strong enough to resist nationalist appeals. Communist leaders in Serbia, who for so long successfully manipulated or suppressed nationalist tendencies, exploited these same tendencies to maintain power in the first elections. First, the Kosovo Albanians and then the Croatians were the victims of highly nationalist Serbian attacks. Croatia's own fragile democracy was never given a chance to demonstrate that the minority Serbian population would be treated fairly before war with Serbia broke out.

Slovenia was an exception in the former Yugoslavia. Here, the society had evolved – even during the communist period – in such a way as to produce a reasonably informed citizenry. It is also apparent that the relative homogeneity of Slovenia had reduced the pressures on a civic culture that itself was not yet fully formed.

# II

The second development need for these societies in transition is what broadly could be called pluralism. This is achieved through a proliferation of intermediary organizations capable of giving effective voice to an informed citizenry. Social engineers cannot artificially construct such institutions. The region's Communist parties tried to create Orwellian associations whose purpose was to reinforce state control by inhibiting natural pluralist inclinations, but in the end they failed. Meaningful pluralism derives its democratic character and strength from a strong civic culture.

Journalist William Echikson in his excellent book, *Lighting the Night*, credits intermediary organizations with bringing down communism. According to Echikson:

> This amazing success did not come overnight as a gift from Mikhail Gorbachev. Rather it came after long years of struggle, building up hundreds of independent organizations, everything from the self-proclaimed journalists' union to a private boy scout group...Slowly, surely, these grassroots groups chiseled away at communist power...until it collapsed like a fragile house of cards.

Echikson's analysis does not apply equally to the Balkan nations, or even to East Germany. In these countries, little pluralism existed during the communist period. The various Protestant churches provided safe havens in East Germany, but few other organizations existed except for those tightly controlled by the state. The same could be said of Romania, Bulgaria, Albania and portions of Yugoslavia. Yugoslavia's relatively open economy and appeal to Western tourists helped overcome the isolation, as did the existence of elites in many of the republics who took advantage of the Tito regime's more liberal approach to communism.

Only in Central Europe did people join together formally to express their discontent, first to each other and then more widely. In Poland, the Catholic Church helped create and protect many groups. In Hungary, reform-minded communists tolerated a relatively open university system and a large number of professional and entrepreneurial associations. And in Czechoslovakia, the Church of Slovakia and the strong cultural heritage of Bohemia encouraged the creation of dissident organizations.

This is not to say that in Central Europe outside assistance and encouragement were not needed. Many of the new groups did not yet have the resources nor the capability to play the role expected of them during the electoral phase of their transitions. European and American counterpart organizations proved crucial to their survival and development.

# III

As is documented elsewhere in this book, creating a viable election system to produce results that reflected the will of the people was an essential first step in the transition process in these countries. For the most part, the elections of 1989 and 1990 accomplished their purpose. In Central Europe, legitimate governments were selected by the people, at the expense of Communist parties throughout the area. The results in the southern tier were not so clear as the first elected governments in Bulgaria, then Romania and Albania collapsed within months of the elections.

Electoral reform continued to be a serious topic in the region in early 1992. Some countries initially settled on systems that resulted from the roundtable negotiating process wherein various parties sought concessions that played to their strengths. Often these negotiations produced compromises between majoritarian systems that led to a small number of strong parliamentary parties and proportional representation systems that tended to assure the representation of significant minority groups. Some nations chose pure proportional systems, some preferred majoritarian systems and some selected mixed systems. But always debate raged over the trade-off between efficiency and representativeness.

Several countries adopted the use of electoral thresholds requiring parties to reach a certain level of popular support — usually 4 or 5 percent — before they could qualify for parliament. These thresholds ultimately sifted out small parties from parliaments. The thresholds also encouraged the formation of democratic coalitions, which could theoretically stand more successfully against still-unified but reconstituted Communist parties.

The chapters of this book that examine the elections in these countries assess their relative strength in three ways: 1) the degree to which the will of the people was expressed in free and fair elections; 2) the representativeness of the results; and 3) the turnout and the extent to which voter alienation or apathy played a role.

With respect to the first criterion — the ability of the system to produce free and fair results — most countries in the region had developed systems technically capable of achieving this minimal goal. Intimidation seriously compromised the election process in Romania, but this was more the result of recidivist forces willing to use threats and an electorate unschooled in democratic choice than flaws in the election machinery *per se*. This problem was detected in the 1990 Bulgarian elections as well, though the process was not compromised as seriously as in Romania. Where intimidation was attempted and where civic culture was weak, the electoral process yielded questionable results that did not provide candidates and parties with the legitimacy needed to govern.

Many of these countries also produced representative parliaments. This was certainly true in the Central European states, as much due to the representativeness of the original opposition coalitions as to the electoral systems themselves. In Bulgaria, where ethnic parties were legally prohibited, a predominantly Turkish-origin party emerged as the third largest party as a result of the 1990 elections. In the Serbian republic of Yugoslavia, on the other hand, the election law was so skewed against minorities that a significant minority — the Kosovo Albanians — chose to boycott the process. In Romania, the Democratic Union of Hungarians in Romania, representing an 8 percent minority, received 7.5 percent of the vote and became the largest opposition party. This is not meant as a tribute, as the Romanian electoral process was seriously distorted in other ways.

Non-participation was a serious problem in the region because it reflected voter alienation. Poland had a 60 percent turnout in its first presidential election. In many Hungarian districts, the requisite 50 percent turnout was not reached in the first elections, requiring rescheduling under the law. Turnout was high in the CSFR (95 percent) and Bulgaria (92 percent).

Whether high or low, turnout did not seem to correlate to the degree to which an electorate was prepared to perform its role in the electoral process. High turnout in Romania, for reasons cited, did not produce meaningful results. Low turnout in the Polish elections resulted from voters frustration and anger over the effects of the economic reform program and the confusing political debate. Apparently the non-voters did not see themselves as able to effect change at the polls. In both cases, voter education programs designed to motivate voters, acquaint them with their responsibilities and enhance their confidence in the system were badly needed but lacking. Where this civic education work was conducted systematically, as in Bulgaria, pre-election polling and subsequent election results reflected a more sophisticated selection process by the voter as well as higher turnout.

# IV

The new political parties of the region, as well as those with historic antecedents, face considerable odds as they seek to strengthen themselves. Many parties have emerged from the larger coalitions formed to oppose the communists. The fragmentation of the coalitions coincided with the collapse of the communist threat. Poland's Solidarity spawned more than 70 parties that competed in the October 1991 elections. The Civic Forum of the Czech lands has broken apart in preparation for elections in June 1992. The Union of Democratic Forces of Bulgaria divided into four parts before the October 1991 elections, although the post-communist Bulgarian Socialist Party remained united. The Democratic Party of Albania, functionally equivalent to umbrella movements in other countries, was formed in December 1990. It was already showing serious fault lines a year later.

A major problem facing these parties was described in a November 11, 1991 editorial from the news magazine *Information from Slovenia*. This editorial stated in part:

> ...we generally have inadequate politicians rather than inadequate programs, because there is less word about programs than personal characteristics. This is a legacy of the one-party system, in which nobody considered the programs, but rather the persons executing them...We have a multiparty system, but we are behaving as in a one-party system...Reflect on how often you hear that as a small nation we should unite. We will not allow others to think differently, much less to let something positive evolve from these opposing views.

Little discussion regarding new ideas was occurring inside the councils of individual parties. It is a given that political parties that do not debate issues and are not organized democratically will not contribute to the democratic society within which they seek approbation through the electoral process. This is why NDI emphasizes in its training seminars such issues as communication within the party, democratic selection of candidates and party leaders, issues and public opinion research, message development, and coordination between those holding elected office and their non-elected party colleagues.

In the spring and summer of 1991, NDI conducted a series of party building seminars in Stirin, Czechoslovakia with the European Studies Center. The project's goal was to facilitate contacts among parties of common ideology, bringing together the Eastern and Western European parties of the Liberal, Christian Democratic and Social Democratic camps. In the same period, NDI sought to create ties among younger politicians through programs with the Democracy After Communism Foundation in Budapest. These programs exposed the new parties of the region to the nuts and bolts of politics. They also placed emphasis on the development of idea politics as opposed to the personal variety. One benefit is that Western European parties have begun to create stronger ties with their ideological soulmates in the East, offering needed support and  beginning the process of politically integrating Europe.

# V

As the West learned long ago, winning elections and administering a government are very distinct matters. The talents needed to appeal to an electorate are not the same as those required to make a bureaucracy respond or a parliament function smoothly. Yet in a new democracy if an elected government seems chaotic and fails to address people's problems, not only the government, but also the democratic system, stands to lose.

The importance of process was one significant outcome that could be observed in the post-election environments of Eastern and Central Europe.  The recently gained freedoms inspired long, unencumbered and often passionate debates,  frequently over the procedures to be followed in conducting the debate.  Lack of respect for the newly created government structures and the obvious desire of some for more power caused executives to overreach into parliamentary domains.  Conflicts arose that might have been avoided had clearer procedures and rules existed.

NDI worked to strengthen parliaments in the region with the help of Western European parliamentarians and in conjunction with a U.S. Congressional task force, chaired by Rep. Martin Frost, established to provide material aid — communications equipment, computers, research facilities and rules handbooks.  Much more assistance is needed to invigorate the capacity of political parties to function inside parliamentary bodies and to develop the means to pursue their ideas through legislation and to communicate them to their constituents.

Creating responsive and well-managed local government is another challenge facing these new democracies.  Some of the nations elected local governments, but have yet to enact legislation that fully defines the powers and relationships of these authorities to national structures.   Still other countries are struggling to educate newly elected municipal officials to manage cities and towns in ways previously unknown to highly centralized societies.

At all levels of government, officials were finding it difficult to make decisions.   Healthy governmental institutions within a democratic framework must facilitate not only open debate, but decision-making as well.  Procedures that are so liberal as to obstruct the will of the majority or to thwart a developing consensus are not adequate for a modern democratic state.  Debate must reach closure.  Talking is an important part of democracy, but talking interminably is a dangerous disease that can threaten the system itself.  Time limits must be set and votes scheduled to move the process along.  These principles are being learned, but learning takes time and threats such as economic collapse and environmental degradation require immediate government action.

One temptation has been for executives — presidents — to usurp parliamentary power.  During 1990 and 1991, such attempts were prominent, in varying degrees in Poland, Hungary, Czechoslovakia, Bulgaria, Albania and Romania.  These moves produced a healthy reaction from the threatened institutions and the resulting debates reinforced the importance of constitutionalism and the rule of law.


# VI


By early 1992, considerable progress had been made in Eastern and Central Europe toward developing the institutions essential to secure, stable democracies.  It will take a full generation, however, for even the Central European democracies to assimilate the essentials of a democratic political and civic culture and to make regression seem utterly impossible.  Democracy-building work must rank high among the priorities of these governments for the foreseeable future.

Many observers, including some who have contributed to this book, have referred to the events that transformed the region as "revolutionary."  The transitions seemed so dramatic, the changes so definitive.  But revolutions usually result in the expulsion of the *ancien régime* by violent means — by bullets, not by ballots. The elections of 1989-90 were far from revolutionary — they principally helped resolve societal conflicts and ended the communist era. They were vehicles for reconciliation, not revolution.

In all of these countries, post-Communist parties, former communist leaders and vast bureaucracies of the past continue to play a role, to the chagrin of many former dissidents. Preoccupation with the past, and with those who collaborated with the old regimes, has created strong pressures for retribution that may threaten newly forming democratic norms. It remains to be seen how far these pressures will push new politicians to compromise democratic principles. Yet, the felt need to cleanse these societies and to punish those who violated human rights must be satisfied in some way.

The nations of the region and Western governments alike must remain realistic about the time needed to develop democracy and must avoid worrying excessively about how economic difficulties might result in authoritarian or fascist forces gaining power. Pessimism and negative self-fulfilling prophecies will not motivate citizens, investors, aspiring politicians or new entrepreneurs.

The hierarchy of democratic development described here could be applied to any society moving from authoritarianism to democracy. But two other pressures imposed themselves as well on the politics of these transitional European societies: 1) the need to restructure centrally planned economies and to create markets and 2) the need to mitigate ethnic tensions and conflicts. The success of the Eastern and Central European democratic experiments rests on the ability of their fragile political systems to address urgently these two issues.

Newly elected leaders are reminded daily of the vital political dimension of economic reform. Economic markets consist of both material and human resources. It is these human resources — consumers, entrepreneurs, workers — who are in need of support and development. And, as the new leaders told their people, this can only be done in an environment of freedom and democratic practice.

The ethnic strife in the region, as noted earlier, is in part caused by the absence of a strong civic culture. Democratic values emphasizing the concept of citizenship are, in many respects, absent. Yet the conflicts remain real and it is not possible to wait a generation for a civic culture to form.

One remedy gaining support is accelerated integration, both East-West and East-East.  If the Hungarians living in Romania and the Germans living in Poland, the Poles living in Lithuania, the Turks living in Bulgaria and the Serbs living in Croatia begin to feel part of a larger community perhaps they would see opportunities for new solutions, as have the ethnic minorities of Western Europe.

As part of this accelerated integration, several steps have been taken.  The Commission on Security and Cooperation in Europe (CSCE) framework has been expanded and a new office established in Warsaw to strengthen democratic institutions.  Efforts are underway to further strengthen CSCE's capabilities to deal with ethnic conflicts.  The Council of Europe has already admitted many Eastern and Central European nations as members.  The Council has formed a commission to focus on the region and to offer new ideas for integration.  Eastern and Central European countries that are now Council members are being encouraged to ratify the treaties committing them to European human rights standards and to the jurisdiction of the European Court for Human Rights.  Some observers suggest that associate membership in the European Community be accompanied by the election of non-voting legislators to the European Parliament, who would serve in this capacity until full membership is extended.  These and other suggestions are still under discussion, but as war rages between Serbs and Croatians and as other flash points are being closely watched, Europeans are sensing the urgency of proceeding toward political integration even before economic integration can be considered.

The triumph of human nature over communism created real euphoria in the region and in the democratic world.  The elections that followed provided an appropriate climax to the drama.  However, the hard work of consolidating democracy and reforming the economic system soon commenced and the euphoria disappeared. These nations must work on all of their democratic development needs simultaneously; work that will take a generation.

If anti-democratic elements emerge as tomorrow's leaders, anointed by the electoral process, the history books may look more critically at the first elections and the early stages of the transition. In early 1992, the prospects looked good despite the long, difficult road ahead.  The initial elections produced a new generation of political leaders, infused with hope and vowing never to lose their hard-won freedoms. Their road is still long and arduous, but they have begun the journey with an awareness of the potential rewards and a keen understanding of the costs of failure. For unlike many of us who offer help, these are people who have lived without democracy.

# APPENDIX

# EAST GERMANY

### Parliament Election Results
### March 1990

| Party | Percent of Vote | Seats Won |
|---|---|---|
| Alliance for Germany - Total | 48.1 | 192 |
|     Christian Democratic Union (40.9/163) | | |
|     German Social Union (6.3/25) | | |
|     Democratic Awakening (0.9/4) | | |
| Social Democratic Party of Germany | 21.9 | 88 |
| Party of Democratic Socialism | 16.4 | 66 |
| Federation of Free Democrats | 5.3 | 21 |
|     (Liberal Democratic Party, | | |
|     Free Democratic Party, and | | |
|     German Forum Party) | | |
| Bundis 90 | 2.9 | 12 |
|     (New Forum, | | |
|     Initiative for Peace and Human Rights, | | |
|     and Democracy Now) | | |
| Democratic Farmers' Party | 2.2 | 9 |
| Green Party and Independent Woman's League | 2.0 | 8 |
| Other | 1.0 | 4 |

Eleven parties contesting the election did not win any seats.

# HUNGARY

## Election Results*
## March 1990

| Party | Percent of Vote | Constituencies | | | Seats Won (total) |
| | | Single Member | Region | Nation | |
|---|---|---|---|---|---|
| Hungarian Democratic Forum | 24.7 | 114 | 40 | 10 | 164 |
| Alliance of Free Democrats | 21.4 | 35 | 34 | 23 | 92 |
| Smallholders Party | 11.8 | 11 | 16 | 17 | 44 |
| Hungarian Socialist Party | 10.9 | 1 | 14 | 18 | 33 |
| Federation of Young Democrats | 8.9 | 2 | 8 | 12 | 22 |
| Christian Democratic Peoples Party | 6.5 | 3 | 8 | 10 | 21 |
| Agrarian Alliance | 3.2 | 2 | 0 | 0 | 2 |
| Independents | 0.0 | 6 | 0 | 0 | 6 |
| Candidates from two parties | 0.0 | 2 | 0 | 0 | 2 |

*Percentages based on votes cast for regional party lists.

# SLOVENIA

### Presidential Election Results (First Round)
### April 1990

| Candidate - Party Affiliation | Percent of Vote |
|---|---|
| Milan Kucan LCS - Democratic Renewal Party | 44.4 |
| Joze Pucnik - DEMOS | 26.6 |
| Ivan Kramberger - Independent | 18.5 |
| Marko Demsar - Liberal Party | 10.5 |

### Presidential Election Results (Run-Off)
### April 1990

| Candidate - Party Affiliation | Percent of Vote |
|---|---|
| Milan Kucan LCS - Democratic Renewal Party | 58.6 |
| Joze Pucnik - DEMOS | 41.4 |

### Collective Presidency Election Results
### April 1990

| Winning Candidates - Party Affiliation | Percent of Vote |
|---|---|
| Ciril Zlobec - Socialist Alliance | 52.2 |
| Ivan Oman - DEMOS, Slovene Farmers' Union | 46.2 |
| Matjaz Kmecl LCS - Democratic Renewal Party | 38.2 |
| Dusan Plut - DEMOS, Greens of Slovenia | 38.1 |

## SLOVENIA

### Chamber of Municipalities
### Election Results
### April 1990

| Party | Seats Won |
|---|---|
| DEMOS - United Opposition | 50 |
| Liberal Party | 16 |
| LCS - Democratic Renewal Party | 5 |
| Socialist Alliance | 5 |
| Italian Community | 1 |
| Hungarian Community | 1 |
| Independent candidates | 2 |

### Chamber of Associated Labor
### Election Results
### April 1990

| Party | Seats Won |
|---|---|
| DEMOS - United Opposition | 29 |
| Liberal Party | 10 |
| LCS - Democratic Renewal Party | 19 |
| Socialist Alliance | 6 |

The remaining 16 seats went to independent candidates and the
Free Slovene Trade Unions and the Chambers of Economy.

## SLOVENIA

### Socio-Political Chamber Election Results
### April 1990

| Party | Percent of Vote | Seats Won |
|---|---|---|
| Democratic Renewal Party | 17.3 | 14 |
| Liberal Party | 14.5 | 12 |
| DEMOS - Total | 54.8 | 47 |
|    Slovene Christian Democratic Union (13.0/11) | | |
|    Slovene Farmers' Union (12.6/11) | | |
|    Slovene Democratic Union (9.5/8) | | |
|    Green Party of Slovenia (8.8/8) | | |
|    Social Democratic Union of Slovenia (7.4/6) | | |
|    Slovene Tradesman's Party (3.5/3) | | |
| Socialist Alliance | 5.4 | 5 |
| Others | less than 2.5 | 2 |

# ROMANIA

## Presidential Election Results
## May 1990

| Candidate - Party Affiliation | Percent of Vote |
|---|---|
| Ion Iliescu - National Salvation Front | 85.1 |
| Radu Campeanu - Liberal Party | 10.2 |
| Ion Ratiu - National Peasant Party | 4.3 |

## Senate Election Results
## May 1990

| Party | Percent of Vote | Seats Won |
|---|---|---|
| National Salvation Front | 67.0 | 92 |
| Hungarian Democratic Union of Romania | 7.2 | 12 |
| National Liberal Party | 7.1 | 9 |
| National Peasant Party | 2.5 | 1 |
| Romanian Ecological Movement | 2.5 | 1 |
| Romanian Unity Alliance | 2.2 | 2 |
| Romanian Ecological Party | 1.4 | 1 |
| Others | — | 1 |

# ROMANIA

## Assembly of Deputies Election Results
## May 1990

| Party | Percent of Vote | Seats Won |
|---|---|---|
| National Salvation Front | 66.3 | 263 |
| Hungarian Democratic Union of Romania | 7.2 | 29 |
| National Liberal Party | 6.4 | 29 |
| Romanian Ecological Movement | 2.6 | 12 |
| National Peasant Party | 2.6 | 12 |
| Romanian Unity Alliance (RUA) | 2.1 | 9 |
| Agrarian Democratic Party | 1.8 | 9 |
| Romanian Ecological Party | 1.7 | 8 |
| Socialist Democratic Party | 1.1 | 5 |
| Others | — | 20 |

# CZECHOSLOVAKIA

### Federal Assembly Election Results*
### House of People
### June 1990

| Czech Republic - Parties | Percent of Vote | Seats Won |
|---|---|---|
| Civic Forum | 53.2 | 68 |
| Communist Party of Czechoslovakia | 13.5 | 15 |
| Christian Democratic Party | 8.7 | 9 |
| Movement for Self-Governing Democracy - Society for Moravia and Silesia | 7.9 | 9 |

| Slovak Republic - Parties | Percent of Vote | Seats Won |
|---|---|---|
| Public Against Violence | 32.5 | 19 |
| Christian Democratic Movement | 19.0 | 11 |
| Communist Party of Czechoslovakia | 13.8 | 8 |
| Slovak National Party | 11.0 | 6 |
| Coexistence, Hungarian Christian Democratic Movement | 8.6 | 5 |

*Percentages based on first scrutiny of ballots.

# CZECHOSLOVAKIA

### Federal Assembly Election Results*
### House of Nations
### June 1990

| Czech Republic - Parties | Percent of Vote | Seats Won |
|---|---|---|
| Civic Forum | 50.0 | 50 |
| Communist Party of Czechoslovakia | 13.8 | 12 |
| Christian Democratic Party | 8.8 | 6 |
| Movement for Self-Governing Democracy - Society for Moravia and Silesia | 9.1 | 7 |

| Slovak Republic - Parties | Percent of Vote | Seats Won |
|---|---|---|
| Public Against Violence | 37.3 | 33 |
| Christian Democratic Movement | 16.7 | 14 |
| Communist Party of Czechoslovakia | 13.4 | 12 |
| Slovak National Party | 11.4 | 9 |
| Coexistence, Hungarian Christian Democratic Movement | 8.5 | 7 |

*Percentages based on first scrutiny of ballots.

## BULGARIA

### Grand National Assembly Election Results
### June 1990

| Party | Percent of Vote | Seats by PR | Constituencies Won June 10 | June 17 | Seats Won (total) |
|---|---|---|---|---|---|
| Bulgarian Socialist Party (BSP) | 47.1 | 97 | 75 | 39 | 211 |
| Union of Democratic Forces (UDF) | 36.2 | 75 | 32 | 37 | 144 |
| Movement for Rights & Freedoms (MRF) | 6.0 | 12 | 9 | 2 | 23 |
| Bulgarian Agrarian National Union (BANU) | 8.3 | 16 | 0 | 0 | 16 |
| Fatherland Party of Labour | 0.6 | 0 | 0 | 1 | 1 |
| Social Democratic Party | 0.1 | 0 | 1 | 0 | 1 |
| Alternative Socialist Party | 0.3 | 0 | 0 | 0 | 0 |
| Independents | 0.0 | 0 | 0 | 0 | 4 |

# Contributors

**Madeleine Albright** President, Center for National Policy. Former William H. Donner Research Professor of International Affairs and Director of Women in Foreign Service Program, Georgetown University. Member, Board of Directors, National Endowment for Democracy, 1991-present. Vice-Chair NDI Board, 1985-90. Leading expert on foreign policy and on Eastern and Central Europe. Participated in NDI-sponsored international observer delegations in Hungary and Czechoslovakia.

**Genaro Arriagada** General Secretary, Christian Democratic Party, Chile. Former Chairman, Campaign for the No. Former Chairman, Radio Cooperative Radio Station. Former Visiting Scholar, John F. Kennedy School for Government and Woodrow Wilson International Center for Scholars. Author, *Pinochet: the Politics of Power* and several articles on civil-military relations and political transitions. Participated in NDI training program and observer delegation in Bulgaria.

**J. Brian Atwood** President, National Democratic Institute for International Affairs. Executive Director, Democratic Senatorial Campaign Committee, 1983-84. Dean, Professional Studies and Academic Affairs, Foreign Service Institute, 1981-82. Assistant Secretary of State for Congressional Relations, 1978-81. Participant in NDI training programs and international observer delegations in Bulgaria, Hungary, and Poland.

**Shlomo Avineri** Professor of Political Science, Hebrew University, Jerusalem, Israel. Author, *The Social and Political Thought of Karl Marx* and *Hegel and the Modern State*. Former Director-General, Israeli Foreign Ministry. Participated in NDI training programs and international observer delegations in Czechoslovakia, Hungary and Yugoslavia.

**Eric C. Bjornlund** Senior Program Officer, National Democratic Institute for International Affairs. Associate, Ropes & Gray, 1984-88. Author, "The Devil's Work: Judicial Review under a Bill of Rights in South Africa and Namibia," Stanford Journal of International Law, vol. 26, num. 2. (1990).

**Robin Carnahan** Managing Partner, Carnahan & Associates. NDI representative in Czechoslovakia and Hungary, February-June 1990.

**Thomas Carothers** Associate, Arnold & Porter. Former visiting scholar, Woodrow Wilson Center. Author, *In the Name of Democracy: U.S. Policy Toward Latin America In the Reagan Years* (1991). Participated in NDI-sponsored international observer delegation to Romania.

**Judith Corley** Associate, Perkins Coie, specializing in election law. Chief, Office of Public Communications, Federal Election Commission, 1975-81. Participated in NDI-sponsored international observer delegation to Czechoslovakia.

**Andrew Ellis** Central and Eastern Europe Director, GJW Government Relations, and Central and Eastern European correspondent, European Library of Political Programmes, Berlin. Secretary-General, British Liberal Party and Liberal Democrats, 1985-89. Observed 1990 elections in Bulgaria, Czechoslovakia, Hungary, Poland and Slovenia.

**Larry Garber** Senior Counsel for Electoral Processes, National Democratic Institute for International Affairs. Author, *Guidelines for International Election Observing* (1984) and numerous articles on elections, election processes and election observing. Adviser, U.S. delegation to the June 1990 CSCE meeting in Copenhagen, Denmark. Participated in NDI-sponsored pre-election and international observer delegations in Bulgaria, Czechoslovakia, Hungary and Romania.

**Daniel P. Gordon** Attorney, U.S. General Accounting Office. Author, "Limits on Extremist Political Parties: A Comparison of Israeli Jurisprudence With That of the United States and West Germany," Hastings International and Comparative Law Journal (1987). Observed 1990 elections in East Germany.

**Maya Latynski** Program Associate, European Institute, Woodrow Wilson International Center for Scholars. PhD. candidate, Georgetown University Department of Government. Author of many articles on Poland and Eastern Europe. Observed 1989 and 1990 elections in Poland.

**Edward McMahon** Senior Program Officer, National Democratic Institute for International Affairs. Foreign Service Officer, U.S. Department of State, 1981-91. Coordinated NDI election observing missions and programs in Yugoslavia.

**Thomas O. Melia**  Program Director, National Democratic Institute for International Affairs.  Associate Director, Free Trade Union Institute, AFL-CIO, 1986-88.  Legislative Assistant for Foreign and Defense Policy, Senator Daniel P. Moynihan, 1980-86.  Coordinated NDI programs in East and Central Europe during 1989-91 and participated in pre-election missions and international observer delegations in Bulgaria, Hungary and Romania.

**Antonio Nadais**  Assistant Professor, Constitutional Law and Political Science, Lisbon Law School.  Former Legal Advisor, Portuguese Constitutional Court.  Participated in NDI-sponsored pre-election mission and international observer delegation in Bulgaria.

**Fred W. Reinke**  Associate, Milbank, Tweed, Hadley & McCloy. Fellow, Robert Bosch Foundation, West German Ministry for Intra-German Relations and at the Bundesbank in Frankfurt, 1987-88. Author, "Treaty and Non-Treaty Human Rights Agreements: A Case Study of Freedom and Movement in East Germany," Columbia Journal of Transnational Law, vol. 24, num. 3 (1989).  Observed 1990 elections in East Germany.

**Antonio Vitorino**  Judge, Constitutional Court of Portugal.  Professor of Law, Lisbon Law School.  Former Member of Parliament.  Vice-Minister of Administration and Justice for Macao, 1986-87.  Vice-Minister for Parliament Affairs, 1983-85.  Participated in NDI programs and international observer delegations in Bulgaria, Czecho-slovakia and Hungary.

# The National Democratic Institute for International Affairs

The National Democratic Institute for International Affairs (NDI) was established in 1983. By working with political parties and other institutions, NDI seeks to promote, maintain, and strengthen democratic institutions in new and emerging democracies. The Institute is chaired by former Vice President Walter F. Mondale and is headquartered in Washington, D.C.

NDI has conducted democratic development programs in more than 40 countries. Programs focus on six major areas:

*Political Party Training*: NDI conducts multipartisan training seminars in political development with a broad spectrum of democratic parties. NDI draws expert trainers from around the world to forums where members of fledgling parties learn first-hand the techniques of organization, communication and constituent contact.

*Election Processes*: NDI provides technical assistance for political parties and nonpartisan associations to conduct voter and civic education campaigns, and to organize election monitoring programs. The Institute has also organized more than 20 international observer delegations.

*Legislative Training*: In Eastern Europe, Latin American and Africa, NDI has organized legislative seminars focusing on legislative procedures, staffing, research information, constituent services and committee structures.

*Local Government*: Technical assistance on models of city management has been provided to national legislatures and municipal governments in Central and Eastern Europe and the Soviet Union.

*Civil Military Relations*: NDI brings together military and political leaders to promote dialogue and establish mechanisms for improving civil-military relations.

*Civic Education*: NDI supports and advises nonpartisan groups and political parties engaged in civic and voter education programs.

# National Democratic Institute for International Affairs

# Selected NDI Studies

- *Albania: 1991 Elections to the People's Assembly*
- *Bangladesh Parliamentary Elections, February 27, 1991*
- *The October 13, 1991 Legislative and Municipal Elections in Bulgaria*
- *The June 1990 Elections in Bulgaria*
- *Democratization in Cameroon: International Delegation Report (1991)*
- *Chile's Transition to Democracy: The 1988 Presidential Plebiscite* (English and Spanish)
- *The Commonwealth of Independent States: Democratic Development Issues and Options (1992)*
- *Peaceful Transitions and the Cuban Democratic Platform: Report of an International Conference* (1991 English and Spanish)
- *1990 Elections in the Dominican Republic*
- *The 1990 National Elections in Guatemala*
- *The New Democratic Frontier: A Country by Country Report on the Elections in Central and Eastern Europe*
- *The 1990 General Elections in Haiti*
- *The Hungary Transition 1989-91*
- *Nation Building: The U.N. and Namibia (1990)*
- *The October 1990 Elections in Pakistan*
- *The May 7, 1989 Panamanian Elections* (English and Spanish)
- *Voting for Greater Pluralism: The May 26, 1991 Elections in Paraguay*
- *Reforming the Philippine Electoral Process: 1986-88* (Reissued Summer 1991)
- *The May 1990 Elections in Romania*
- *An Assessment of the Senegalese Electoral Code (1991)*
- *The October 31, 1991 National Elections in Zambia*